Selves at Risk

SELVES
AT RISK

Patterns of Quest in Contemporary American Letters

IHAB HASSAN

The University of Wisconsin Press

The University of Wisconsin Press
114 North Murray Street
Madison, Wisconsin 53715

3 Henrietta Street
London WC2E 8LU, England

Printed in the United States of America

Library of Congress Cataloging-in-Publication Data
Hassan, Ihab Habib, 1925–
    Selves at risk: patterns of quest in contemporary American
letters/Ihab Hassan.
        248 pp.   cm.—(Wisconsin project on American writers)
        Includes bibliography and index.
        1. American prose literature—20th century—History and criticism.
2. Quests in literature.   I. Title.   II. Series.
PS374.Q47H37   1990   89-36082
818'.50809'353—dc20   CIP
ISBN 0-299-12370-7

S

We Americans are the peculiar chosen people—the Israel of our time. . . . We are the pioneers of the world; the advance-guard sent on through the wilderness of untried things, to break a new path in the New World that is ours.

  — Herman Melville

If you are ready to leave father and mother, brother and sister, and wife and child and friends, and never see them again—if you have paid your debts, and made your will, and settled all your affairs, and are a free man—then you are ready for a walk.

  — Henry David Thoreau

O we can wait no longer!
We too take ship, O soul!

  — Walt Whitman

Old men ought to be explorers
Here and there does not matter
We must be still and still moving . . .

  — T. S. Eliot

Contents

x   Contents

Acknowledgments

Chapter 2 appeared, in another version, in *Contemporary Literature* 29, 4 (Fall 1988); and some pages of other chapters in *Michigan Quarterly Review* 27, 1 (Winter 1988) and *American Literary History* 1, 1 (Spring 1989). An earlier overview of my topic appeared also in Malcolm Bradbury and Sigmund Ro, eds., *Contemporary American Fiction* (London: Edward Arnold, 1986). I am grateful to the editors of those journals and books, most particularly to Malcolm Bradbury who, as friend, artist, fellow critic, stimulated my ideas about literature and culture over the years.

I remain grateful to the Vilas Trust Fund and the University of Wisconsin in Milwaukee, specially to Dean William Halloran of the College of Letters and Science, for their enduring support of my research; and I thank Yuan Yuan for his cheerful and thorough assistance in that research.

Allen Fitchen, Director of the University of Wisconsin Press, invited me to contribute to the Wisconsin Project on American Writers, which he initiated. I much appreciated his tactful insights and patience.

Selves at Risk

In-Quest:
A Synoptic Introduction

I am afoot with my vision . . .
                    — Walt Whitman

Much of the extraordinary ignorance of most Americans about what
has been happening elsewhere . . . is due to the fact that their eyes
and ears — their writers — have stayed home.
                    — Edward Hoagland

1

THIS IS a book about quests in contemporary American letters, and about contemporary reality. These quests are of a particular
kind. They solicit adventure — I would call them "questures," but we have
had critical neologisms enough.* They also affirm essential values even
as they assay new modes of being in the world. Spirit, effort, peril constitute these journeys, in fiction or nonfiction, as does the great wager with
death. Such journeys put articulate selves at risk, selves that may incur
failure or folly but always spurn the glossy ironies, the camp and kitsch
of our day.

Still, one may ask: Quest? Adventure, in the fading glare of our century? In this era of satellites and supersonic jets, of the ubiquitous Mc-
Donald's and pervasive Panasonic? In our coddled jacuzzi culture, our cybernetic, if not quite cyborg, society of acronyms and first names, where
acedia measures lives between hype and fix? Indeed, the very name of
quest may strike some as quaint, lacking as it does deconstructionist brio,
Marxist bravura, or feminist coloratura.

Yet the spirit of quest endures, unquavering, with stiff upper lip. It endures, moreover, confident of its future and proud of its (largely British)
pedigree. From rain forests, across oceans, steppes, savannahs, saharas,
to the peaks of the Andes or Himalayas, men and increasingly women still
test the limits of human existence. They test spirit, flesh, marrow, imagi-

*Henceforth, *in this work,* I will use quest and adventure freely, interchangeably, though
the terms may not be identical in other contexts.

3

nation, in a timeless quest for adventure, for meaning really, beyond civilization, at the razor edge of mortality. And they return, with sun-cracked skin and gazes honed on horizons, to tell the tale.

Indeed, seekers can be eloquent, even loquacious. I limit myself in this book, therefore, to postwar American prose writers whose works reshape the traditional genre of quest in hybrid forms. In a way, we are, both reader and author, in quest of an ideal text of quest. Though we may never find such a text, we may in the process develop a working concept, an effective sense, of the enterprise. We may also discover in these vicarious voyages compelling images of our own concerns. And who knows but that we may take some pleasure in works uncommonly blessed with style, the vivid, verbal grace of human beings under pressure?

Already, the reader notes, certain qualities of quest have begun to emerge: hope, movement, danger, exposure to otherness in alien cultures or natures, all rendered in a distinct personal voice. And since the authors I address all write in the first person about the present—no historical quests or romances here—their works have the timbre of autobiography. Still, the word quest evokes projects as various as those of Parsifal, the Pilgrim Fathers, and Indiana Jones. Thus quest, metaphor of life itself, of life even beyond death, requires from us sharper demarcation.

I have taken quest here in its singular sense, though from the Argonauts to the Astronauts seekers have also journeyed in groups. But "superalpinists" now scale Everest alone, dispensing with oxygen if not with faith, thus confirming Salman Rushdie when he says: "the myth more often seems to require the existential purity of a single human being pitted against the immensity of the universe. . . ."[1] At the same time, I have not considered quest simply as a personal matter, a private transaction between an individual and the universe. Rather, I have viewed quest as a vital, symbolic option in the postmodern world, a focus of choices and constraints in American society, and, beyond that, as a signal to us all about risk, strangeness, achievement, the terrible splendors of self-renewal. Therefore, I have eschewed quests that are mainly interior, those night journeys through the inverted forests of the soul. For once, D. H. Lawrence missed the mark when he wrote: "Superficially, the world has become small and known. . . . There is no mystery left, we've been there, we've seen it, we know about it. We've done the globe, and the globe is done. . . . Yet the more we know superficially, the less we penetrate vertically. . . . There still remain the terrifying under-deeps, of which we have utterly no experience."[2] But the mystery remains, and it is both "vertical" and "horizontal," private and public: in *both* dimensions quests persist, discovering spirit in action, making meaning.

2

The public aspects of quest and adventure merit our first attention, for they reveal a central, historical tendency in the West. Michael Nerlich traces this tendency back to the high Middle Ages, perceiving there the beginning of a "systematic glorification of the (knightly, then bourgeois) adventurer as the most developed and most important human being," a glorification that "defined the inalienable fundamental condition of human existence."[3] This "ideology of adventure," Nerlich argues, transgresses boundaries of class, abets change, tolerates uncertainty, and entails confrontation with others, "other races, other languages, other names, other necessities, other desires, etc."[4] All this leads to our modernity, the climax, Nerlich insists, of that dynamic, innovative impulse no society can stifle in its individuals without becoming sterile.

The ideology of adventure finds its preeminent instance in the American experience. As Todorov put it: "the discovery of America, or of the Americans, is certainly the most astonishing encounter of our history. We do not have the same sense of radical difference in the 'discovery' of other continents and of other peoples. . . ."[5] Discovered first by Europeans, America perpetuated the quest on its own continent; later, it repatriated the quest to Europe, Africa, Asia, repatriated, as it were, the American Sublime together with its native versions of cultural imperialism. In the process, America constructed its own histories, myths, and legends, its own ethos of quest, in and out of literature.

Certain commonplaces of criticism reverberate still in our minds. American literature, critics have said, is largely autobiographical, a literature of the Self, enacted most often on the margins of society, from Poe's Arthur Gordon Pym through Melville's Ishmael, Twain's Huck Finn, and Whitman's Myself, to Salinger's Holden Caulfield or Bellow's Augie March. It is also, we are often told, a symbolic, visionary literature, less social than metaphysical, with a prepossession for myth and romance. Its bias is for innocence, evasion, solitude, wonder, change, errancy, as the titles of even scholarly books intimate: *The American Adam, The American Newness, The Imperial Self, The Reign of Wonder, Errand into the Wilderness, The Virgin Land, A World Elsewhere, Radical Innocence.* Finally, it is a literature, though Adamic, of extremity, of intense and brooding modernity, as D. H. Lawrence insisted.

Such critical commonplaces shift with the moods of historical revisionism, as if we know "now" better than "then," see things more clearly — in fact, we see them only otherwise.[6] Yet even revisionist works confirm quest in the American grain. The quest moved west, absorbing that dire and dazzling energy Europeans expended in their colonial empires. The quest, as Myra Jehlen has noted, also translated time into space. "The most interesting aspect of the general belief in a national destiny to expand ever westward is one we tend to overlook, perhaps because we take it for granted," Jehlen says; "the American teleology cites the will of heaven and the human spirit, but it rests its case on the integrity of the continent"; and so Americans traveled restlessly, leading "lives in a state of perpetual landing."[7] Moving out, the quest also found its need for otherness in the wilderness, and found its motives in the eternal search of misfits, outlaws, scalawags, crackpots, vagrants, visionaries, individualists of every stripe, for something they could hardly name: El Dorado, the New Jerusalem, the Earthly Paradise, the Last Frontier. "Philobats" (walkers on their toes), as Gert Raeithel argues in his psychohistory of *voluntary* American immigrants, they formed weak attachments to objects, persons, places; they relished stress, movement, exposure, transgressive fantasies.[8] Yet Americans could no more exempt themselves from history than from power or desire. Their quests, therefore, reveal certain social attitudes, historical patterns, that we also need to ponder.

Here Martin Green's *The Great American Adventure* proves pertinent. Green reviews classic adventures, from Cooper to Mailer, and discerns in them particular features — and I would say manners. These include a pagan, anti-intellectual, antipacifist outlook; a masculinist, often misogynist, stance; a concept of manhood linked to nationalism, patriotism, America's Manifest Destiny; and a strong sense of caste, if not class, led by military aristocrats *and* democratic woodsmen (hunters, trappers, Indian fighters) who magnificently possess the frontier virtues of valor, self-reliance, knowledge of the wilderness, and, above all, a rude *ecological ethic*. Thus, for Green, venturesome quests mark "the highest achievement of American literature," a counterpart to the "Great Tradition" (F. R. Leavis) of the European novel.[9]

In any event, though adventure became secular in the last century, possibly anti-Christian, it often took a spiritual, even mystic, turn. As Green says: "Although hunting is an activity of the aristo-military caste, being a hunter in the American sense is in some ways not a caste activity, in that it takes place in a non-social space, outside the frontier of society. . . . Just for that reason, however, it represents more vividly the sacramental function of the man of violence. . . . Thus, if the hunter fails to represent the social aspect of caste, he nonetheless represents its religious aspect vividly."[10] The religion in question is, I believe, "natural," the kind we sometimes see shimmer through the paintings of Thomas Cole, Frederick Edwin Church, Winslow Homer, or Albert Pinkham Ryder.

Spirit was never a stranger to violence, of course, the violence of nature first, the sacramental violence also of the hunter or primitive warrior who on behalf of his tribe breaks the taboo against killing. Indeed, some historians of the American frontier have come to consider the notion of "sacramental violence" as crux. Thus, for instance, Richard Slotkin claims that "the myth of regeneration through violence became the structuring metaphor of the American experience." He continues: "an American hero is the lover of the spirit of the wilderness, and his acts of love and sacred affirmation are acts of violence against that spirit and her avatars."[11]

Slotkin's use of the feminine pronoun with reference to nature is instructive. The American hero loves nature but must also violate "her," either profanely—exterminating the buffalo, wasting the land—or sacramentally.[12] This ethos also affects the hero's attitude toward women, as Leslie Fiedler has famously argued in *Love and Death in the American Novel*. For quest always tempts the hero to abandon hearth, family, friends, leave society behind, a willed alienation aggravated by frontier conditions which released one kind of desire (freedom) only to constrain another (love).

We can plausibly conclude, then, that the historic experience of America proved singularly congenial to the spirit of quest. That experience provided an alternative to European colonialism, provided a colonialism within, a dramatic, often destructive encounter that became, through dime novels and Hollywood movies, an international myth: the myth of the Indian, the myth of the Frontier and the Wild West. Similarly, the "journey centeredness" of that historic experience offered "matter, form, directional association for the literary imagination," offered a mythic focus for all the contradictions of American democracy and empire.[13] It is as if the "complex fate" of which Henry James spoke at the turn of our century really entailed, more than a confrontation between Europe and America, a spirited adventure into the uncharted wilderness both of the New World and of the Old Adam, Caliban, whom Lawrence derisively invoked:

Ca Ca Caliban
Get a new master, be a new man.[14]

3

Lawrence might as well have invoked the new American woman. For quest also concerns gender, and in this concern touches all the sexual complexities of America.

Women, of course, rarely engaged in adventurous quests or explorations before the end of the eighteenth century. Increasingly, though, they have become intrepid travelers—witness Leo Hamalian's *Ladies on the Loose,* Mary Russell's *The Blessings of a Good Thick Skirt,* and Elizabeth

Fagg Olds's *Women of the Four Winds.* Still more recently, women have undertaken daunting tasks: Libby Riddles won the solo Alaska Dog Sled Race, covering 1,135 miles; Enda O'Coineen crossed the Atlantic alone in a rubber dinghy; Pam Flowers reached, in fifty-four days, the North Pole by a route hitherto impassable; Jan Reynolds skied down 24,757-foot Mount Mustagata in western China; and Julie Tullis perished *after* conquering K2.

The tradition of errant women, though, was largely British; Americans, male or female, expended themselves on their own westering frontiers.[15] Later in the nineteenth century, some doughty Americans—Fanny Bullock Workman, Annie Smith Peck, Delia J. Akeley, Marguerite Harrison, Louise Arner Boyd—ventured far, high, and wide, founding the Society of Woman Geographers in 1925. But the historical climate of strenuous travel was already changing, affecting its appeal to women. Elizabeth Fagg Olds puts it thus:

> The new women travelers were largely American. And they were different from most of their predecessors, who had tended to be romantic dreamers, more intrigued by the exotic aspects of travel, the "spell of the East," for instance, and with the novelty of independence than driven toward defined goals. The new women explorers, by contrast, were highly goal oriented, single-minded, and stoutly dedicated to specific objectives. They freed themselves from their Victorian upbringing to organize and lead expeditions of their own, with institutional or other backing if possible, but in any case asserting themselves as serious explorers.
>
> They are important as a transitional group in the evolving advances of women, for they were the direct forerunners of today's trained women scientists and field workers. Although themselves heirs and successors to their Victorian counterparts, they cast off, as soon as possible, the quaint and inhibiting sidesaddles, flowing skirts, long tresses, and veils of their sisters. But they were not yet modern, either. Having after all been born in the Victorian era, they donned their knickers with misgivings, rode astride but wore concealing robes or jackets, and bivouacked with their porters and bearers with uneasy apologies. But meanwhile they managed to explore some of the earth's most unlikely spots, encounter adventures as wildly improbable as their predecessors' and contribute much to our knowledge of people, customs, and geography.[16]

This new attitude, "stoutly dedicated to specific objectives," encourages science more than quest.[17] Also, pure motion in space, without inner need or visionary gleam, without a quality of awareness that gives resonance to narrative, indeed without narrative itself, can not serve us as model for quest. Hence the relative scarcity, in *Selves at Risk,* of postwar American women writers, writers of the order, say, of Freya Stark, who was English and traveled in another age.

But the question of gender in quest does not arise only in the recent history of women. The question inhabits myth, and is charged with contradictions. Male seekers have traditionally kept aloof from women, only to discover the woman within. Inspired often in their adventures by some actual woman, these mythic heroes also used their journeys against the "other sex," to liberate themselves from social and erotic bonds. With clear intuition, Paul Zweig summarizes the paradox: "This is where the adventurer discoveres the elusiveness of woman. She is the house from which he frees himself in order to give birth to himself as a pure male. But she is also the means within him by which he escapes. And she is still more: her various incarnations appear before him as occasions for adventure, mysteries beckoning to him out of the obscure fertilities of chance."[18] Thus hoping to reinvent himself arduously as a man's man, the questing hero ends, as we shall see, by sublimating his "femininity" into a cosmic vision.

It is not essential for us to speculate here on the differences between men and women regarding their inherent character or behavior. Such speculations usually draw on a large, common fund of ignorance and prejudice, recycle debates about nature and culture, and finally expend themselves in ideological fictions of resentment or self-esteem. Some ideas about gender, though, are relevant to quest; they enjoy reasonable consensus, and so warrant review. Only men, for instance, seem to have hunted, headed tribes, made war, and sought some form of violence to validate themselves.[19] Men also seem more prone than women to catastrophic fantasies, feelings of insecurity, hence to striving and strain.[20] They generally evince, as Walter J. Ong puts it, a higher degree of "adversativeness," restlessness, solitude — also, paradoxically, of extreme bonding — a larger need for self-redemption.[21] In their stance toward risk, men also differ from women:

> Margaret Hennig and Anne Jardim in *The Managerial Woman* (1977) put very pointedly what countless proverbs, folktales, and literary works express about the human experience of male and female agonistic attitudes across the world: "Men see risk as loss or gain; winning or losing; danger or opportunity," while women "see risk as entirely negative. It is loss, danger, injury, ruin, hurt. One avoids it as best one can. . . ."[22]

Risk and contest, Ong further argues, also relate to "othering," differentiation between individuals or species. This process of differentiation creates the "I," the self, which exists both in connection with other "I's" and "in a state of terrifying isolation"; thus when "the human ego is threatened with dissolution, often there is nothing like a good nonlethal fight, a contest, to get it back together again, even if the contest is lost."[23]

How do these ideas about gender illumine the subject of quest? In so far as quest entails isolation, combat, delight in risk and strain, it expresses a *traditionally* male aspect of the human character, and this may also account for the relative paucity of female quests, *quests as here defined.*[24] To moot the "biological" or "social" character of this tradition, moot its origin, is futile. In all things human, biological evolution and social conditioning have become inextricable, their separation, in favor of one or the other, an egregiously ideological act. Nor is the "individual" more or less a fiction than "society," since in all things human, again, idiolect, sociolect, and biolect continually interact.

But the decisive point about gender in the literature of quest envisages the near future rather than the distant past. If literary narratives now turn inward, as Erich Kahler has argued, if the oral stage of epic feats now yields to more subtle introspections, can we also conclude that quest, like American culture itself, has become "feminized"? I am tempted to answer with an ambiguous "yes." Ong, I think, is in the main right: "Narrative centered on raw male combat, such as the Western or the typical television whodunit, is today usually regressive, for it can no longer be made to carry the serious psychic load of combat stories in oral cultures."[25] But history, we should also recall, is often "regressive," and cultural fashion even more so — witness *Rambo I, II,* and *III,* and all the arts of nostalgia in our space age. Moreover, contemporary quests may signal a renewal of literature, a restitution of belief, a way past the wasteland of our ironies and ideologies. Thus Zweig would argue against Ong: "The very movement inward, which undermined the traditional framework of adventure, created in its place the medium for a new exploit, and a new simplicity. . . . We have circled back to a level of primitive certainties."[26]

Have we? It remains to be seen whether this "new simplicity" will prove wish or prophecy, and whether a "level of primitive certainties" can still provide a base for the mixed, multiform, anfractuous communities of the future.

4

The wish for a "new simplicity," though, betrays our lacks, betrays the conditions of American society from which seekers flee and to which they return. What conditions? One may as well ask: which American "society"? Nearly half a century has elapsed since the end of the last world war, and America has suffered seismic changes, suffered ruptures, reversals, restorations on a planetary scale. What rubrics or abstractions, then, can describe these years? None, of course, though hints of our collective energies may be found among the fading stamps, peeling labels, of the last decades.

Since the war, we have been told that America — successively, sometimes concurrently — became conformist, "a lonely crowd" (David Riesman); that it entered an "age of discontinuity" (Peter Drucker); that the "greening of America" (Charles Reich) was at hand; that the "coming of a post-industrial society" (Daniel Bell) was already fact; and that the republic had yielded to a "culture of narcissism" (Christopher Lasch); still, "astral America" (Jean Baudrillard) remained a "haloed energy" of simulacra, affecting the future.[27]

In all this, beneath the rubrics and abstractions, there is much to offend men and women of spirit, much to drive them out. Kitsch and hype, boredom and banality, sterility and satiety, spurious values everywhere, the arrogance of pervasive bureaucracies, the cheery cretinism of media, crime, pollution, deprivation, and overcrowding, nature itself on the wane, the prospect of high-tech genocide, the rust of dreams, the ashes of failure — all these surround them. Threatened in their autonomy, they choose to test their purpose elsewhere. Can they win through to the divine, or at least to their own version of reality?

The maladies of civilization are, of course, nothing new; we have simply become inured to their facts. Our most brilliant cities are more menacing than jungles — homicide, rape, drugs, cancer, heart failure. They seethe with anger while inhibiting its expression, until anger reaches the flashpoint.[28] They, the best evidence of our civilization, generate motley freedoms while incarcerating millions within their crumbling walls. Can we wonder that C. L. R. James makes both Ellis Island and Melville's doomed *Pequod* his metaphors of American society, American cities?[29] They, the most vital evidence of our culture, sustain myriad arts while thriving on death. Can we wonder that Al Alvarez considers contemporary artists as masters of suicide or degeneration who "survive morally by becoming . . . an imitation of death in which their audience can share."[30]

The authors in *Selves at Risk* "imitate death," confront it, in other, more salubrious ways. They leave, for a time, "civilization," *their* civilization, and move east or south rather than west. In doing so, they do not deny the crisis of American society, which they rightly perceive as part of a world crisis, a geopolitical spasm. Rather, they engage the crisis by trying to face it in themselves; and if they flee somewhere, they still carry it with them, hoping to resolve it in encounters with otherness, especially that gray, gluey otherness within. The risk they take, though, is not only of death; it is also of failure, repetition, the secular and unoriginal sin of self.

But what crisis precisely is this? In a sense, the crisis is permanent — call it the human condition. In another sense, our discontents have grown with modernization, which inspired John Donne to write in 1611:

And freely men confess that this world's spent,
When in the Planets, and the Firmament
They seek so many new; then see that this
Is crumbled out again to his Atomies.
'Tis all in pieces, all coherence gone;
All just supply, and all Relation.

("An Anatomy of the World")

Hundreds of bristling tomes have since tried to explain the anatomy of our world — alienation, fragmentation, dehumanization, etc.— nor is the end of explanations in sight. This is due to the changing character of modernity itself, its willed and intrinsic fugacity. Modernity "deinstitutionalizes," as Arnold Gehlen put it, destabilizes, and so permits the extremes of isolation and collectivism, subjectivity and enforced totality. "'Tis all in pieces," Donne said, but also all compacted together in mass movements and fanatic ideologies. For Gehlen, therefore, the crisis is "a total one, in the sense that the basic coordinates themselves of the interpretation of the world have become doubtful."[31]

Gehlen exhibits the conservative's sense of decline in the West, and his understanding of recent, cybernetic society is scant; yet his conclusion about the "coordinates of interpretation" accords with Lyotard's desuetude of "master narratives" in the postmodern world and my own concept of "indetermanence."[32] Certainly after the creative, and inevitably destructive, convulsions of the sixties, canons, authorities, values, "relations" of every kind came into deeper (Donnian) doubt. Not only that but the social ecology of America, indeed the very existence of a coherent society, turned moot. For Baudrillard, society became invisible to the rational eye, like an impacted black hole in space, or else visible only as a "hyperreal" frenzy of "simulacra," a vertigo of paralyzed images.[33]

5

Within this motley world — archaic here, postindustrial there, hybrid and decolonized nearly everywhere — seekers go their sundry ways, their very powers of motion fraught with political as with spiritual import. As Mary Louise Pratt has shown about traditional travel narratives, they always codify the Other, and express fantasies of dominance over peoples and even landscapes. Inevitably, often unwittingly, the very information they produce is locked in a particular ideology which legitimizes their explicit or implicit violence. This is not to say that all such narratives express the same ideology; in fact, Pratt admits, "European penetration and appropriation" in these tales "is semanticized in numerous ways that can be quite distinct, even mutually contradictory."[34]

None is exempt from ideology, as it is now fashionable, and inane, to say. In any case, the ideology of contemporary displacements draws on other, more postmodern, assumptions. Whether seeker, explorer, or simply traveler—and we must distinguish the first from the others—we have all become tourists, Dean MacCannell claims. This is because "a complex and sometimes arduous search for an Absolute Other is a basic theme for *our* [my italics] civilization," a search predicated on the expansionist, if not imperialist, tendency of modernity, predicated too on "mass leisure, especially international tourism and sightseeing."[35]

But the seeker is, of course, no ordinary "tourist." He, sometimes she, does not respond to ads saying: "Spend 21 days in the land of the Hatfields and McCoys for $378, living in with some of the poorest people in the U.S. in Mingo County, West Virginia"; nor does he go to Kenya and cry: "Let us shoot at every living thing we can find today and see what bag is possible in one day."[36] Again, the seeker rarely imitates the "human cougar," the tough, independent loner-drifter whose habitat was mainly the American West; nor does he appear simply as an individualist, intent on his own selfish gains, the kind of person that the gregarious authors of *Habits of the Heart* condemn as a "cancer" in American society.[37]

The seeker, as I hope to show, has many faces. But he is not characterless or faceless. He is certainly self-reliant, tolerant of risk. He is mobile. He seeks meaning, even if danger must attend his pursuit; he intuits that individuals need and consume meanings far more than products. And he suspects that the sacred, as Mircea Eliade would say, camouflages itself in that pursuit. Though contemporary life shields him from hazard, he feels that his best moments blaze in peril, or at least insecurity. He disdains vicarious jeopardy, pseudo risks, packaged by prurient media or proffered by amusement parks. He knows unreal America.[38] He knows, therefore, that in venturous quests he may recover reality, constitute significance, maintain his vigor, all in those privileged moments of being when life vouchsafes its most secret rewards. Is this not the whole sense of Emersonian experience?

In all these stirrings, the seeker may not be fully conscious, wide awake. He becomes so only in his story, more precisely in the author's narrative and art. Yet in the *literature of quest*—the quest itself does not come within our purview—the author is often himself the seeker, or at least in imaginative and spiritual cahoots with his errant hero. This accounts, as I noted, for the autobiographical resonance of literary quests. Given the crisis of value, authority, belief in the West, the crisis of discourse itself, where may words finally come to rest but in the dying flesh? How else join autobiography to myth, beliefs to the world? How else speak to the cosmos?

Beliefs—their scope, glory, corruption—are what these selves at risk test and tempt. Like William James, they "will count mystical experiences if they have practical consequences," and "will take a God who lives in the very dirt of private fact—if that would seem a likely place to find him."[39] Their "will to believe" impels them through jungles, over glaciers, across deserts or swamps; and though they may never find what they seek, and may forsake their hope, they leave behind them a verbal trace of some inner pain or radiance to make our journey in this "half-saved, half-wild" universe more right.

6

But who speaks in these pages beside the writers I write about? I do, of course. A word then about my bias. All writing is refined avoidance, a mode of autobiography. I can not speak of my own "quest" here, though I may note that *Selves at Risk* has been itself both an expression of my displacements—from Egypt to America, from engineering to literature, from criticism to paracriticism and back—and a displacement of some "true" expression I have not yet found. I have been, and so remain, amateur of change, addicted to travel and avant-gardism, forms of restlessness. The first is desire in space, the second in time; or perhaps I should say desire *of* space, desire *of* time, which our lives mask or transpose. This is a kind of radical innocence, the human project to conquer death. Conquer how? By defiance? By death itself? By a rage for life?

No one feels that he, that she, has lived fully enough, and when I read stories of genuine quest and adventure, this feeling, beyond envy, jabs some vital part. But I have no talent for regret, and I push my life as I can. There is something existential in this attitude—call it an existential pathos—which affected my first book, *Radical Innocence* (1961). This pathos returns, perhaps, in *Selves at Risk* (1990), mutant, recursive, altered irrevocably by time. A critical sympathy for certain authors and texts also recurs here, breaking through postmodern theories and distractions.

How do I read these authors, these texts? Not transparently, I hope, but neither according to any prescriptive ideology or theory. If that be "ideology" too, then it's mine.[40] But is "everything ideological," as goes the slogan? Ideologies differ greatly with regard to their claims, values, procedures, their overt and hidden exactions; they cry for discrimination. Some require us to denounce parent and child to the state, or to torture; others persuade us to avoid violence to all life. What prevents us from making such crucial distinctions in the humanities, especially in the study

of literature? Perhaps it is GRIM, acronym for the Great Rumbling Ideological Machine. This is an Orwellian machine, grinding out slogans and
theories — no one asks when "theory" is theory, when not — and scattering
all pavid spirits in its path. True, racism, sexism, imperialism surround us,
as do the neglect of poverty and abuses of power. But GRIM finally concerns itself less with these dire realities than with its own "ideospeak," its
own ideological clang.

In *Selves at Risk,* I neither argue for or against theory nor address a
particular "community of scholars" — this book must take its chances with
whoever reads it. I also try to heed the languages of texts, follow the "itin-
erary of the signifier"; but language also means to its users, and I concern
myself urgently with meanings, all kinds of meanings, stable, shifty, or
complex. Not Deconstructionist, Marxist even less, not a "straight" Humanist reader, I construe the books of our time with the discipline of my
experience, construe them finally as they move me and as I imagine they
move some readers. Still, no frame of intellectual tolerance is infinite, and
mine has its grains, knots, and warps. I confess: my bias is for an independent critical stance.

But what can "independent" mean in a transactive, semiotic, cybernetic
age, rife with simulacra, rampant with global cargo cults? It does not
mean, in any case, "robust" nineteenth-century individualism, from Andrew Carnegie to Dale Carnegie. It means, rather, a tough-minded, Emersonian "whim," to which I will return in later chapters. It means resistance
to one's own immediate community, not only to the Kremlin or the White
House, the KGB or the CIA, but also to "the herds of independent minds"
(Harold Rosenberg) that surround us. It means a certain agility, mobility,
nimbleness of spirit, what Lyotard calls *"sveltesse,"* with regard to all
systems. It means less a position than a process, a continual struggle among
perspectives. It means a recognition of difference, heterogeneity, a way to
inhabit the space of otherness. It means an acceptance of marginality, knowing how to skate on edges. It means a cheerful skepticism of solidarity,
of the raised voice, pointed finger, clenched fist. It means a distinctive style,
in writing, thinking, acting, in being in the world. It means an ability to
choose, answer, and perhaps to love. Can we attain these, in the West,
without some felt sense of self? I think not: hence my title, *Selves at Risk.*

The authors I engage here — some less canonical than others, all brightly
accomplished, and I quote from them copiously for that very reason —
exemplify different aspects of quest. But their exemplifications remain selective, refractions of the human spirit in stress. This makes *Selves at Risk*
selective too, not an exhaustive survey of a field. The book, rather, is a
small imitation of a quest, going over quests, or more precisely, going over
accounts of quests, re-covering them, in search of its own idea of quest.

Thus the book seems to be, in Aristotelian terms, an imitation of an imitation of an action. This is safe enough as adventures go, though all writing also makes its acquaintance with death: one ages in writing as one traverses the time of a book.

The book proceeds in three parts. The first explores some general issues pertaining to quest; here, and particularly in Chapter 2, is occasionally dense discussion of the topic. The second reviews, in fiction and nonfiction, works that begin to define the idea of quest. The third, more leisurely in pace, comprises three exemplary writers, Paul Bowles, Paul Theroux, and Peter Matthiessen, who develop that idea. Brief prefaces summarize the arguments of each part. Thus, in describing the structure of *Selves at Risk*, these précis may also hint at the syntax of quest. Introduction and Conclusion try to frame what must remain finally frameless, the radical aspirations of human beings. These aspirations, despite the epigraph from Edward Hoagland, are still in the American writer's keeping.

Part 1
Contexts
of Quest

Quests are horizons of personal desire, but that horizon also circles the world. Put another way, quests, even in narrower focus, illumine the concerns of men and women in society; they mirror the human universe.

In Part 1, therefore, I examine some contexts of quest: literary, philosophical, psychological, and geopolitical. I inquire, in Chapter 1, about the formal properties of quest as literature, its generic affiliations with myth, adventure, romance. In Chapter 2, I moot the question of the self, challenged now by sundry theories, and try to recover a pragmatic, a working concept of self, which sustains all our pursuits. Next, in Chapter 3, I review various motives of quest, those mysterious urgencies that impel men and women to far errands in the wilderness. But what is the politics of that "wilderness" now? This is the question I address in Chapter 4, address it in a world both planetized and tribalized, wherein powers, cultures, histories continually clash.

The contexts of quest, then, are also contexts of all human aspirations, and of the miseries to which we are heir in the postmodern world. Still, may not the idea of quest itself, personal quest in the face of high-tech genocide, hint at a larger destiny for our race? The hint, implicit in this first part, emerges, I hope, with ever greater insistence in Selves at Risk.

Chapter One
Quest as a Literary Mode:
The Forms of Quest

I distinguish in Literature a genre of major significance to me, which
would include those works where the [bull's] horn is present in one
form or another, where the author assumes the direct risk either of a
confession or of a subversive work, a work in which the human condition is confronted directly or "taken by the horns". . . .
— Michel Leiris

W 1

HAT IS QUEST, and what forms does it take? Ety-
mology leads to Latin *quaerere,* to ask or seek; and in English, meanings
cluster around substantives like search, inquiry, inquest, expedition, pursuit, venture, chivalrous enterprise, and even the collection of alms. There
is movement in the word, restlessness, the itch of want. There is a roving
curiosity in some fabulous or emblematic space, seeking knowledge —
knowledge of being, knowledge as being, some gnosis of a dangerous or
ultimate kind. Yet uncertainty shadows quest. A self, often solitary, is at
risk, and self-realization of the highest kind is the rare reward. But doubt
and strain contend there, even when the effort becomes its own mystery,
its own end or balm. How, then, define quest?

As always, definition proves elusive, asymptotic, insufficient to the
mind's need. What possessed Captain Ahab, lured Sinbad the Sailor, drove
the Wandering Jew? Was Odysseus or Alexander a leader, adventurer,
seeker? And closer to our time, Lindbergh and Hemingway — were they
merely celebrities or questers beyond fame?[1] What was Mishima, with his
exorbitant desire for purity, when he says: "I gladly go to meet the mes-
senger from the ends of the earth . . . and in the instant of my departure,
I abandon everything that is comfortable and familiar"?[2] And T. E. Lawrence, who became bound to his desert myth like Prometheus to his rock?

In another day, quest may have been defined by its genre, the forms
it takes; or if not defined, its ambiguities contained. But the idea of genre
has become questionable, as has the concept of literature itself. This has
prompted Alastair Fowler to claim that "variations in *paideia* mask a greater

difficulty in the concept of literature: namely, the instability of its generic structures."[3] Indeed, such instability often permits "individual works [to] convey literary meaning."[4] But what happens when the instability becomes almost a norm, as it has become in the febrile, experimental clime of the last hundred years? How judge by genre?

Our moment seems congenial to "carnivalization," proliferating in parody and pastiche, paracriticism and paraliterature, crossings of every kind.[5] Canons open, definitions blur, margins shift, leaving no clear line between inside and outside, text and context. Deconstructive terms like "trace," "difference," "supplement," "remainder," "ornament," "*parergon,*" and "*hors d'oeuvre*" contest all the binary concepts of the humanist tradition. Thus, in "The Law of Genre," Derrida argues for an "impurity" or "principle of contamination" lodged "within the heart of the law itself," making it a "mad law," even if madness fails to define it.[6]

How, then, engage contemporary quest as a literary mode, verbal construct? Perhaps by adverting briefly to its cognate historical types: myth, epic, and romance; the literature of travel and adventure; autobiography; conceivably the picaresque novel; certainly narratives of the American frontier; perhaps even the Sublime, transcending the human. Though these may not be clearly identifiable in postwar American quest — and are themselves impure genres — they help recall its provenance and transmutations, help reveal the particular energies of its evasive form. Thus, perhaps, may we gradually imagine, if not define, the mapless region of quest.

2

Quest reverts to myth which still pervades our social existence, informing our knowledge and arts. Originally, quests related to such narratives as the shamanistic flight, the hero's night journey, his search for ultimate knowledge. Later, these narratives provided the structures and archetypes of epic, romance, and picaresque, inspiring to this day the gothic novel, science fiction, the detective story, all manner of travel and action tales that find analogues in the great epics of the world.

We, of course, shun myth nowadays, preferring ideological "demystification." Yet myth inspired the masters of modernism, and impressed crucial thinkers — Nietzsche and Heidegger, for example — since Vico. Vico himself discovered the new historical science in the postulate that "the first gentile peoples, by a demonstrated necessity of nature, were poets who spoke in poetic characters."[7] Myths were the "civil histories" of these primordial poets; "tropic speech" was their first speech; metaphor constituted "the primary operation of the human mind."[8] And "when the golden bough" of life was "torn from its trunk" another grew in its place because

nature thought poetically.[9] For Vico, then, mythopoiesis was the necessary angel, the indwelling power of history.

More than a century later, James Frazer offered, in *The Golden Bough,*
a dramatic compendium of human destiny under the twin aspects of a
dying and rising god; and the old masters of psychoanalysis—Freud, Jung,
Rank, Roheim, Ferenczi, others—probed the archetypes of myth, dream,
and art. At the same time, the magi of literary modernism found in myth
a renewed sense of their world and word. Thomas Mann spoke for many
when he said, in "Freud and the Future": "The myth is the foundation of
life, the timeless *schema,* the pious formula into which life flows when it
reproduces its traits out of the unconscious."[10] A literary theory of myth
would later follow, propounded by such diverse critics as Joseph Campbell, Philip Wheelwright, Leslie Fiedler, and Northrop Frye. "And so it
was," writes Campbell, "that . . . the old horizons were dissolved and the
center of gravity of all learning shifted from the little areas of local pride
to a broad science of man himself in his new and single world."[11] In this
"broad science," or rather, in this mythic tapestry, we can pick out the
brilliant thread of quest.

The thread runs through Campbell's classic work, *The Hero with a
Thousand Faces.* Though Campbell knows that "no final system of interpretation" can apply to myth, he proposes a pattern, a "monomyth," of
separation, initiation, return: "A hero ventures forth from the world of
common day into a region of supernatural wonder: fabulous forces are
there encountered and a decisive victory is won: the hero comes back from
this mysterious adventure with the power to bestow boons on his fellow
man."[12] It is this "mysterious adventure" that also bears the name of quest,
a journey inward as well as outward—there are parallels between heroes,
artists, and mystics—a perilous journey of attainment and re-cognition.
Finally, the hero and his daemon become one. "The two . . . are thus
understood as the outside and inside of a single, self-mirrored mystery,
which is identical with the mystery of the manifest world. The great deed
of the supreme hero is to come to the knowledge of this unity in multiplicity and then to make it known."[13] This knowledge is at once sacred
and profane—spiritual, oneiric, erotic, martial—a knowledge of at-one-
ment within the great cosmogonic cycle.

In the ancient epics, those closest to the primary vision of myth, quest
and adventure are indeed inextricable, inextricable like life and death. In
the *Gilgamesh,* for instance, the titular hero, one-third man and two-thirds
god, strives mightily to attain everlasting life, only to fail when a serpent
steals from him the sweet flower of immortality. Beauty, strength, fame
will not suffice, though Gilgamesh possesses them all in supreme measure;
nor wisdom even, if it cannot bring the conquest of death. In despair he

cries out to Utnapishtim, the only man to escape the Flood and achieve immortality:

> Why should not my cheeks be starved and my face drawn? Despair is in my heart and my face is the face of one who has made a long journey. . . . Enkidu, my brother whom I had loved, the end of mortality has overtaken him. I wept for him seven days and nights till the worm fastened on him. . . . For this I have wandered over the world, I have crossed many difficult ranges, I have crossed the seas, I have wearied myself with travelling; my joints are aching, and I have lost acquaintance with sleep which is sweet. . . . I have killed the bear and the hyena, the lion and panther, the tiger, the stag and the ibex, all sorts of wild game and the small creatures of the pastures. . . . Oh, father Utnapishtim, you who have entered the assembly of the gods, I wish to question you concerning the living and the dead, how shall I find the life for which I am searching?[14]

The epic hero ventures, suffers, overcomes; but death, or rather a deep knowledge of something beyond life or death, seems always the true object of his quest. His heroic self aspires to what is not itself, yet often remains entrapped in fame, glory, just another version of the self.

Adventure, I have said, is essential to epic quests, though raw action is seldom their goal. The *Gilgamesh* begins: "I will proclaim to the world the deeds of Gilgamesh. This was the man to whom all things were known; this was the king who knew the countries of the world. He was wise, he saw mysteries and knew secret things, he brought us a tale of the days before the flood. He went on a long journey, was weary, worn out with labour, returning he rested, he engraved on a stone the whole story."[15] Indeed, Gilgamesh is a gnostic of love, history, nature, and dream, and epic *writer* no less than warrior or king.

In the most resonant quests or adventures, then, we find a spiritual element, an ontic affirmation, an urge first to transgress, then to restore the order of Creation in pure moments of being. As Paul Zweig luminously remarks: "The gleams of intensity which invest . . . [such moments] have an otherworldly quality, as if a man's duel with risk were not a 'vacation' at all, but a plunge into essential experience. . . . Adventure stories transpose our dalliance with risk into a sustained vision."[16] The vision can be demonic; for the true mythic quester predates the ordinary hero, standing outside the circle of social obligations. He offers us the disturbing "spectacle of the self-determined man who defends not us, but himself. His inner destiny is his law. He reclaims for man an area of the forbidden ground."[17] He conquers the underworld because he contains it in part; the problem is inserting him into a human world, into society, a problem persisting to our day.

All this may suggest an archetypal pattern, though archetypes, like

myths, now seem suspect, without ontological, without even psychological, ground. Yet their historic weight presses on us all, and their exemplary
recurrence in the world's literature is what we call *tradition,* perpetuated
by readers and writers as they attend continually to compelling forms of
their past. That is why Eliot adverts in *The Waste Land* — is it not our modern epic? — to Jessie Weston's work on the Grail. That is also why Jessie
Weston herself concludes:

> The Grail story is not *du fond en comble* the product of imagination, liter-
> ary or popular. At its root lies the record, more or less distorted, of an ancient
> Ritual, having for its ultimate object the initiation into the secret of the sources
> of life, physical and spiritual. . . . The study and the criticism of the Grail
> literature will possess an even deeper interest, a more absorbing fascination,
> when it is definitely recognized that we possess in that literature a unique ex-
> ample of the restatement of an ancient and august Ritual in terms of imper-
> ishable Romance.[18]

Origins and influences aside, literature lives on fathomless interactions
with its verbal past. Weston's "imperishable Romance" becomes for Northrop Frye a great order of literature in which "romance, tragedy, irony,
and comedy are episodes in a total quest-myth."[19] Frye, we know, articu-
lates this "total quest-myth" into cycles of Comedy (Spring), Romance
(Summer), Tragedy (Autumn), and Irony (Winter), and identifies its protagonist, in declining order, as the divine hero of myth, the human hero
of epic or romance, the *alazon* or *miles gloriosus* of tragedy, the *eiron* of
comedy, and the *pharmakos* or victim of farce and satire.

But the erudite taxonomy of Frye concerns us less than his perception
of quest-romance as central to both the formal and historical schemes of
literature. For Frye, "quest-romance has analogies to both rituals and
dreams. . . . Translated into dream terms, the quest-romance is the search
of the libido or desiring self for a fulfilment that will deliver it from the
anxieties of reality but will still contain the reality. . . . Translated into ritual
terms, the quest-romance is the victory of fertility over the waste land."[20]
Episodic in structure, because adventure is intrinsic to its plot, quest takes
naturally a sequential or processional form. Four phases mark the hero's
journey: *agon* or conflict, *pathos* or death struggle, *sparagmos* or (provisional) dismemberment, and *anagnorisis* or recognition of a newborn
world. The enemy — giant, behemoth, leviathan — is a demonic power, associated with winter, darkness, sterility, the old world of sin and death. These
motifs of quest command us because "they impart the mysterious rapport
with nature that so often marks the central figure of romance," because
they enact "a greater degree of metaphorical identification," because they
recount the essential dialectic of existence, which sometimes "means that

subtlety and complexity are not much favored."[21] Hence the apocalyptic or messianic undertone of quest, in epic or romance, in Scriptures as well.

Quest, then, "looks forward" to literature, and "looks back" to myth, though it may also contain imaginative elaborations that Northrop Frye calls, in *The Secular Scripture,* fabulous. Frye's distinction between mythic and fabulous stories clarifies the development of quest. The former, embodying the significant concerns of a society, "transmit a legacy of shared allusion"; the latter, aimed to entertain or amuse, "meet the imaginative needs of the community." [22] The latter, however, permit a greater degree of inventiveness, of individual creativity, precisely because their fictions carry a lighter weight of beliefs. Still, mythic narratives may become fabulous when one culture supersedes another, as in the case of classical myths in Christian societies, or biblical stories in a secular world. The quest romance moves in the space between the mythic and the fabulous, moving historically toward the latter, until realistic fiction threatens to usurp its place. But quest is also dialectic, as Frye sees: "romantic" and "realistic" modes continue their interplay; the novel itself is but displaced-quest or "parody-romance."

For Frye, then, quest-romance has become a "secular scripture," or better, *a dialectic element of literature.* It retains, in various measure, its primordial powers, inward with death, dream, danger, and desire. At once archaic and prophetic, populist and elitist, collective and individual, it marvelously recreates the possibilities of the present, wherein past and future meet. It offers a vision of humanity reconciled to nature and reconciled to itself in fraternity. At its best, Frye says, it aspires to great literature: "the genuine infinite as opposed to the phony infinite," as opposed "to the endless adventures . . . of the wandering of desire."[23] At its best, it may even hint of silence, the real silence that "is the end of speech, not the stopping of it," the "last Sabbath vision in our greatest romance."[24]

3

In *The Progress of Romance through Times, Countries, and Manners,* Clara Reeve demonstrates the relevance of romance to the corpus of world literature since 1785. But romance, quest, adventure, are also *narrative,* which is nothing less than a way of representing reality, of experiencing and sharing it in a distinctly human mode; they remind us that literature itself may be an essential category of existence, like time and space, precisely because story prefigures death.

This is the burden of Walter Benjamin's signal essay "The Storyteller." Great authors, when narrative, differ least from the anonymous tellers of tales, Benjamin argues; thus they render *experience*—a talismanic word for him—and offer counsel "woven in the fabric of real life," offer true wisdom.[25] Thus the decline of storytelling in the modern world is really a decline in the value of experience itself, coinciding with the rise of the novel, a *book* by a solitary author to a solitary reader, neither of whom able to attest his most inward concerns. More basic still is the devaluation of eternity. Benjamin puts it thus:

> The idea of eternity has ever had its strongest source in death. If this idea declines, so we reason, the face of death must have changed. It turns out that this change is identical with one that has diminished the communicability of experience to the same extent as the art of storytelling has declined.[26]

In a brilliant swerve, Benjamin goes on to compare the involuntary sequence of images that flit before a dying man's eyes, revealing to him the ineffable narrative of his life, with the authority at the very source of story. Thus the real storyteller is also "the man who could let the wick of his life be consumed completely by the gentle flame of his story. . . . The storyteller is the figure in which the righteous man encounters himself."[27]

Story, word, deed, death thus seem of one imagination and one memory compact. For a seeker or adventurer also speaks; and when the danger passes, Zweig says, "the adventurer, like the mystic, is left stranded in the slower world of time. Then words are needed to clothe his idleness. . . . They help to preserve his identity through the *little death* which follows the climax."[28] Hence the double action of an adventurer's story, perhaps of Story itself, both recovering and defeating time, the former in the run of worldly narrative, the latter in the stillness of some transcendent intuition or sacred repetition, the ecstasy of eternal recurrence.

4

Yet just as Benjamin historicized death, so must we now briefly historicize quest in literature, historicize even its transports and epiphanies. The novel, we have seen, displaced romance, the novel itself being displaced romance. This entailed the introversion of quest, culminating with the hieratic art of James, Proust, Joyce, Faulkner, and Kafka. At the same time, however, that the novel pursued its high, modernist destiny—it had begun as a lowly, rowdy picaresque and was to prove child of many destinies—romance and adventure maintained themselves in another, more popular, tradition. The two traditions continually crossed, creating endless mutations of "romance" and "realism," "fictional" and "empiric" modes, "high" and "popular" culture, "sacred" (revealed) and "secular" (imaginative) scripture, the very lack of any symmetry in these diads betokening the anarchic energy of narrative.[29] Thus Zweig is right to insist that in "the transformed shape of popular romance, 'adventure' preserves itself from the corrosions of novelistic morality," even though the "cross-fertilization between novelistic narrative and popular fantasy" had become particularly intense in the nineteenth century.[30]

Certainly one such hybrid genre is the traveler's tale, akin to quest, adventure, and autobiography, partaking of fact and fantasy in various measure. The genre is ancient; Roman prose writers like Petronius, Lucian, and Apuleius developed the first-person journey narrative which, once interiorized, could become confession or autobiography.[31] Earlier even, the *Odyssey* tested its hero more in travel than in battle. By the start of the nineteenth century, in any case, more travel and adventure books had been written, and eagerly read, than any other kind of literature. Fluid as genre, travel then pervaded the novel, leading one scholar to remark: "With writers such as Céline and Bellow the fictional protagonist becomes a traveler like the great travelers of all time — Marco Polo, Columbus, Pinto, Cook. With writers such as Naipaul and Raban, the travel book and the novel become one form, as they did sometimes with Challe, with Sterne, and with Smollett in the eighteenth century."[32]

The idea, the sense of motion, refers with particular force to American writers, disposed to quests, errands, journeys, to romances that in their symbolic action transpose space and time, dream and reality, nature and history. Though aware of their precedents in the Bible, classics, or European literature, these authors recalled the "journey-centeredness" of their historical experience, putting voyages to their own artistic use.[33] For voyages are translations, carryings across physical or psychic boundaries; they are metaphors as the etymology of that word (Greek *metapherein,* to transfer) proves; sometimes, they are even hyperboles of the unspeakable, the Sublime. Between the Old and the New World, wherever these may be, there are real and figurative transactions, transumptions in space, time, and language, to which every American is heir.

American fiction, then, in one of its large, vivid strains, opted for "the territory ahead"; for a verbal "world elsewhere"; for fabulous, folkloric, and mythic forms; for a perpetual "reconstitution of romance within the novel"; for pursuit of the true "IT . . . the self in its wholeness."[34] "Whatever else the Great American Novel may be," Janis Stout maintains, "it has been, throughout its history, a fiction zestfully committed to motion and to the free, transcendent individual."[35]

This commitment, however, did not always elicit the zest of writers after Henry James. Some, in fact, attributed to it the diminishment of consciousness in American letters, a growing impoverishment of imagination. Thus Wright Morris:

In the nineteenth century the writer took to the woods or the high seas, literally as well as figuratively. In the present century the same flight is achieved through nostalgia, rage, or some such ruling passion from which the idea of the present, the opposing idea, has been excluded. In the American writer of genius the ability to function has been retained—with the exception of James—by depreciating the intelligence.

For more than a century the territory ahead has been the world that lies somewhere behind us, a world that has become, in the last few decades, a nostalgic myth. On the evidence, which is impressive, it is the myth that now cripples the imagination, rather than the dark and brooding immensity of the continent. It is the territory behind that defeats our writers of genius, not America.[36]

Morris's opinion may have been too gloomy, as I hope to show. Already, in the sixties, Leslie Fiedler discerned, in *The Return of the Vanishing American,* a New Western without nostalgia or defeat, a kind of hallucinatory adventure—witness Ken Kesey's *One Flew over the Cuckoo's Nest*—skirting madness, and suggesting rebirth in the Future, not the Past. In our own moment, writers "taking to the woods" have produced a literature of remarkable vivacity, rich in its figurative transactions between mental states, between cultural worlds.

5

Such figurative transactions enliven not only American but nearly all modern travel literature. Hence the interest of a work like Robert Byron's *The Road to Oxiana*—the British remain the most enterprising, certainly the most prolific, travelers—which provides, Paul Fussell claims, "opportunities for the richest kind of imaginative genius to exercise itself."[37] Hence, too, the editorial in a special travel issue of *Granta,* which imputes to its texts "the sheer glee of story-telling, a narrative eloquence that situates them, with wonderful ambiguity, somewhere between fiction and fact," and concludes that "if there is a revival in travel writing, this ambiguity—this generic androgyny—is partly responsible for it."[38]

Some critics, we have seen, would contend that the golden age of travel ended perhaps with the first, certainly the second, world war. It was an age without passports, without jets or packaged tours, an age of privileged, clever, and eccentric travelers, scouring zanily their receding empires. This prompts Fussell to distinguish wryly between the explorer, the traveler, and the tourist—all of whom, I believe, touch variously on the motive of quest. "All three make journeys," he remarks, "but the explorer seeks the undiscovered, the traveler that which has been discovered by the mind working in history, the tourist that which has been discovered by entrepreneurship and prepared for him by the arts of mass publicity."[39] If explorers met high adventure (and were knighted too), travelers could at least entertain high hopes of misadventure; tourists merely consumed.

Quest, I have insisted, engages spirit and risk. Travelers, of course, may move in an exotic space, and travel itself may become a quest for strangeness, for the self in some *other* guise or disguise. Travelers cross borders too, and this recalls the debased equivalent of the moment in romance when the outsetting hero defeats or conciliates, in Joseph Campbell's terms, "the 'shadowy presence' that guards the hero's passage out of his own land and lets him through the gate into his adventures."[40] Indeed, touched by some modern malady, wounded somehow or infirm, travelers may also travail in an obscure spiritual cause, as if called by the echo of myth.

Whatever the call, we may wonder: who speaks, and in what kind of speech? Here we return to the question of genre. Travel narratives, more than quest romances, are a species of auto-bio-graphy. In them, a first-person narrator serves at the same time as vagrant, witness, hero, writer. A traveler goes "there," sees, acts, records. He may give himself to these functions unequally, and this will shape the story. He may identify closely with the material — landscape, legend, people — or may hold aloof; this, too, will shape the story. He may recount his tale as adventure, memoir, meditation, or combine them all as Hemingway does when, within the imbrications of *The Green Hills of Africa,* he offers his Statement on American Literature. Or he may give us a kind of poetry, as do many travel writers, thus raising travel to the condition of verbal performance.

The traveler we read is, after all, a *writer.* Who speaks? A seeker or adventurer, perhaps, but above all an *artist.* This artist often takes the strangeness and solitude of travel as an allegory of the human condition. "The writing travellers — Theroux, Chatwin, Thubron and the rest — offer themselves up as a type of estranged modern hero, willing to travail *stylishly* [my emphasis] on our behalf and, like Ulysses, return to report that Abroad is Abroad and Home is Home," says Jonathan Raban, himself a traveling writer.[41] But the journey becomes also symbolic of the writing process itself, and of the artist's own quest for self-understanding.[42] In this symbolic perspective, inner and outer world, letter and deed, merge.

Indeed, writing and travel engage in profound collusions, as Michel Butor perceives in his brilliant, elliptic essay on the subject. We all recall the childhood truisms: every story is a journey, every book a galleon, every page a window on neverland. But the truisms go deeper. Travel requires reading the signs and manners of foreign places; and reading itself requires travel or displacement as the eyes move across the page, as the mind flies beyond every word on the page. Travel is also writing. Romantic voyagers —

Chateaubriand, Lamartine, Gautier, Nerval, Flaubert — were often bookish writers; books frequently inspired their trips; and since they were writers, they often read on their trips, wrote journals, and later produced books
of their own. Butor says: "They travel in order to write, they travel while
writing, because, for them, travel *is* writing."[43] Besides, most travelers mark
(write on) the lands they visit; they name or disfigure them in some clear
or hidden way. Finally, writing itself is a kind of travel, a text of secret
displacements. "If reading is a crossing — even if it often pretends to be
only an erased passage through the cloud of whiteness — writing, always
the transformation of reading, is necessarily even more so."[44] Even as
Butor writes two words in a sentence, the earth turns, traveling also in space
with its writer.

6

Quest is adventure, adventure travel, travel autobiography: is this not a
continuum of selves, or perhaps personae, at various degrees of risk?

Autobiography is, of course, the singular voice of literature. That voice
has become of late both rasping and rife. All manner of autobiographies
vie for our attention in factual or fictional, "factional" or "fictual," guise.
Why this greed for self-witness? Perhaps because we live in a self-regarding
age; perhaps because through autobiography we deny the obsolescence of
the self in mass society; perhaps because we lack consensus in our values,
and so must ground our deepest articulations on the self, on death itself,
the invisible ground of every autobiography.

But perhaps, too, we choose autobiography because it expresses all the
ambiguities of our postmodern culture. In the current climate of our ironic
self-awareness, autobiography has indeed lost much of its innocence. It
has become the vehicle of our epistemic evasions, our social and psychic
vexations. The innate contradictions of autobiography emerge to confirm
the cunning of our knowledge. This is evident in the questions that both
writers and critics — theoreticians all — of autobiography now ask.[45] Here,
schematically, are some queries they present in their perscrutations of the
mode:

Can a life ever be translated into words? Is there no irreconcilable tension between word and deed? Was John the Apostle or Goethe nearer the
mark, one proclaiming the Word, the other the Act (*die Tat*)? Is autobiography simply *écriture* as Barthes says; or do words, like "white ants," devour the body, "the pillar of plain wood" which is life incarnate, as Mishima
claims?[46]

Can a life still in progress — the dead don't write autobiographies, they
only have biographies written about them — ever grasp or understand it-

self? Can it predict a future, that particular event of the future which would permit it to organize retrospectively its past? Isn't autobiography, therefore, doubly partial, twice biased, in the sense of being both personal and incomplete, partisan and fragmentary?

Again, is there any hope of distinguishing between fact and fiction in autobiography, any more than we can distinguish between them in our media? Isn't memory sister to imagination, kin to nostalgia, desire, and deceit? Isn't memory sometimes even an agent to mendacity, meant consciously to mislead or manipulate history?

Therefore, isn't autobiography a labor of self-creation no less than of self-cognizance or self-expression, itself a quest rather than the record of a quest? Isn't it a mask, the mask of an absent face, that becomes actually the face we show and others see? Hence, doesn't autobiography affect the real, dying subject, as if words could change the life they presume merely to describe?

Put another way, isn't autobiography shifty in that a first person present (I, now) pretends to be a third person past (he/she, then), and in the process alters both characters? Or is it rather that we all continually live in a dimension that is not wholly past, present, or future, but a blend of them all, a dimension that autobiography simply makes explicit, rendering it into speech?

If so, isn't every reader a vicarious autobiographer, a reader become writer in the shared act of cultural understanding, in the common shadow of human mortality? Isn't every autobiography, as Gertrude Stein put it, "everybody's autobiography"? Or do the *conventions* of autobiography finally prevail to make it a way of reading the written self of another?

At the same time, isn't all autobiography both an act of dying (pretending to round off one's life in writing) and also a wager on immortality (aspiring to remembrance through print)? Isn't it a counterfeit personal ending as well as a pseudo eternity?

And precisely how does autobiography transform the most private confession — from Augustine through Rousseau to Elizabeth Taylor — into public expression, the "mirror of an age," as we grandly say? How can the most prurient or idiosyncratic document offer us a vivid sense of its epoch?

Last, cutting across previous queries, how do we ourselves, in this time and in this place, write our knowledge of this writing, write the history and theory of autobiography as genre?

Such conundrums, no doubt, betray our graphomania, betray also the convolutions of autobiography as a cultural form. The more critics attend to it, the more its form escapes them. The more they heed the written self, the more they incline to disperse, dissolve it, "yet another version of the principle of absent presence, pervasive in contemporary literature."[47] Despite it all, the autobiographical imperative endures, particularly in America where, as Kazin says, "the experience of being so much a 'self'— constantly explaining oneself and telling one's story—is as traditional in the greatest American literature as it is in a barroom."[48] And so does the self itself, as we shall see in the following chapter, endure.

7

We can suppose, then, that quest, adventure, travel, and autobiography coalesce in a contemporary, hybrid mode that conveys both the perplexities of the postmodern condition and the ancient, visionary powers of myth. This mode, defying any comfortable distinction between fiction and fact, employs the sophisticated resources of narrative to raise fundamental problems of human existence, problems personal, social, and metaphysical.

But is the mode only contemporary, really new? Literary historians can trace it to old epics and romances, or at least to Cervantes, at the dawn of the novel. They are not wrong to trace it so. For contemporary quest assumes the imaginative freedom of romance, its liberation of desire; but it assumes as well the modern novel with all its reflexive and nonmimetic techniques since Proust, Joyce, Faulkner. (Witness, in the germane form of autobiography, the preponderance of poetic over historical modes in the last hundred years.)[49] At the same time, contemporary quest reacts against the postmodern assumptions of "exhaustion," finding in certain re-membered forms, re-newed values, the sources of its own "replenishment."[50]

Central to this renewed quest, moving as the quest moves, the center itself still and moving, we discover "the hero with a thousand faces," an ontological voyager, a doer, sufferer, over-reacher, at once an alien and founder of cities, another version of ourselves. Thus the "I" that speaks to us through contemporary quest is both knowing and naive, historic and primordial, worldly and ghostly; in it, as in Grail romances, individual, social, and cosmological elements fuse. An "I" speaks; its words constitute reality even as they confess its current entrapments; its confessions draw us into a circle of experience that remains exotic to us.

An "I" speaks, yet the words of quest also hint their own abolition in death, in silence, in extreme spiritual risk—abolition in all those final states that make literature itself superfluous. "What difference does it make who is speaking?" Michel Foucault asks.[51] None, in one way; and all the difference in the world, the difference that matters, if abolition of self is to matter, in another, more interesting, way.

Chapter Two
The Subject of Quest:
Self, Other, Difference

Here's for the plain old Adam, the simple genuine self against the whole world.

—Ralph Waldo Emerson

In my case, the effort for these years to live in the dress of Arabs, and to imitate their mental foundation, quitted me of my English self, and let me look at the West and its conventions with new eyes: they destroyed it all for me. At the same time I could not sincerely take on the Arab skin: it was an affectation only. Easily was a man made an infidel, but hardly might he be converted to another faith. I had dropped one form and not taken on the other, and was become like Mohammed's coffin in our legend, with a resultant feeling of intense loneliness in life, and a contempt, not for other men, but for all they do.

—T. E. Lawrence

1

W HO SEEKS, and in seeking speaks? The question is, in large part, autobiographical: it concerns a vital and articulate self. But the self itself is now in dire question, declared a "fiction" by a variety of contemporary theories. A fiction? Perhaps an effective fiction, more durable than all the theories that proclaim it so. Call it an eidolon, blooded, sweaty, and rank with the rage of history. But what of the other, everything that the self is not? Is it a fiction too, though of another kind? If so, how represent differences (between the self and all its others), differences of language or culture, race or gender, differences of desire?

Such queries, though intractable, point to the radical subject of quest, a risking, writing, written subject. The risk is double: first to a historical, *writing*, dying subject in the world, next to a *written* subject, alive to us only in a verbal text, alive so long as readers recall or read, an interpretive risk. This chapter addresses these and other risks of the self, the self mainly as a historical and narrative function in literature.

2

Consider first the written self. Its field is autobiography in the broad sense. We have already glimpsed some general complexities of the form in an earlier chapter; here we need only focus on certain difficulties of the "I" in autobiographical narratives.

The issues, though legion, center on the textualization of the autobiographical self, its dispersal into language, depriving it of any ontological status within or without the text. Autobiography is thus "de-faced;" and death itself becomes, as Paul de Man says, "a displaced name for a linguistic predicament," that of personification or "prosopopoeia of the voice and the name."[1] For de Man, then, autobiography "is not a genre or a mode, but a figure of reading or of understanding that occurs, to some degree, in all texts."[2] Hence, de Man avers, all texts are autobiographical and, by the same token, "none of them is or can be."

The argument is somewhat precious, and pragmatically untrue. If prosopopoeia "is the trope of an autobiography, by which one's name . . . is made intelligible and memorable as a face," all figures of prosopopoeia are not identical.[3] Nor can autobiography be explained by a single figurative feature—a displacement of death—which purports to disfigure the self and dissolve the genre. Most readers, in fact, *continue to read certain texts as autobiographies,* welcoming an encounter with an *imagined* life, a subjectivity, other than their own. They may read rhetorically, as de Man invariably does; but they may also read passionally, experientially, responding to a felt reality, a reality neither "present" nor "absent," neither immediate nor intrusively mediated. In brief, they read, as the best readers read, with their own sense of death (or self) alive to them, and in doing so experience new possibilities for both self and otherness. Janet Varner Gunn puts it aptly:

> the reader experiences the autobiographical text as an occasion of discovery: of seeing in the text the heretofore unexpressed or unrecognized depth of the reader's self—not as a mirror image, nor even as a particular manifestation of some shared idea of selfhood, but as an instance of interpretive activity that *risks* display. What the reader finds displayed is that vulnerability which makes it possible to celebrate the finitude of his or her own selving.[4]

Advocates of "the death of autobiography," however, may demur, adducing the discourse of psychoanalysis, the "talking cure." In that discourse —here we cross from the written to the writing, from the textual to the dying self—the patient's autobiography is a narrative, enmeshed in dream, wish, memory, in fact and fantasy, rumor and reflection. Exhaustive analysis, as Freud admits, may not lead to "real occurrences" but rather reveal "products of the imagination . . . which are intended to serve as some kind of symbolic representation of real wishes and intents," the ineluctable "truth of phantasies."[5] Who, then, really speaks? What remains of the sovereign subject among this conscious and unconscious débris? What becomes of autobiography? Gregory Jay wittily answers: "After Freud, autobiography is not the tale of things done, but of meanings made and unmade: every action is a symptom, every statement a symbol, every narrative a dream of desire," and "death yields the profit of the autobiographical speculation, as *la mort propre* becomes *l'amour propre.*"[6]

Good enough. But we should not dazzle by a deconstruction that explodes all "essentialist" notions, leaving every urgent question hanging sullenly in the air. The self may rest on no ontological rock; yet as a functional concept, as a historical construct, as a habit of existence, above all as an experienced or existential reality, it serves us all even as we deny it theoretically. The self represents something to us, even when we select some aspect of it to act. We do the same in reading or writing texts. "To seek the personal focus of an autobiographical truth," Francis Hart observes, "is to inquire what kind of 'I' is selected, how far the selected 'I' is an inductive invention and how far an intentional creation, and whether one single or one multiple 'I' persists throughout the work."[7] Even Roland Barthes, toward the end of his life, saddened by some obscure sense of failure, sought to "escape from the prison house of critical metalanguage," and to write in a simpler, more compassionate idiom, testifying to his private experience in the limpid space of *La Chambre claire.*[8]

This intimates an ethical, perhaps spiritual, element in the question of the self. The element is pertinent to the literature of quest, particularly American quests, which assume a voluntarist, sometimes visionary, stance, pertinent as well to autobiography, especially American autobiographies wherein the dream of self-creation becomes moral imperative no less than historical fact. Thus Albert Stone, in his capacious study of American autobiography, remarks: "To stress the self as the creator of history—even, at times, as the fabricator of fantasies—maximizes one's freedom from circumstances and social stereotype. In this way, an ideal self always coexists with an actual—that is, a determined—historical reality."[9]

The status of this ideal self may be only fiduciary or metaphoric, contingent on some trust. But trust makes the foundations of our lives, in history, religion, or art—the art of self-witness, the art of quest or risk. Without a confident sense of (well)being in the world, without a sense of self, we risk to lose the world and mutilate the lives we touch, lives both in literature and in the flesh.

3

Trust, however, must be adequate to its occasion. Any fiduciary grounding
of the self must reckon with shadows, ambiguities, clinging to it throughout the ages. I mean the Western self, not only in autobiography or writing of any kind, but also in that larger, terrible perspective we call history.

From the start, it seems, men have indulged their "frenzy of renown":
extreme and transcendent gestures of self-affirmation meant to conquer
mortality. This "dream of fame in Western society," Leo Braudy says, was
ever "inseparable from the ideal of personal freedom"; it also occupied
"that strange and vitally important area where matters of the spirit and
matters of the flesh meet."[10] In such extreme gestures, of Achilles or Alexander say, the human condition finds a blazing, if momentary, focus. Most
often, the gestures are performed on foreign ground; the hero must forth,
as in the case of Achilles or Alexander, and of Odysseus even more. Great
deeds require risk and displacement, even if they require, in the end, a
prodigal return.

But the heroic self has always elicited our ambivalence, shades of envy,
admiration, resentment, doubt. Diogenes ordered Alexander out of his
sun, and Plato placed the self in metaphysical chains. The Judeo-Christian
tradition—witness the Book of Job, the Epistles of Paul, the *Confessions*
of Augustine—cast black suspicion on the self. Buddhism, we know, went
farther still, denying the individual self any reality. Indeed, the task of all
mysticism, East or West, has been to empty out the self, void it utterly,
in an expectancy both fierce and tranquil.

This stubborn ambivalence toward heroic self-assertion reflects itself,
with softer shades, in our attitude toward narcissism, which Paul Zweig
engagingly traces in *The Heresy of Self-Love*. Zweig focuses on "the West's
millennia-long fascination with Narcissus; deploring his inhuman solitude,
admiring him as a figure of fulfillment and transcendence," Zweig concludes:

> In the speculative fantasies of the Gnostics, in the programmatic self-
> indulgence of the Medieval Brethren of the Free Spirit, in the almost object-
> less love poems of Provence, in Adam Smith's theory of self-interest, in the
> radical social criticism of the nineteenth century, we find the same cult of self-
> love, along with the same foreboding that self-love will undermine the teeter-
> ing fabric of sociability.[11]

Zweig discloses his own stance toward Narcissus in the subtitle of his book:
"A Study of Subversive Individualism." Surprisingly, Narcissus proves to
be a figure of serene resistance, of meditative renitence, opposing everything current, common, collective, a mirror, so to speak, of the "ambiva-

lent warfare—call it a dialectic—between subversive individuals and the large, moralized embrace of society. . . ."[12] In this "ambivalent warfare," as we shall see, seekers continually engage, as does Zweig himself in two other works, *The Adventurer* and the autobiographical *Three Journeys,* which excellently engage the subject of quest.

I do not mean, of course, to convey in a few pages the history of the Western self—such a history is far too various, devious, capacious.[13] I mean simply to elicit a few implications of the written self in autobiographical narratives, including adventure and quest; and to link these implications with a historic equivocation toward the idea of self. In the last century, that idea endured more powerful, more resonant, provocations from Kierkegaard, Marx, and Nietzsche.

Kierkegaard, we know, proposed a subjectivity so inward, solitary, and radical as to be nearly indefinable, except perhaps with respect to God; the crowd was ever Kierkegaard's untruth. This subjectivity could dissolve itself in masks: the "pseudonymity of anonymity" of Johannes de Silentio, Johannes Climacus, Frater Taciturnus, Victor Eremita, Nicholas Notabene, Constantine Constantius, Inter et Inter, a chorus of ventriloquists casting doubt on every uttered sound, every written word.[14] For Kierkegaard himself, the "real" Kierkegaard, true despair was always despair of self, the universal sickness unto death. Nonetheless, the self remained for him a zone of dialectical freedom. "For the self is a synthesis in which the finite is the limiting factor, and the infinite is the expanding factor . . . ," he wrote. "The self is in sound health and free from despair only when, precisely by having been in despair, it is grounded transparently in God."[15] This revokes the Enlightenment, or more precisely, drastically revokes its secular, bourgeois idea of the self, which permitted the identity of thought and being, a "chimera of abstraction."

Marx assaulted that idea in the name of another god, History, though it failed him. Proclaiming the dictatorship of the proletariat, the dissolution of class, and the abolition of property, he chose to define the individual as an "ensemble of social relations."[16] Unlike Vitruvian Man, this "ensemble" could not hold the center; society obeyed impersonal, material forces; class conflicts determined history; the collective was destiny. Otherwise the fate of the self was illusory freedom or inevitable alienation. Individualistic theories seemed to him "Robinsonades" (from Robinson Crusoe). And though he valued in principle personal development, opposing reifications of every kind, he also diminished the self to itself, shrinking its domain in both theory and practice. The self became simply a "product" rather than, say, accident, invention, pattern, process, or mutation, more plausible metaphors of the self than the mechanistic idiom of "production" that dismally prevails in critical discourse today.

No two thinkers could have been more dissimilar than Nietzsche and Marx, yet both concur in the deprecation of the self. "The 'subject' is only a fiction: the ego does not exist at all," Nietzsche famously wrote; and again: "The assumption of one single subject is perhaps unnecessary; perhaps it is just as permissible to assume a multiplicity of subjects. . . ."[17] Nietzsche, we note, negates the self as an ontological fact or originary cause; he does not deny it conative, affective, or functional powers. Indeed, the self appears as an expression, one of many, of the "will to power," a self scattered among the multitudinous languages that constitute it, and that it constitutes. Invented, projected, discursive—here are premonitions of Freud and Lacan—the self must be construed like any discourse. Yet, for all that, the self remains a creature of the primary "will to power," corrupted and perverted by the ascetic ideals of the Judeo-Christian tradition which turned man into a "torture chamber," a "pining and desperate prisoner," sick of himself.[18]

Nietzsche looks back to Kierkegaard, forward to Freud. Like many thinkers of our own century, he perceives the self as a "fiction," or rather as a linguistic phenomenon. Unlike them, he endows it with a dynamism, a conatus, that they, recalling the "blood-dimmed tide" (Yeats) of two world wars, hesitate to concede. To these belated thinkers we must now look for the most current challenges to the questing self.

4

Who is Oedipus? Or what does Freud want? We have already referred to his "truth of phantasies" in the talking cure. This "truth," truly an enigma, reposes on Freud's own conception of the individual (ego, id, superego) as a largely unconscious entity, in the grip of instinctual drives. Freud himself struggled heroically to win a larger domain for the conscious ego, a struggle he believed himself to have finally lost. Dream, myth, art, slips of the tongue could disclose flickers of the unconscious; sublimation could, in some measure, relieve the instincts; but the self—a term he largely avoided —remained at best a tragic battleground between Eros and Thanatos, eternal "giants that our nurse-maids try to appease with their lullaby about heaven."[19] Autonomy, coherence, self-mastery, even simple happiness, proved to be dubious fictions, the past of an illusion. And was not the ego itself the silent abode of the death instinct?[20] How then give the Adamic self any credence, let alone sovereignty?

Presumably, the self was always largely unconscious—or did it become so only after Freud? The question is not entirely frivolous. Our perceptions of the self, the models we make of it, affect our self-apprehension, self-presentation. In the last hundred years, as we have seen, the self took a linguistic turn. This turn was nowhere sharper than in Freud's most arcane disciple, Jacques Lacan, who construed the grammar of the self and read its "lettered unconscious" in the "patient's Word." Born in a mirror, as the infant first recognizes its specular image, "the I is precipitated in a primordial form, before it is objectified in the dialectic of identification with the other, and before language restores to it, in the universal, its function as subject."[21] This Lacanian self, first specular then textual, remains heterogeneous, multiple, indeterminate, quite like a signifier jostling among the infinite signifiers of the Symbolic Order. Hence the phenomenon of *aphanisis,* the subject's "fading," its alienation or "fundamental division."[22] *Aphanisis* rumors the end of reflexive certainty, the quietus of the Cartesian *cogito.*

The rumor is widespread among linguists, ethologists, literary critics, among philosophers who welcome the "death of the subject" with a certain personal glee. Arguing that self and language are coextensive, coeval, Emile Benveniste simply prefers to situate the former in the latter rather than to deny subjectivity. "It is in and through language that man constitutes himself as a *subject,* because language alone establishes the concept of 'ego' in reality," Benveniste says in a formulation that has become nearly apophantic since Ferdinand de Saussure distinguished between *langue* (impersonal codes) and *parole* (personal utterance).[23] Claude Lévi-Strauss makes his point more grandly: "If there is one conviction that has been intimately borne upon the author . . . during twenty years devoted to the study of myths . . . it is that the solidity of the self, the major preoccupation of the whole of Western philosophy, does not withstand persistent application to the same object, which comes to pervade it through and through and to imbue it with an experiential awareness of its own unreality."[24] And Barthes banishes the authorial self, the author as semiotic agent. "In France," he remarks, "Mallarmé was doubtless the first to see and to foresee in its full extent the necessity to substitute language itself for the person who until then had been supposed to be its owner. . . . the text is henceforth made and read in such a way that at all levels the author is absent."[25]

The consensus — or is it conformity? — of opinion on this subject seems preternatural; the Demiurge of Language, unleashed in Gaul, reigns over the Western mind. In no small measure is this due to Jacques Derrida. If human reality can be conceived and read as a text without boundaries, so can the self. This *dé-bordement* of textuality, Derrida says, "forces us to extend the accredited concept, the dominant notion of a 'text' [to] . . . everything that was to be set up in opposition to writing (speech, life, the world, the real, history, and what not, every field of reference — to body or mind, conscious or unconscious, politics, economics, and so forth)."[26]

But this *dé-bordement* must also efface names, signatures. For as signs disperse in the great system of *différance* which is the (Universal) Text, so must discrete identities circulate: that is, find and lose themselves, "repeat" themselves, against the background of death, oblivion. As Derrida says in *La Carte postale:* "The proper name . . . returns to efface itself. It arrives only through its own effacement."[27] This, of course, is a hypothetical effacement, which never prevented anyone from answering to his or her name.

The self, we see, suffers disgrace abounding. It has become an essentially contested category, continually revised, devised, supervised, or denied. The denial seems most persuasive regarding an ontological, originary, coherent self. After putting everything in doubt, consciousness ends, reflexively, by turning that doubt upon itself. "When God and the creation become objects of consciousness, man becomes a nihilist," J. Hillis Miller says. "Nihilism is the nothingness of consciousness when consciousness becomes the foundation of everything."[28]

In fact, our straits are not quite so desperate. Miller, like the gifted French sophists of our day, is not sufficiently pragmatic, historical. His fallacy, like theirs, is an intellectualistic fallacy in thinking that logic invariably grounds practice. Though the self may find no basis in theoretical analysis, it is very well able to dispense with such basis. The self, as I argue, finds justification in lived and effective reality.

5

In our lived reality, no power seems more menacing than the power of the other, everything the self perceives as alien to itself. I come now to this other because it confirms the functional self; and also because it marks, in the literature of quest, a crucial encounter between American and non-Western cultures.

The idea of the self may be moot, its history long, convoluted, dappled. But just as the pronoun "I" seems to occur in nearly every language, as Marcel Mauss maintains — "there has never been a human being," he says further, "without the sense not only of his body, but also of his simultaneously mental and physical individuality" — so also is the idea of otherness ubiquitous.[29] The self lives in its pronoun or name, which may invoke totems or ancestors; the other may bear a name or remain unnameable. The self, a persona, may wear a mask, *be* a mask; the other wears a mask of a different kind or assumes the selfsame mask. Through all its evasive or sinister representations, the other endures — in us.

We transact these representations continually, and in doing so mold our lives, both private and public. We also write what Clifford Geertz calls "the social history of the moral imagination." Such writing, though, is not always benign; we lose much in translation between texts, more even between selves or cultures. Yet the imperative to transact otherness remains a moral imperative. "To see others as sharing a nature with ourselves is the merest decency," Geertz says. "But it is from the far more difficult achievement of seeing ourselves amongst others, as a local example of the forms human life has locally taken . . . that the largeness of mind, without which objectivity is self-congratulation and tolerance a sham, comes."[30]

But what really is this other? Freud might answer, a Mother's Breast; Sartre, the Gaze of Another; Lacan, the No/Name of the Father; a physicist, Nature; a tribesman, *Manna;* a theologian, the Numinous; a romantic, "all things counter, original, spare, strange" (Hopkins); everyone, Death. And "the Man in the Street"? We know his retort: Blacks, Indians, Gays, Women, Jews, Nazis, Communists, Khomeinis, finally Satan—usually within. The other? Its aspect is always Difference, perhaps not quite so fugitive as Derrida's *différance,* yet still dialogical, shuttling between terms. In human discourse, we know, every I implies a Thou; the language animal is not monologous. But this duality is shifty. Benveniste says:

> It is a duality which it is illegitimate and erroneous to reduce to a single primordial term, whether this unique term be the "I," which must be established in the individual's own consciousness in order to become accessible to that of the fellow human being, or whether it be, on the contrary, society, which as a totality would pre-exist the individual and from which the individual could only be disengaged gradually, in proportion to his acquisition of self-consciousness. It is in a dialectic reality that will incorporate the two terms and define them by mutual relationship that the linguistic basis of subjectivity is discovered.[31]

Self and other, then, can not be simply merged; nor can their antinomy be simply reified. Do they "exist"? In fact, they often conflict and even war. This is difference in action, difference perceived, imagined, believed, difference realized rather than theorized. Such differences structure societies, generate ideologies, and make for the horrors of history. Such differences also impel the counterideologies of liberation, which sometimes yield to formulaic outrage.[32] The exigencies of morality and politics, which these ideologies assume in their own case to be the same, transform difference into an instrument of power and concern. Thus, for instance, Trinh T. Minh-ha writes about "Third World" woman:

> After all, she is this Inappropriate/d Other [on the cover of the magazine, Other is under erasure] who moves about with always at least two/four gestures: that of affirming "I am like you" while pointing insistently to the difference; and that of reminding "I am different" while unsettling every definition of otherness arrived at.[33]

This claim may not precisely conform to Benveniste's "dialectic reality," but it enacts everyone's adult fantasy, rendered here with a particular historical accent. This is difference as self-assertion, played out as a no-loss game (hence its fantasy).

Even in reading, the concept of difference shifts from grammar to rhetoric, from logic to interest. Taking her cue from Derrida and de Man, Barbara Johnson argues that at the heart of difference resides an uncertainty which only power can resolve. "What is often most fundamentally disagreed upon," she observes in *The Critical Difference,* "is whether a disagreement arises out of the complexities of fact or out of the impulse of power."[34] The impulse of power in language, the transition from its cognitive to its performative functions, becomes the overriding theme of her later work, *A World of Difference,* which admits, like its opening epigraph from Alice Jardine, that difference can not be thought, let alone maintained, without violence, aggressive or defensive.

Here is the point I have wanted to make: neither the concept of difference nor the sense of alterity can wholly diffuse or empty the self. That task may devolve only upon love, ecstasy, mystical union. Yet in current theory as in everyday practice, some differences we do honor, some forms of alterity we do respect. These, as I have said, manifest themselves in liberation or anticolonial movements *before* they appropriate Truth, Justice, Freedom, appropriate a Universal Signifier and so become oppressive themselves. Deference for difference or alterity also manifests itself in certain thinkers (Martin Buber, for instance, Emmanuel Lévinas, Georges Bataille, Jacques Derrida) and in certain recent works (Michel de Certeau's *Heterologies,* Tzvetan Todorov's *The Conquest of America,* Jean-François Lyotard's *Le Différend*). Still, their philosophical tact with regard to difference, their willingness to preserve it, can not finally obviate the tenacity of purpose, the *dur désir de durer* of the self.[35] Our own desires, it seems, always contaminate the otherness of others even as we name its unnameability.

6

Let me recapture, once more, the central threads of this chapter. The self has endured many challenges, both in history and, crescively, in writing. Such challenges, however, serve only to redefine the self, as it has been redefined before in diverse moments and cultures. In the twentieth century, the challenges, proposing a purely textual self, became more subtle and persistent. Yet these provocations fail, on the whole, to reckon with the conative powers of the self, its effective function and experienced identity.[36]

Such an identity need not presume unity or coherence; nor does ego integrity preclude the linguistic qualities of the self. Paul de Man counts "at least four possible and distinct types of self: the self that judges, the self that reads, the self that writes, and the self that reads itself."[37] But the acute "methodological difficulties" he discerns are, in practice, mediated daily by every schoolchild, playing or reading. For human identity no more depends on singleness or homogeneity of psychic states than corporal identity depends on homogeneity in the body's cells. Life works in wholes though seemingly riddled with holes.

Theorists, psychologists of identity, may offer us, therefore, more serviceable models of the self than deconstructionists can afford. Refining the concepts of Erikson, Winnicott, and especially Heinz Lichtenstein, Norman Holland limns a model of human identity composed of theme and variations, much like a sonata, much like any work of art. The self maintains an intense, if unnamed, awareness of itself through great changes, from infancy to death; it creates for itself a unique "style."[38] Defining identity as a compound of agency, consequence, and representation, Holland perceives in each person a dynamic pattern, biological, psychological, social, semiotic. The pattern stubbornly perdures, governed by an instinct for self-preservation, by "an identity principle . . . stronger than desire or the drive for pleasure"; the pattern continues even in the style of an individual's death.[39]

Studies of aging confirm that same variable persistence of self. Thus, for instance, Sharon Kaufman speaks of "cognitive themes," areas of meaning derived from experience, that "explain, unify, and give substance to perceptions" even in extreme age.[40] Drawing on George Herbert Mead's "symbolic interactionism" as well as her extensive interviews with the elderly, she concludes: "How does one maintain a sense of self that integrates 70 years or more of diverse experience . . . ? I have found that in the expression of the ageless self, individuals not only symbolically preserve and integrate meaningful components of their pasts, but they also use these symbols as frameworks for understanding and being in the present."[41] In short, meaning, integrity, even health, derive from *the ability to continue being oneself through longevity.*

The insight may seem too simple, too "nostalgic" or "naive," as some critics would no doubt claim. Yet it also invokes the sense of an *inhabited self,* constituted without the mannered aporias, paradoxes, paralogies that poststructuralists "deploy" when they "demystify" the "fiction of self-hood."[42] The insight envisages as well the heightened sense of a self at risk, even when the self seeks to write that risk, writing in the "shadow of the bull's horn"; for in "mortal danger," in those bounded moments radically discontinuous with the "regular course of a human destiny," the true artist and adventurer discover their "profound affinity."[43]

But the survivor self finds allies in other quarters. As the editors of a recent anthology called *Reconstructing Individualism* put it: "reconstruction does not imply a return to a lost state [the *summum malum* of contemporary criticism] but rather an alternative conceptualization . . . of subjectivity, enriched by the chastening experience of the last century."[44] Thus, despite deprivations in contemporary "regimes of knowledge and power," despite facticities in the administered life of consumer societies, complex efforts still aim to recover "individual experience, choice, and initiative," leading the editors to aver that "the figure of the individual has not been discredited or dissolved so much as displaced and transposed."[45]

Even Marxists, rarely in the vanguard of Western thought nowadays, have begun to show some interest in a reconstituted self. Fredric Jameson, for instance, deplores "the militant anti-humanism" of various structuralisms, and their "humiliation of the old-fashioned subject"; "for the death of the subject," he continues, "if it might be supposed to characterize the collective structure of some future socialist world, is fully as characteristic of the intellectual, cultural, and psychic decay of post-industrial monopoly capitalism as well."[46] Elsewhere, Jameson acknowledges that "the lived experience of individual consciousness as a monadic and autonomous center of activity is not some mere conceptual error," but partakes of reified bourgeois history, a history we have long waited for Marxism to terminate.[47]

7

Walter Benjamin may have been right: "In the world's structure, dream loosens individuality like a bad tooth"; and this "loosening of the self by intoxication," he continues in a mixed trope, inspired many modern artists, especially surrealists.[48] The dissolution of self in dreams — always dialectic, a process of loss and recovery — may pertain to seekers and adventurers as well. It makes, George Simmel says, for a sense of dreamlike displacement, as if life were "experienced by another person," as if the organizing self were acting on behalf of something else: "we could appropriately assign to adventure a subject other than the ego," he writes.[49] This points to a vital paradox of the self: its inexhaustible capacity for both self-assertion and self-abnegation. Hence the adventurer's mystic genius, which Simmel thus describes: "If it is the nature of genius to possess an immediate relation to these secret unities which in experience and rational analysis fall apart into completely separate phenomena, the adventurer of genius lives, as if by mystic instinct, at the point where the course of the world and the individual fate have, so to speak, not yet been differentiated from one another. For this reason, he is said to have a 'touch of genius.'"[50] Here we verge on Freud's "oceanic feeling," which radically redefines the relation of self to other, self to itself.[51] We no longer know where center and circumference of self may lie, unless, like Giordano Bruno's God, they lie everywhere, nowhere. Yet we do know, with some of the ferocity vouchsafed to spiritual tempers, that the self is neither the garrulous chimera nor the Chirico-like, rubble-strewn lot that certain theories now propose.

That the self's final hosanna draws power from its denial, Emerson best shows; the singer of self-reliance sang of a supra-individual reality, sometimes raucously, even more. Strains of contradiction and discord abound in his chant. He could wail: "I am not united, I am not friendly to myself, I bite & tear myself. I am ashamed of myself."[52] He could ask: "What is the aboriginal Self, on which a universal reliance may be grounded? What is the nature and power of that science-baffling star . . . ?" He could growl: "The individual is always mistaken." And he could exult: "Standing on the bare ground — my head bathed by the blithe air and uplifted into infinite space — all mean egotism vanishes. I become a transparent eyeball; I am nothing; I see all; the currents of Universal Being circulate through me; I am part or parcel of God."[53]

Somehow, any commentary on the self — ascribing absence or presence, difference or identity, ascribing even contaminations between self and other — must consider this sequence of Emerson's reflections, consider it not as a sequence, since Emerson himself unsequences it at every turn, but as emblems in the Book of Self, a book made of our body and the world and no one knows what more. For they are emblems of a "power" Emerson himself names many times, grimly or ecstatically, without being able finally to give it a name.

We may not know what self is, but the body knows. The body shows when the self is false, when, for instance, we put a foolish smile on our face "in company where we do not feel at ease, in answer to conversation which does not interest us." Then, Emerson says, the "muscles, not spontaneously moved but moved by a low usurping wilfullness, grow tight about the outline of the face, with the most disagreeable sensation."[54] This is not behaviorism, a mechanism of the heart, but a pragmatic sense of how things act on the eye, on all five organs of the mind. For as Emerson asserts, the self is act — life "is not intellectual or critical, but sturdy"; the self is human power in transience or transference — "all things glitter and swim"; the self is agonism, antagonism, acquiescence, transcendence — and finally that very singular human effort, whatever the risks of failure, perpetually to substitute being for seeming.[55]

This looks to William James, with whom I shall presently conclude. But first and last, where do we stand now regarding the subject of quest? No doubt the question will remain moot, a provocation or mystery, like

Language, the Unconscious, God. Sartre and Lévi-Strauss quarreled about the subject, Derrida quarreled with both, then Lacan quarreled . . . How can these polemics, spite and glory of the Western mind, end? How can logic resolve us here? All these "attacks" on the self, all these theories, unproven and unprovable, what cognitive or epistemic authority do they claim? What evidence of verity can they offer? On what do they rest but warrantless reductions, contested arguments, faddish consensus, historicized beliefs? Can an intellectual fiction (a theory of the subject) void a lived fiction (the experienced self) in the face of death? Where do deconstructions stop? Certainly not where "the buck stops" (the White House), but as certainly where tact, need, purpose, commitment, where desire and history, demand deconstructions to cease if only to commence again.

> From a mere masquerade to the mask, from a role to a person, to a name, to an individual, from the last to a being with metaphysical and ethical value, from a moral consciousness to a sacred being, from the latter to a fundamental form of thought and action—that is the route we have now covered [in tracing the self]. . . . Who knows even if this "category," which all of us here today believe to be well founded, will always be recognized as such? It was formed only for us [in the West], among us. . . . We have a great wealth to defend; with us the Idea may disappear. Let us not moralize.[56]

Thus Marcel Mauss about the self, in 1938. Much has changed since then, notably that confident "we" (the West) entrusted, entitled, to defend the self. But the energies that self organizes—organizes well or ill, with genius, waste, or malice—abide. So does the self as pragmatic act, less fiction than function, a felt agency, personal memory, fiducial force, positing value in the world and immanent in its own effects. The self simply *interests* us, whether in life or in literature. It interests us, especially, in autobiographical narratives of quest or adventure wherein an individual at risk enacts our life in myth. Thus, in the end, the genius of the self derives its practical powers from an inexpugnable will to be and to believe which, as William James eloquently shows, is pivot and fulcrum to all human actions; for "truths cannot become true till our faith has made them so."[57] As an organizational function, if not entity, "the Self," James thought, may remain "incidental" to nature and "the causal order generally"; yet that same gratuitous self, neither object nor subject only but both at once, could continually find its "pragmatic equivalent in realities of experience."[58]

No, the self is no mysticism: it empowers this discourse, any counter-discourse, and all the vastations of history.

Chapter Three
The Motives of Quest:
Between Desire and Vision

Passage indeed, o soul, to primal thought!
— Walt Whitman

You may learn now what you ought to know:
That every journey begins with a death. . . .
— James Fenton

W
1

HY SEEK? Quests, we have seen, touch on many
things: adventure certainly, autobiography, exploration, speculative journeys, even tourism in an age of packaged kitsch. Nor are they alien to
violence, aggression, intimacies of death, the hunter's or warrior's steely
instinct. Quests touch also the alchemies of artistic creation and the mystic's *via negativa,* which they probe in their radical curiosity about inner
reality; they are imagination and spirit in action.

We must approach the motives of quest, then, with indirection if not
discretion, wander about a bit, glance at many things. I do not believe we
can fathom those motives: this were to fathom existence itself, a quest
about quests. But we can glimpse how adventurers, thinkers, poets articulate for themselves, or others, the motives of quest. Thus I commence with
the testimony of adventurers, review some thinkers — Ortega y Gasset, Konrad Lorenz, Michael Balint, Sigmund Freud, Friedrich Nietzsche, William
James — who illumine divers aspects of quest, and end with poetic meditations concerning quest *in language.*

2

Quests call us to something other, something more, than pure peril. But
danger swells in their nature, journeys beckon in their call. Why, then, do
men and women assay such fanatic tasks, taking rabid risks? In their harsh
exigency, they, too, reveal an aspect of quest.

Consider the adventurer, most often solitary, sometimes in groups. Dick

Rutan and Jeana Yeager fly around the world in nine days, nonstop and without refueling, cramped in the coffinlike cabin of a giant dragonfly called *Voyager*. Francis Chichester circumnavigates the globe in *Gipsy Moth IV* at the age of sixty-five; John Fairfax rows across the Pacific in an open boat, wrestling sharks with a long, bright knife; and David Lewis sails solo from Sydney to Cape Town, across the Roaring Forties, into the world's most dreadful seas. Reinhold Messner climbs the fourteen highest peaks, all above eight thousand meters, *without* oxygen; Bruce Klepinger leaves his wife and medical research in Kansas to climb a thousand mountains and lead expeditions around the world, traveling more than Columbus, Cook, and Amundsen together; Hillary and Tenzing Norkay live in legend. Then there are all those trekkers across the Empty Quarter and Hindu Kush, wanderers in the plains of Patagonia, outbacks of Australia, rain forests of Amazonia, deserts of Mongolia, blinding icecaps of the Poles. Some prefer to travel in time: Thor Heyerdahl recapitulates mythic journeys in *Kon-Tiki* and *Ra II,* and Tim Severin emulates Saint Brenden (supposed to have crossed the Atlantic in a sixth-century ox-hide ketch) and impersonates Sinbad the Sailor in an Arab dhow. Others: Chuck Yeager, John Glenn, Neil Armstrong. And those indomitable women, in "a good thick skirt," riding, hiking, climbing, sailing everywhere. From Margery Kempe, dictating her travel accounts to a friar in 1436, to Christina Dodwell, Robyn Davidson, Naomi James, and Judith Chisholm in our own day, they venture where few men or gods would go.[1] What goads them all, what bears them through?

No single answer, of course, will suffice. Adventurers have adduced heredity, adrenalin, whim, boredom, rage, loss, rivalry, eroticism, and maladjustment to civilization; the search for fame, self-worth, wholeness, enlightenment; a mysterious nostalgia for otherness; the lure of things difficult and strange; the urge to confront fear, death really, and to master, if only for a moment, their singular fate. Their motives may be, as we have seen, ultimately ontological, some profound affirmation, hope of rebirth, under the twin aspects of cosmic harmony and heroic strain. At the center lies some fierce satisfaction, a moment of inviolate existence, a primal intensity beyond self or risk.

But words like "boredom" or "rage" are too abstract to render the ineffable experience of the adventurer in extremity. Perhaps nothing can render that experience. Perhaps the adventurer, sniffing death, can hint it best. The last entries of Robert Falcon Scott are justly famous:

Wednesday, January 18, 1912.
. . . Great God! This is an awful place and terrible enough for us to have laboured to it without the reward for priority. . . .

Now for the run home and a desperate struggle. I wonder if we can do it.

Thursday, March 22 and 23.

— Blizzard bad as ever — Wilson and Bowers unable to start — to-morrow last chance — no fuel and only one or two of food left — must be near the end. Have decided it shall be natural — we shall march for the depôt with or without our effects and die in our tracks.

Thursday, March 29.

— Since the 21st we have had a continuous gale from W.S.W. and S.W. We had fuel to make two cups of tea apiece and bare food for two days on the 20th. Every day we have been ready to start for our depôt *11 miles* away, but outside the door of the tent it remains a scene of whirling drift. I do not think we can hope for any better things now. We shall stick it out to the end, but we are getting weaker, of course, and the end cannot be far.

It seems a pity, but I do not think I can write more.

R. Scott

Last entry.

For God's sake look after our people.[2]

Here is also Bonington, at harrowing length, on David Lewis's more recent voyage around Antarctica:

The waves reared up, chaotic, boiling white, like huge breakers on a reef; foam and wind-blown sleet made it difficult to tell where ocean ended and sky began. The roar of breakers intermingled with the high-pitched scream of wind in the rigging, as the little boat was hurled up onto the crest of a wave, before lurching crabwise down into the trough, where for a few strange moments she was becalmed, sheltered by the breakers around her from the noise of the wind. But somehow that only amplified the crash of collapsing rollers; sooner or later one of these must hit *Ice Bird*.

Once already, the boat had been knocked down; the self-steering vane had vanished and what little sail he had left up had been ripped away. David Lewis was now crouched, braced on the wet bunk in the cabin, his state of mind not so much fearful as beyond fear, for there was very little he could do to control his fate. He still clutched the tiller lines, which he could operate from within the shelter of the cabin, but the boat barely answered to their call.

Then suddenly, at about two in the morning, it happened. It was like a gigantic hand that picked the boat up, tossed and then rolled it; everything went black, water roaring in, clothes, tins, books tumbling around him; he was lying on the roof, then almost in the same instant on the floor amongst the swilling waters and flotsam of what had been his home. By the light of the sub-Antarctic dawn he saw that the fore hatch had been ripped away, but when he struggled from under the table that had collapsed on top of him and poked his head out of the hatchway, his worst fears were confirmed. The mast had been ripped out of its seat in the huge vortex of the roll and was trailing over the side, held only by the festoons of knotted rigging. . . .

By now his boat was a piece of flotsam, adrift in the Southern Ocean. Somehow he had to find a way of building a jury mast. Protecting his hands with wet woollen gloves, he salvaged a ten-foot-long spinnaker pole, somehow erecting it, and staying it with what was left of the rigging and some old climbing rope. But it could only take a pathetic amount of sail, barely enough to keep him under way, as *Ice Bird* plodded, crabwise, towards his haven of the Antarctic Peninsula. It was a desperate, yet hopeless struggle for survival, for he still had 2500 miles to go and, at that speed, he would have run out of water long before he got there. And yet he kept struggling on, spending up to fourteen hours at a time operating the tiller lines from the shelter of the cabin, to claw his way in the right direction, tacking painfully, first north-east, then south-east, to gain a few precious miles. The numbness of his hands had now given way to intense and growing agony. They were soft, swollen, beginning to suppurate. He took massive doses of antibiotics to stop them becoming gangrenous but even touching anything was agonisingly painful. Despite this he had to bail out twenty or thirty bucketfuls of bilge water each day, struggle with the Primus stove, go out on deck to readjust his pathetically inadequate sail or repair the fragile mast. The position was hopeless. He commented in his log:

A shutter has closed between a week ago when I was part of the living and since. Chance of survival negligible but effort worth it in spite of pain and discomfort. These last are very great. Must go on striving to survive, as befits a man. Susie and Vickie without a daddy is worst of all.[3]

Unlike Scott, Lewis survives, with no more sentimentality in either — though we may sense its nearness — than in a sliver of blue ice.

But the question, at once impertinent and unappeasable, returns: why? Perhaps we do well to consider the answers of adventurers themselves. Once again, here is Bonington:

The basic satisfaction of climbing is both physical and mental — a matter of co-ordination similar to any other athletic attachment. But in climbing there is the extra ingredient of risk. It is a hot, heady spice, a piquance that adds an addictive flavour to the game. It is accentuated by the fascination of pitting one's ability against a personal unknown and winning through. Being master of one's destiny, with one's life literally in one's hands, is what gives climbing its fascination.

It also gives a heightened awareness of everything around. The pattern of lichen on rock, a few blades of grass, the dark, still shape of a lake below, the form of the hills and cloud mountains above might be the same view seen by the passenger on a mountain railway, but transported to his viewpoint amongst a crowd, he cannot see what I, the climber, can. This is not an elitist ethic, but rather the deeper sensuous involvement that the climber has with the mountains around him, a feeling heightened by the stimulus of risk.

These are the elements of adventure that I have discovered in climbing — the physical satisfaction of having complete command over one's body, a sense of risk in the process, an awareness of beauty and the exploration of the unknown. At its most satisfying this would mean one of the rapidly dwindling unknown parts of the world, but almost equally satisfying is a personal unknown, even if others have trodden that path before.[4]

There it all is: pride, risk, curiosity, self-sufficiency, strenuous will, but also a "coordination," some sensuous apprehension of being, beyond egoism. In quest for adventure, the self opens for an instant to the great light, however mean its motives may seem back on the ground, back of the mind.

Wonder in a man of action may appear ingenuous, and this reminds us that not all seekers are poets. Still, a writer-adventurer like Bonington can bring us closer to the challenge of impossibility on which he thrives. He can reveal the inner climate of adventure: its terrible solitude, grinding efforts, romantic yearnings; its elations and despairs; and always that preternatural determination, embodied in strong, capable hands, eyes honed on horizons. He can also expose the outer conditions of adventure: the envious fascination of ordinary citizens, the skepticism or venality of sponsors, the glamour of media and their hype. And he can attest to the ecological ethic of adventure, its simplicity, its minimal use of force.

Ultimately, adventurers, who come from every profession, background, and class, move in a unique, dreamlike space. "On an expedition or a voyage," Bonington writes, "the rest of the world with all its power politics, threats of war or recession, or more personal problems of money, pressure of work, family obligations—all vanish in this tiny microcosm."[5] Some may call it escape, others an access to higher consciousness. Thus Bernard Moitessier, sea mystic, spurns all records and rivalries; circumnavigating the world solo without a stop (Chichester had stopped), he disdains winning the Golden Globe race, and, still making no landfall, sails on through the Southern Ocean. Some would say he went sea-crazy; he thinks: "when one is months and months alone, one evolves."[6] Before such purity, one falls silent.

But adventure also defies purity. Donald Crowhurst lied consistently about the position of his *Teignmouth Electron* until he disappeared, his boat found ghosting in the Atlantic. Nor are adventurers in the heterocosm exempt from human contradictions. They may dream of home on their desperate journeys, only to depart again, like Tennyson's Ulysses— "Made weak by time and fate, but strong in will / To strive, to seek, to find, and not to yield"—as soon as they return. They value their friends, spouses, children, only to embrace solitude, value their health only to place their bodies in extreme jeopardy. They celebrate life, even immortality, though death marks them as his favorites.

No doubt death lies near the center of their awareness—as it does, somehow, in every human animal. But the impulse is neither "death wish" nor "masochism." Adventurers walk on the margins of life, counting to *live* on the thinnest edge; their world is not the shuttered world of the suicide. Intuitively, they submit themselves to Conrad's "destructive element," and with their exertions find a larger life. They do more than seek for paradise or the Hesperides, more than touch the "coasts of illusion." They grasp at something that Freya Stark knows how to grasp:

> So far as my personal object in life goes, I should wish to attain two things: first the confidence of more time, not to be confused within the narrow limits of one life; secondly, the sense of death as a new and wonderful adventure. . . . to risk one's life seems to me the only way in which one can attain to a real (as distinct from a merely theoretic) sense of immortality unless one happens to be among lucky people in whom faith is born perfect.[7]

In the end, though, the motives of adventure and quest remain not only plural but diaphanous, obscure. From Pytheas, who started out from Massilia (Marseilles) in the fourth century B.C., through Ibn Battuta, who wandered seventy-five thousand miles over a lifetime, to Christina Dodwell in our day, adventurers, though often eloquent, have refused to define their "long desire."[8] Dodwell puts it simply thus: "I travelled in much the same way that other people stayed still—it was the way of life that suited me. As for purposes and goals in life, I didn't have any."[9] Perhaps this is another way of saying what Bonington says: "Man's quest for adventure is not so much 'because it is there'; the answer lies concealed, mysterious, in the complexity of man."[10] And woman, of course.

3

This originary mystery invites even as it defies our knowledge—ethology, psychology, sociology, philosophy—to clarify its nature.

Risk, aggression, violence, no less than that miraculous, bonding intelligence we call language, have informed human evolution. The lion, the saber-toothed tiger, the great white shark feared no predator during the Ice Ages; they were large, fierce, and rare. But it took more than ferocity, more even than intelligence, to change our own ecological niche in the last hundred thousand years—and keep changing it upward, so far. Could this "ecological mobility" (Colinvaux) be due to our questing curiosity, a radical human restlessness; or to an "ability to confront risk and take chances . . . basic to our biological success" (Keyes); or again, to a native "adversativeness" that provides "a paradigm for understanding our own existence" (Ong)?[11] And were these gifts and skills honed during aeons of hunting?

The "hunting hypothesis"—that man is "man, and not a chimpanzee, because for millions upon millions of evolving years we killed for a living" —remains opaque, factious.[12] But Ortega offers some illuminating remarks on the subject in his *Meditations on Hunting.* Knowledge, he says, is active search. Like Socrates in Plato's *Republic,* the philosopher "hunts," posted behind a thicket with watchful mind: "By the devil!" Socrates cries. "I think we have a track, and I don't think it will escape us now."[13] The real hunter, though, faces an absence: the beast's. Hence the constant vigilance for what-is-not-yet-there, what-may-never-be-there. Hunting, then, is live pursuit conducted in empty space; it is expectation in action. This pursuit still recapitulates for us in play, mock vacations from the twentieth century, permanent possibilities of being human. Such possibilities demand unique attentiveness for their realization:

> [The hunter] does not believe that he knows where the critical moment is going to occur. He does not look tranquilly in one determined direction, sure beforehand that the game will pass in front of him. The hunter knows that he does not know what is going to happen, and this is one of the greatest attractions of his occupation. Thus he needs to prepare an attention of a different and superior style — an attention which does not consist in riveting itself on the presumed but consists precisely in not presuming anything and in avoiding inattentiveness. It is a "universal" attention, which does not inscribe itself on any point and tries to be on all points. There is a magnificent term for this, one that still conserves all its zest of vivacity and immanence: alertness. The hunter is the alert man.[14]

Quite so, as is the true adventurer, true seeker.

This alertness, though, can not be wholly innocent, devoid of will and remembrance, free of aggression and violence. Like the "hunting imperative," "aggression" in human beings is ideologically moot. The ethologist Konrad Lorenz makes the best case for it, contending that aggression is a useful biological instinct, not a "death wish" as Freud claimed. Lorenz joins Freud, however, in tracing assorted human maladies to aggressions that find no channel for sublimation or "militant enthusiasm." Lorenz concludes:

> We do not know how many important behavior patterns of man include aggression as a motivating factor, but I believe it occurs in a great many. What is certain is that, with the elimination of aggression, the *"aggredi"* in the original and widest sense, the tackling of a task or problem, the self-respect without which everything that a man does from morning till evening, from the morning shave to the sublimest artistic or scientific creations, would lose all impetus; everything associated with ambition, ranking order, and countless other equally indispensable behavior patterns would probably also disappear from human life. In the same way, a very important and specifically human faculty would probably disappear too: laughter.[15]

May not quest or adventure provide fit, and sometimes sublime, expression for human *aggredi?*

The energy of adventure is perhaps also kin to the violence of war. True, seekers and adventurers are most often *isolatoes,* walking, sailing, flying alone; they want no power or dominion over others; they contemn conquistadors. Yet many of them seem possessed of a warrior's mystic rage, like Cuchulain who exterminated the sons of Nichta in battle while still a boy—he was "cooled off" by a troop of young, naked women carrying three barrels of cold water—and in his prime fought the sea for seven days and nights; he became, Paul Zweig says, "the intense berserker radiance of his acts."[16]

We have glimpsed in an earlier chapter this heroic or shamanistic fury; here we need only note the hidden nexus of violence and quest. For violence is not purely mythic; it is historical as well, a shaping cultural force in nearly every tribe or society of our world. *Weem,* ritual war among the Dani of New Guinea, for example, sanctions their various institutions. It has persisted among them since the Stone Age, and they can envisage no end to it. "Without it, the culture would be entirely different; indeed, perhaps it could not find sufficient meaning to survive except parasitically as the novelty of missionaries or policemen," write two anthropologists who observed the Dani in their remote Central Highlands.[17]

Our concern here is not the desperate and stupendous question of war in the modern world; it is rather the historical fact that certain kinds of violence seem to have been constitutive, decisive in the psychic and cultural economies of human organizations.[18] The Dani, who indulged in no adventures or quests, consumed much of their energy in ritual aggression. Others, like the Vikings, may justify their depredations as exploration, preceding Columbus to the New World. Kipling credits them with the wanderer's metaphysical itch:

> What is a woman that you forsake her,
> And the hearth-fire and the home-acre,
> To go with the old gray Widow-maker?
> . . .
>
> Yet when the signs of summer thicken,
> And the ice breaks, and the birch-buds quicken,
> Yearly you turn from our side, and sicken—
>
> Sicken again for the shouts and the slaughters.
> You steal away to the lapping waters
> And look at your ship in her winter-quarters.
>
> ("Harp Song of the Dane Women")

Others still, neither Dane nor Dani, may find ways to sublate their violence into more spiritual quests.

The intrepid seeker, at any rate, often draws on inner resources unavailable to a military hero like Audie Murphy, who fell prey to boredom, anxiety, a terrible emptiness at the end of his days. Still, their motives cross, entwine. William Broyles, Jr., movingly asks: "How do I explain—to my wife, my children, my friends—that I loved war as much as anything before or since?" Broyles, a writer and Vietnam veteran, adduces many things: comradeship, intensified experience, heightened sexuality; escape from the ambiguities of ordinary life; the anarchic or erotic exhilaration of untrammeled destruction; the sheer joy of being alive on the great, grisly scene of death; even a weird beauty recovered from the ugliness of war, its mud, blood, excrement, and putrefying flesh. Such feelings may not move all questers, though many would consent to Broyle's ontic insight:

> For all these reasons, men love war. But these are the easy reasons, the first circle, the ones we can talk about without risk of disapproval, without plunging too far into the truth or ourselves. But there are other, more troubling reasons why men love war. The love of war stems from the union, deep in the core of our being, between sex and destruction, beauty and horror, love and death. War may be the only way in which most men touch the mythic domains in our soul. It is, for men, at some terrible level the closest thing to what childbirth is for women: the initiation into the power of life and death. It is like lifting off the corner of the universe and looking at what's underneath. To see war is to see into the dark heart of things, that no-man's-land between life and death, or even beyond.[19]

Psychologists and sociologists, however, resort to another idiom when they theorize about extreme jeopardy. Reviewing divers psychoanalytic theories, Samuel Z. Klausner contends that even civilians seek conflict or risk to master deeper anxieties (Otto Fenichel), to achieve a higher integration of their personality (Erik Erikson), or to test out alternative values (Gregory Bateson). Thus stress seeking proves to be a kind of "voluntary tropistic behavior," which can become an end in itself, requiring cycles of planned ventures and egoistic satisfaction, a forceful bid for autonomy. Such autonomy may have anarchic or sociopathic elements. But the stress seeker also serves, as well as subverts, society. "More fundamentally," Klausner argues, "the stress-seeker manifests the active energies that society identifies with its constructive development. In this, he contributes to the general optimism that society will indeed have the strength to achieve its goals."[20]

Does the adventurer, then, preeminently a stress seeker, define a particular psychological type? In *Thrills and Regressions,* Michael Balint distinguishes between "ocnophils" (literally, shrinkers, lovers of hesitation) and "philobats" (lovers of thrills, walkers on their toes). The latter, much like American immigrants, form weak attachments to objects, persons, places; they relish movement, vertigo, transgressive fantasies. The former cling, seek security in objects and people, accept limits, finding huge expanses horrid, preferring *terra firma* over *"das ozeanische Gefühl"* (Freud). Balint's distinction is like all suggestive dichotomies — including Nietzsche's between the Apollonian and Dionysian — mainly heuristic. But it also puts in relief the *ideal* character of the adventurer ("philobat"), his proclivity for hazard, excitement, violence, or adversity as "fun." In him, a "mixture of fear, pleasure, and confident hope in the face of an external danger . . . constitutes the fundamental elements of all *thrills.*"[21] Throughout, an enhancement of the ego takes place, a conquest of doubt and deficiency. Like the mythic hero, Balint says, the philobat sallies forth from the safety of home (mother and Mother Earth), achieves momentary triumph in the world, returns.

This return accounts for the iterative, even obsessive, drive of the adventurer; Odysseus must hoist sail again. Though Balint departs from Freud, substituting "object relations" for traditional libido theory, both stress the cyclical process of mastery, the compulsion to overcome some primary loss or trauma through repetition. Freud, we know, tells the story of the child who played a game — *fort/da* (gone/there)! — with a wooden reel, simulating disappearance and recovery. In doing so, he reenacted his mother's departures and returns. "At the outset he was in a passive situation — he was overpowered by the experience," Freud observes; "but, by repeating it, unpleasurable though it was, as a game, he took on an *active* part. These efforts might be put down to an instinct for mastery acting independently of whether the [repeated] memory were in itself pleasurable or not."[22] Freud then proceeds with a further interpretation: the game is also the child's revenge on his mother, as if to say, "All right, go away, I don't need you anyway!" — an act, that is, of covert aggression.

From this nursery game, a *fort/da* of babes, Freud draws the most ominous conclusion for the human race. The compulsion to repeat, though it may serve the urge to master reality, reveals a more primitive and elemental drive that sets aside the pleasure principle. This is Thanatos, primordial death, which aggression also serves. Dismally, Freud concludes in *Beyond the Pleasure Principle:* "we shall be compelled to say that 'the goal of all life is death' and, looking backwards, that 'what was inanimate existed before what is living'!"[23] We are in the realm of shadows, a cosmic Manichean drama acted out by Eros and Thanatos, which founds our civilization and its discontents. "And it is this battle of the giants that our nurse-maids try to appease with their lullaby about Heaven."[24]

We may appear to have wandered far from our topic; we are actually close to its heart. Whatever we choose to believe of Freud's speculative theories — and in one version or another, they inform the work of Balint, Erikson, Fenichel, among others — they signal the ontological motive of quest, its cunning complicities with childhood, and its entanglements with anxiety or desire. The theories further expose the unappeased need for adventure, and touch a deep "wound"—like Hemingway's?—on which I must touch in later chapters.[25] But this is not a disabling wound; quite the contrary, it often inspirits human beings, impels them to high and rare attainments.

4

I turn now to two modern thinkers who place quest in ampler perspective: Friedrich Nietzsche and William James. Quick to life's perils, they also sound its meaning, its sense on surface and in depth.

"Live dangerously!" Nietzsche cries in *The Gay Science,* and the cry echoes, becoming vicious or trite, in innumerable mouths. But what does it mean, to live dangerously? At the anguished center of Nietzsche's life is a quality one needs to call courage. This is a gay and cruel and tragic courage, an ecstatic courage, voluptuous sometimes yet inward with despair, a defiant, metaphysical courage. It makes proud meaning of "nothing"; for as Nietzsche knew, man would rather take the void for purpose than be devoid of purpose. And it shows itself ultimately in *bearing life,* repeated in an "eternal recurrence" of agonies, errors, exultations.[26] Yet Nietzsche advocates no mere stoicism or endurance; he wants also to *overcome* life, impose on being the character of becoming, which leads him to the utopian concept of the *Übermensch.*

The Overman interests us only in so far as he embodies emergent qualities of human existence, qualities we may also associate, rather guardedly, with the adventurer-seeker. What qualities? First, the ability to conquer "the tyranny of pain," both physical and spiritual, a tyranny "even excelled by the tyranny of pride that refused the *conclusions* of pain—and conclusions are consolations. . . ."[27] Next, a radical restlessness that Nietzsche describes in terms recalling Balint: "The spirits who seek rest I recognize by the many *dark* objects with which they surround themselves: those who want to sleep make their room dark or crawl into a cave.—A hint for those who do not know what it is that they seek most, but who would like to know."[28] Also, a ruthless curiosity, a penchant for dangerous, unstable, monstrous things:

> *At the sea.*—I would not build a house for myself, and I count it part of my good fortune that I do not own a house. But if I had to, then I should build it as some of the Romans did—right into the sea. I should not mind sharing a few secrets with this beautiful monster.[29]

Finally, a "nobility," itself evidence of health, an unperverted "will to power," the latter being a "primitive form of affect" to which all the other affects revert.[30]

Nietzsche's notion of nobility is complex — no "blond beast" here — and thoroughly historical. In a moment of impending Western nihilism, nobility becomes an attribute of *chandalas* (outcasts), "the *immoralists,* the nomads of every type, the artists, Jews, musicians," who "determine honor on earth" and are "today *advocates of life.*"[31] It is they who create values, incarnate the highest quantum of power, become the vehicles of valor. But we do well to hear Nietzsche speak in the searing cadences of *The Will to Power:*

> The princes of Europe should consider carefully whether they can do without our support. We immoralists — we are today the only power that needs no allies in order to conquer: thus we are by far the strongest of the strong. We do not even need to tell lies: what other power can dispense with that?

> There is a noble and dangerous carelessness that permits a profound inference and insight: the carelessness of the self-assured and overrich soul that has never troubled about friends but knows only hospitality.

> That one stakes one's life, one's health, one's honor, is the consequence of high spirits and an overflowing, prodigal will: not from love of man but because every great danger challenges our curiosity about the degrees of our strength and our courage.

> The highest men live beyond the rulers, freed from all bonds; and in the rulers they have their instruments.[32]

These scant entries, shards of insight, prescind themselves from Nietzsche's (often contradictory) thought on "The Noble Man," "The Masters of the Earth," "The Great Human Being," "The Highest Man as Legislator of the Future." They highlight a crucial aspect of quest: its pertinence to any larger apprehension of reality, its relevance to the human condition, as it is, as it might become. For what Nietzsche says of "nomads" and "immoralists" applies, uncannily, to adventurers who still embody the ancient, stubborn, redemptive will of men. Here Zweig is apt:

> Nietzsche's philosophy restores the adventurer to the place he has occupied in traditional cultures: no longer an outcast or a criminal, but like Odysseus or Gilgamesh, a source of values, expressing the essentially human adventure of a man engaged in the economy of struggle which is the world.[33]

Pragmatism participates vigorously in this "economy of struggle." Without irony or dogma, evasion or intolerance, William James testifies continually to the openness of existence, its risky and real and unfinished character. There is a touch of anarchism, as he confesses, in his as in Nietzsche's thought. There is much generosity, patience with what others might call disorder in their haste to impose unity on the world. Hence his pragmatic resolve for pluralism, the inevitable hypothesis "of a world im-

perfectly unified still, and perhaps always to remain so."[34] Above all, there
is cheerful assent to the strenuous nature of reality. Famously, James
remarks:

> I find myself willing to take the universe to be really dangerous and adventur-
> ous, without therefore backing out and crying "no play." I am willing to think
> that the prodigal-son attitude, open to us as it is in many vicissitudes, is not
> the right and final attitude towards the whole of life. I am willing that there
> should be real losses and real losers, and no total preservation of all that is.

And this prompts him to quote from the Greek Anthology:

> A shipwrecked sailor, buried on this coast,
>   Bids you set sail.
> Full many a gallant bark, when we were lost,
>   Weathered the gale.[35]

This is an adventurer's creed in "a drastic kind of universe," a universe
from which neither exigency nor freedom can be expelled.

Will is central to James's thought, "will to believe" no less primal than
"will to power." We have a "willing nature," he insists, which includes "all
such factors of belief as fear and hope, prejudice and passion, imitation
and partisanship, the circumpressure of our caste and set."[36] Our total
character and our personal genius — not logic, ideology, system — give us
the "solving word" when we find ourselves on trial. Will, for James, pre-
cedes conception; thinking is for action's sake. This makes for a certain
conative optimism — pessimism for him is a "religious disease," an unsat-
isfiable metaphysical demand, and melancholy a form of repletion. "Need
and struggle are what excite and inspire us; our hour of triumph is what
brings the void."[37] For all that, James opens himself repeatedly to wonder:

> Existence then will be a brute fact to which as a whole the emotion of onto-
> logic wonder shall rightfully cleave, but remain eternally unsatisfied. Then
> wonderfulness or mysteriousness will be an essential attribute of the nature
> of things, and the exhibition and emphasizing of it will continue to be an in-
> gredient in the philosophic industry of the race. Every generation will produce
> its Job, its Hamlet, its Faust or its Sartor Resartus.[38]

In such moments of "ontologic wonder," all theories fall silent, as if lis-
tening intently to hear the pulse of Being beat.

In William James, then, we find a thinker for our thin season, an imagination of risk. Men and women, he pragmatically believes, make sense
of their lives in action, in difficulty and self-exposure; they often find zest,
as he did, in the rough and tumble of existence. As a youth, James joined
Louis Agassiz for fifteen months in an arduous expedition to the Amazon.
He enjoined himself thereafter to ascend to "some sort of partnership with

fate," a Nietzschean declaration of *amor fati,* as Jacques Barzun says, that owes nothing to Nietzsche; James simply wills "to posit life."[39] "Excursive" and experimental in its temper, James's magnum opus, *Principles of Psychology,* struck Barzun as an American masterpiece, quite like *Moby-Dick,* the "narrative of a search" for the elusive mystery of mind, "as momentous for Everyman as anything symbolized by the white whale."[40]

5

So far I have stressed risk in quest, mortal risk. This is an element of search, an internal horizon of reality, rarely experienced as an actual confrontation with death. In any case, the seekers in this book are also writers, indeed artists; explorers still, they exemplify more than the adventurer's invincible will. They think with their bodies and possess a creative curiosity manifest in the best science or art. Their motive, then, is partly cognitive; for danger — the very face of the Unknown — creates the conditions of knowledge.

Elements of adventure, quest, and creativity mingle in their enterprise. Thus Erik Erikson speaks of Luther, Shaw, Darwin, Freud, and William James in terms of a youthful "identity-crisis" befitting a future adventurer or conquistador; similarly, George Simmel insists on the "profound affinity between the adventurer and the artist," and indeed, on the artist's attraction to adventure.[41] And Jacques-Yves Cousteau sees in exploration a profound cognitive adaptation, inducing evolutionary growth through "risk, freedom, initiative, and lateral [i.e., imaginative] thinking"; while Philip Morrison, a theoretical scientist, considers all exploration as "filling in the blank margins of that inner world, that no human can escape making."[42] This cognitive and creative imperative inspires also the seeker.

It inspires particularly the *writing* adventurer, and may even move the best travel writers. Any serious travel writer, Robert Byron says, obeys a sensuous and spiritual necessity, akin to the motive of art.[43] Jonathan Raban makes the point more explicitly: "Why, then, not simply stay home and shut up? Because for me travel is a literary experiment that the writer conducts on himself."[44] This is an experiment in estrangement, "defamiliarization" (*ostranenie* as Russian formalists used to say about art); or rather, an experiment in self-defamiliarization, a trial by otherness. The trial conjures for Raban something uncanny, some aspect of Freud's *Unheimlich,* a product of disorientation. And so Raban concludes:

> To travel is *not to be at home.* In Freudian translatorese it is deliberately to orientate oneself badly in one's environment, and thereby to open oneself to the odd and the uncanny. The famous sharp eye of the traveller — the capac-

ity to notice everything that Henry James named as the first qualification of
the novelist — is the result of a fundamental maladjustment between the traveller and the world he passes through.[45]

Quests, then, imply more than danger and displacement, more even than
cognitive adventure and imaginative exploration. An artist may find in
them, as we have seen, some motive intrinsic to the creative process itself,
to the requirements of narrative pace and space — witness romantic poems
of voyage, from Coleridge's "Rime of the Ancient Mariner," through Baudelaire's "Le Voyage," to Yeats's "Sailing to Byzantium." We do well, therefore, to perpend some of these poets, masters of symbolic motion, fantastic voyagers; for their testimony reveals other nuances of quest, other
intricacies of desire or remorse.

In quest or adventure, I have said, the self opens, ecstatic, opens for
an instant to the great light. This is the urgency in Whitman's lines from
"Passage to India":

> Passage — immediate passage! the blood burns in my veins!
> Away, O soul! hoist instantly the anchor!

But quests also retreat from the light, and darkness and dread may crowd
their path. For every Conquistador of the Spirit, there is an Aguirre, Wrath
of God; for every metaphysical Columbus, an Ahab, striking the sun, or
a Kurtz, mouthing horror on all fours. Rimbaud, pitching derisively in his
"Drunken Boat," feels the rush of terror:

> J'ai vu le soleil bas, taché d'horreurs mystiques,
> Illuminant de longs figements violets,
> . . .
> Mais, vrai, j'ai trop pleuré! Les Aubes sont navrantes.
> Toute lune est atroce et tout soleil amer.
>
> (I've seen the low sun, fearful with mystic signs,
> Lighting with far flung violet arms,
> . . .
> True I have wept too much! Dawns are heartbreaking;
> Cruel all moons and bitter the suns.)[46]

Nor is the impediment to quest always demonic. Ennui, death's drab
double, may loiter along the seeker's way. Hence, Baudelaire in "Le Voyage":

> Amer savoir, celui qu'on tire du voyage!
> Le monde, monotone et petit, aujourd'hui,
> Hier, demain, toujours, nous fait voir notre image:
> Un oasis d'horreur dans un désert d'ennui.

(It's bitter knowledge that one learns from travel.
The world so small and drab, from day to day,
The horror of our image will unravel,
A pool of dread in deserts of dismay.)[47]

Quests may also create fictions of change, illusions of surprise; they may serve to project ourselves in exotic places without genuine transformation. The phenomenon is all too familiar, prompting Dr. Johnson to cite a Spanish proverb: "He, who would bring home the wealth of the Indies, must carry the wealth of the Indies with him"; and prompting Emerson to remark: "Travelling is a fool's paradise. Our first journeys discover to us the indifference of places. . . . My giant goes with me wherever I go."[48] The giant of the self—the "heavy bear," Roethke calls him—attends us everywhere, making true conversion the rarest human event.

That is because memory always casts its shadow across the seeker's path, inescapable shadow of the past. "Once more on my adventure brave and new," cries the poet (Browning), and in that cry we hear both presage and remembrance. Yet *again* the seeker starts. Is the quest, then, merely an invitation to rehearsal? Calvino writes this about his errant compatriot:

> Marco Polo imagined answering (or Kublai Khan imagined his answer) that the more one was lost in unfamiliar quarters of distant cities, the more one understood the other cities he had crossed to arrive there; and he retraced the stages of his journeys, and he came to know the port from which he had set sail, and the familiar places of his youth, and the surroundings of home, and a little square of Venice where he had gamboled as a child.
>
> At this point Kublai Khan interrupted him or imagined interrupting him, or Marco Polo imagined himself interrupted, with a question such as: "You advance always with your head turned back?" or "Is what you see always behind you?" or rather "Does your journey take place only in the past?"[49]

The cities, "invisible cities," Marco Polo describes may be indeed versions of his native Venice. Thus the great and shrewd Khan, himself mental traveler more than conqueror, taunts his visitor: "It was to slough off a burden of nostalgia that you went so far away! . . . You return from your voyages with a cargo of regrets! . . . Meager purchases, to tell the truth, for a merchant of the Serenissima!"[50] Thus, too, in certain journeys, the past seems to await us as the only destination we *can* reach, making every quest an elegy to its own hope.

But the world is really wide and no past is preserved eternally in the amber of regret. The past is what we come to *understand* as our past, a kind of retroactive winning through. And seekers do change when they seek more than change. No one saw this better than Eliot in the Christian transfigurations of the great *Quartets*. Hear now the voice descanting in the rigging of a windblown ship:

> Fare forward, you who think that you are voyaging;
> You are not those who saw the harbour
> Receding, or those who will disembark.
> Here between the hither and the farther shore
> While time is withdrawn, consider the future
> And the past with equal mind. . . .
> .   .   .
>
>   O voyagers, O seamen,
> You who come to port, and you whose bodies
> Will suffer the trial and judgement of the sea,
> Or whatever event, this is your real destination.[51]

6

Eliot's Christian journey defines one crucial dimension of quest, the quest of spirit for reality, a condition of "complete simplicity," uniting "the fire and the rose." Though such quest may be the end of all quests, it is an end lost in many beginnings, leading to many ways and places. Quests remain various, evident in numberless traces. A great silence may attend them or great loquacity, much danger or none. Yet their vital motive is *meaning,* meaning more than transcendence, nostalgia, or thrills.

No doubt, the motives of quest since Jason or Gilgamesh have become interiorized, starting perhaps with the Knight of the Mournful Countenance. But the interiorization of quest and adventure, as we shall see, voids none of their meanings, drains none of their energies. Zweig may overstate a trifle his case: "By blurring the distinction between inner and outer space, by reversing our standards of value and authenticity, we have returned once again to the shamanistic origins of adventure."[52] Perhaps not quite shamanistic, quests do invoke a "new simplicity" even as they move, in our global villages, through technologized space.

Chapter Four
The Space of Quest:
From Culture to Geopolitics

A missionary blamed his African flock for walking undressed. "And what about yourself?" they pointed to his visage, "are you not also, somewhere, naked?" "Well, but that's my face," the missionary objected. "In us," retorted the natives, "everywhere it is face."
— Roman Jakobson

What enterprise is more noble and more profitable than the reclamation from barbarism of fertile regions and large populations?
— Winston Churchill

W 1

HERE SEEK? Quests do not move only in spiritual and solitary space; theirs is also a worldly place wherein myth and politics, dream and reality, continually crash. In their wild innocence, seekers may hear a voice in the wind, depart at dawn one day — trusting others because they so deeply trust themselves — only to find themselves roughly cast between nature and civilization, between races, places, visions, histories. Such seekers pioneer the planetization of the earth, our timeless transhumanization; they encounter their Other, within themselves and outside, without seeking to overwhelm it.

The planetization of the earth may have begun with neolithic hunters, or perhaps with the first outcast who mated elsewhere. But with Columbus, Cabot, Magellan, Vasco da Gama, Drake, the earth became interactive in another way. This was an exuberant and bellicose moment for the West, grievous for other people who gradually fell prey to colonization, excepting some, like the Japanese, so remote, fierce, and cunning as to stay free. Later, industrialization in the West made both its power and *ratio* pervasive, accelerating all histories. By the middle of our century, Heidegger could lament "the complete Europeanization [he did not say Americanization] of the earth and of man," an infection, he claimed, that "attacks at the source of everything that is of an essential nature."[1]

But Heidegger proved impercipient in politics. Curiously, he ignores the

63

fact that his interlocutor (in the dialogue from which I have quoted) is a Japanese thinker, initiate of "silence" and the untranslatable concept of *Iki*, "the breath of the stillness of luminous delight."[2] In their dialogue, we meet the true condition of our world: not planetization only but also retribalization, not simply communication but the incommunicable as well. Where Heidegger saw only "the Europeanization of the earth and man," we perceive now variety, otherness, Lyotard's unspeakable Sublime. Where Heidegger saw only hegemony, we see factions and fractions refusing totality, Lyotard's *différend.*

Indeed, in matters geopolitical, Heidegger and Lyotard stand at the antipodes. The latter postulates radically incommensurable orders of discourse, of cultures, systems, ideas, "phrases" of every kind. Between these orders of *le différend,* there can be no adjudication, unlike orders of *le litige* which, in dispute, recognize a common court of appeals. Hence the silence that signals *le différend,* its pain and unatoned wrong.[3] Hence, too, the impossibility of writing a universal history of mankind, a universal code of knowledge. For every rule *we* apply and every law *we* proclaim is an exercise in power, without legitimacy in the eyes of the *other.*

This inordinately particular condition, however, may exist nowhere except in the minds of purist—I nearly said Cartesian—thinkers. In reality, self and other meet, mingle, embrace, conflict, stand for a moment aversively apart; they influence and contaminate one another. In reality, too, differences are a function less of logic than of desire and power: that is, differences are preserved, ignored, or transacted in accordance with interests on *both* sides. (The French government, for instance, may declare the Iranian more or less *différend* depending on the former's political concerns at the time.) And who, in any case, announces or certifies *le différend?* Where would such a speaker stand among the various orders of discourse?

The difficulties of this acute particularism, a form of negativity really, are stressed by Richard Rorty in his colloquy with Lyotard. Rorty accepts, conversationally, a pragmatism of liberal hope, tolerant of the world's mélange of conflicting values. He sees in that world, perhaps too benignly, as much "unity and transparency of language as a desire to converse rather than fight"; and he is unable, in practice, to distinguish between persuasion and free conviction, rhetoric and logic.[4] Thus Rorty stands genially between the totality of Heidegger and the potentially terrorist fragments of Lyotard.

Terrorism and totalitarianism may be extremes of our geopolitics, but our global condition is more hybrid and haphazard. This is the age of kitsch and cargo cults. If the West has learned *bricolage,* so have its Others in order to survive. "Occident" and "Orient" have contaminated one another. Far from being simply homogenized, Americanized, the world has become an immense warehouse of residues, plundered and preserved by unequal powers. This is what remains to us of the "virgin land," our pristine moiety in the earth.

The point helps us to perceive the space through which seekers move. Thus Gianni Vattimo elaborates the point:

> The great "warehouse of residues" is not so different from that storehouse of theatrical costumes to which Nietzsche compares the "garden of history". . . . The world of man in our time appears more and more as a theatrical storehouse, but without any ludic or aesthetic implications. . . . In such a world there is no "iron cage" (as Weber called it) of total technological organization nor a pure "glorification of the simulacra," which Deleuze has imagined. . . .

The space, then, is not only historical; it is aesthetic, hermeneutic, anthropological as well. As Vattimo concludes:

> Anthropology, like hermeneutics, is neither an encounter with radical Otherness nor a scientific "systematization" of the human phenomenon in terms of structures. It probably will return to its form of a dialogue with the archaic . . . , but in the only way in which the *arche* is given in the era of completed metaphysics: that of residues, marginality, and contamination.[5]

In the contemporary world, then, seekers move, I have said, between nature and civilization, between the West and its Others. In this space, they can not take the occidental datum for granted. History, Science, Culture, the Self, all come for dramatic revision, all suffer "contamination." This is nowhere more visible or anguished than in the ethnographer's enterprise. Alert to the ravages of cultural encounters, he or she can theorize them, a seeker (or perhaps scavenger, or perhaps redeemer) of Difference in alien cultures.

2

Here we must turn to Claude Lévi-Strauss. Few ethnographers have been more reflective, and at the same time more eager to establish mind as an object among the other objects of reality, in its nature a thing among things. Few have attested more poignantly to worlds on the wane. For as his work shows, every mode of cultural converse borders on aggression, and communication seems less a form of sociability than sociability itself "a lower limit of predatoriness." Such difficulties, however, do not induce Lévi-Strauss to abjure the epistemology of Western science "whose absolute superiority," he roundly states, "cannot be denied."[6] The difficulties, rather, educe confession; ethnography places itself in a public light.

This is the project of Lévi-Strauss in *Tristes Tropiques,* a brooding, heroic search for the totally Other among dying Amazonian Indians—the Caduveos, the Bororos, the Nambikwaras, and most remote of all, the Tupikawahibs. In the end, though, the author can only reveal the plight of his profession, which is that of Western civilization itself. As ethnographer, he can understand only what his own culture has already touched; what it has not (nearly nothing) remains to him unintelligible. This is hermeneutics in active predicament.

The woes of Lévi-Strauss come early. "Not for the first time," he admits, "I was experiencing those manifestations of stupidity, hatred, and credulity which all social groups secrete within themselves when history comes too close to them."[7] Such "manifestations" also reflect images of the observer himself, especially of his power—call it "travel power"—which he exercises in the sheer ability to observe, to intrude upon others. What else are those mysterious photographs we bring back from Borneo or Brazil? What else those palmy South Sea atolls we have turned into atomic testing sites or stationary aircraft carriers? What else the dreck we export everywhere, prized excreta of our civilization, even as our own ecological sensitivities increase?

But the exercise of "travel power" also benefits itself in other ways. Even the lone adventurer, to say nothing of the colonizer, "who wishes to wrest something from Destiny must venture into that perilous margin-country where the norms of Society count for nothing"; and, if he succeeds, will acquire new benefits in the very Society whose norms he has flouted.[8] Scathingly, Lévi-Strauss writes: "Lofty and lucrative are the 'revelations' which these young men [explorers] draw from those enemies of Society—savages, snowbound peaks, bottomless caves, and impenetrable forests—which Society conspires to ennoble at the very moment at which it has robbed them of their power to harm."[9] This is, of course, the wager every arrant venturer makes, though perhaps not every seeker bent on higher gains. It is also the wager every ethnographer, in his own fashion, makes. How candid, then, is Lévi-Strauss when he remarks: "Myself the already-gray predecessor of these 'explorers,' I may well be the only white traveler to have brought back nothing but ashes from my journeys"?[10] Ashes? Can he exclude all his books (including *From Honey to Ashes*), the whole system of structuralism, and his intellectual renown from his traveler's wages?

Lévi-Strauss persuades us more when he returns to the radical paradox of ethnography and, as I have insisted, of our own world. Here is the full passage:

> The paradox is irresoluble: the less one culture communicates with another, the less likely they are to be corrupted, one by the other; but, on the other hand, the less likely it is, in such conditions, that the respective emissaries of these cultures will be able to seize the richness and significance of their di-

versity. The alternative is inescapable: either I am a traveller in ancient times, and faced with a prodigious spectacle which would be almost entirely unintelligible to me and might, indeed, provoke me to mockery and disgust; or I am a traveller of our own day, hastening in search of a vanished reality. In either case I am the loser — and more heavily than one might suppose; for today, as I go groaning among the shadows, I miss, inevitably, the spectacle that is now taking shape. [11]

But there are other losses, contraditions, obdurate queries. Consider: the inveterate traveler is a kind of exile, a rebel or misfit at home. Does he not, then, idealize societies other than his own? Can he condone practices elsewhere — cannibalism, torture, slavery, ritual sacrifice, brute exploitation — practices he would resolutely condemn in his own country? Are cultural relativism and cultural chauvinism the only alternatives open to him? Or does he, by implication at least, refuse *all* societies, and so glorify the state of nature? And why did anthropology emerge as a science only in the West? Is that proof of the West's superior rationality — or rather of its guilt toward others, its remorse, which led it, as Lévi-Strauss says, "to compare its own image with other societies, in the hope that they would either display the same shortcomings or help the West to explain how these defects could have come into being"? [12] Finally, isn't every ethnographer, every serious traveler really, a kind of quixotic redeemer, engaged in both comprehending and rectifying all the failures of the human race? Or is he merely a *writer* of other cultures, engaged in self-reflexive poiesis, seeing *himself* as Other, and so "repatriating the exotic"? [13]

Intractable queries. I project them, through *Tristes Tropiques,* to limn the anxious space of quest in our day. As for Lévi-Strauss, his final answers strike me as strenuously naive. Ethnography, he believes, must "rediscover the 'natural Man' in his relation to the social state"; this "natural Man," like Rousseau's Golden Age, lies neither behind nor ahead but within us all. [14] Presumably, Lévi-Strauss would "rediscover" that human abstract within the deep structures of language and myth. Yet having discovered him there, Lévi-Strauss hastens to abolish our species. "The world began without the human race and it will end without it," he announces; for man is but an entropy machine, "brought perhaps to a greater point of perfection than any other," yet finally doomed to decompose all systems within his reach. [15] Fatidic entropology!

Ethnography will not deliver the world, though it may explain some trials of its transhumanization. Nor can it explain the shocking disparities between nations, say Switzerland and Bhutan. What can? But at the very least, ethnography can qualify our romances of the Other, of Nature and Primitivism, romances that sing in every seeker's head. And it can enhance our ecological sense of the earth, that sense every seeker makes part of his quest. Such a sense, though, will not rest on some idea of original innocence or lost purity, since Nature and Primitivism are always constituted by our discourse. Thus ecology, like ethnology or hermeneutics, becomes subject to the law of contamination, which recognizes that anything purely Other is an ideological fiction, meant to encourage our dialogue with the world.[16]

This notion of a contaminated or, better, constituted primitivism, constituted by the entire experience of modernity, which includes imperialism, differs from the primitivism of many artists earlier in our century. Yet the two kinds share a certain anxiety or dis-ease. As William Barrett put it, perhaps too simply, three decades ago: "The tradition of Western humanism has faltered, become questionable. . . . Hence we respond to the archetypal images of prehumanist man, more abstract and impersonal than the features of man as we know him."[17] Those last features, I suspect, were Kilroy's, already everywhere — *our* features.

3

The dis-ease of the West is nonetheless real, prompting men and women to risk their lives far from societies they disavow. Often they elude their own sahib-kind, whom they find more dangerous and repugnant than any "natives," drawn to the latter, perhaps erotically, in associations that racism or simply difference may subtly excite. Often, they themselves "go native," repugning a life they perceive as vapid, sated, noxious, a delirium of boredom and high-tech genocide — culture shock is what they experience on returning *home!* In short, they flee the contemporary world, flee Western history, hoping to discover another time in another place. Their journeys are as much quests as escapes, no less judgments on occidental reality than assays in utopia.

Yet the best among them also realize that "paradise" is made in the mind, precisely to be lost and perpetually regained. They sense, too, that though the plaint "Nothing is left to explore" has been a recurrent plaint for a hundred years, the world has indeed shrunk, putting nature everywhere in dire jeopardy.[18] Contemptuous of worldly power, they feel themselves become its reluctant agents. Thus organized quest leads easily to conquest; we call it imperialism, colonialism. This has prompted Salman Rushdie to quip: "Adventure and politics are best kept apart, rather like uranium and plutonium."[19] The advice is apt though rarely practical; for nuclear politics now permeates the most isolate enterprise, spreading our dis-ease.

Here we touch on something strange: I call it the adventurer's "wound." Frequently this is a literal, if obscure, infection, a mysterious disease like the Grail King's. Herman Melville suffers it in *Typee,* Francis Parkman in *The Oregon Trail,* Ernest Hemingway in *The Green Hills of Africa.* They all endure some debility, some "pathetic" (the word is Melville's) flaw, a failure in their pampered immune systems. It is as if, in each seeker, two organic as well as cultural orders struggle more than meet. Call them Self and Other; or call them the West and all *its* Others, those people it has discovered and deformed in the name of modernization. Thus the "wound," secret agon of the blood, throbs also with infections of the colonial plague. Is this the wound of postwar history, the revenge of the repressed, on an earth caught between enforced planetization and virulent retribalization? Khomeinis, Gaddafis, Abu Nidals, all the world's zealots, spray their answer with Kalishnikovs.

Yet "the wound" is not only external, a gash in history, cicatrix of cultures. "The wound" is also in the traveler's mind, in his divided consciousness, his alienated state. It is in his ambitious gaze, a gaze without innocence, sometimes panoptic, at once wounded and wounding. Encroaching on primal societies, the explorer finds, indeed *brings,* a serpent in every "paradise" — which, always ready, has other serpents waiting there. Being human, he disturbs the pleroma of existence. Being, in addition, a *writer,* he disrupts that pleroma even more. Perhaps this is the "pathetic flaw" of the scribbling adventurer who turns all life into words.

Note, though, who writes, who speaks. It is not the wilderness nor its aborigines. Note who ventures and seeks. It is not the "native." In the Middle Ages, Arabs raided the earth, roamed the seas, and Ibn Battuta rivaled Marco Polo in reach. In the fourteenth century, Ottomans looked on northern Europe much as Europeans were later to look upon the Americas, rich and heathen lands fit mainly for plunder.[20] But it was really in the Renaissance, with the great European voyagers "in search of Christians and spices" (da Gama), that natives became "natives" because they remained where they were born. They were dis-covered, un-earthed; like children, they were not meant to be heard, only seen. The winsome Bushmen and gentle Tasaday may have perfected an irenic mode of existence. But they have not traveled far from the Kalahari Desert or the rain forests of Mindanao — nor far from the Stone Age. It took another kind of curiosity, drive, aggression, ingenuity, restlessness to "speak" them so that we could all hear.[21] And as Western explorers spoke them, everyone heard, everyone changed. This became the discourse of imperialism.

The discourse could be grimly hilarious. Thus, for instance, the bluff Englishman, in Robert Louis Stevenson's *The Beach at Falesá,* comments on his two daughters, born to a Samoan wife: "what bothers me is the girls. They're only half castes of course; I know that as well as you do, and there's nobody thinks less of half castes than I do; but they're mine, and about all I've got; I can't reconcile my mind to their taking up with kanakas, and I'd like to know where I'm to find them whites?"[22] Stevenson's irony was fully conscious; and even Kipling warned his countrymen on Victoria's Diamond Jubilee:

> Far-called, our navies melt away;
> On dune and headland sinks the fire:
> Lo, all our pomp of yesterday
> Is one with Nineveh and Tyre!

("Recessional")

4

The critique of colonialism had begun, and was to reach after the Second World War paroxysms of outrage. Caught in a violent, Manichean history, that critique sometimes merely inverted colonial stereotypes, black become white, evil good, an exercise in tendentiousness—hence the acrimony surrounding V. S. Naipaul who insists on veracity rather than advocacy or apologetics in his reports on the third world.[23]

Outrage can give no license to mendacity, nor can mendacity heal damaged spirits. But neither could the abominations of colonialism remain forever hid. They are indeed exposed, analyzed, censured in a number of brilliant works, ranging from Frantz Fanon's *The Wretched of the Earth* to Edward Said's *Orientalism*. Nor is Western humanism spared, which Sartre exorbitantly calls, in his introduction to Fanon, an "ideology of lies and pillage," an alibi of aggression. Fanon himself clarifies best the sinister exchanges between colonizer and colonized. If the former resorts to the vocabulary of the bestiary (speaking the native in "zoological terms"), the latter ends by introjecting the values of his speaker. Even the native intellectual, Fanon grieves, "throws himself greedily upon Western culture." "He will not be content to know Rabelais and Diderot, Shakespeare and Edgar Allan Poe; he will bind them to his intelligence as closely as possible."[24] I need not remark, a quarter of a century after the publication of *Les Damnés de la terre* (1961), how prophetic Fanon's vision has proven, and also how warped by its own extremity.

There is less violence in Said's view, if not less predisposition. The "Orient," he argues, is a European invention, a form of cultural and political production. Moreover, "European culture gained in strength and identity by setting itself off against the Orient as a sort of surrogate and even underground self"; and it has universalized the claims of its own history, the only World History.[25] Said then reminds us that Flaubert *could* represent the courtesan Kuchuk Hanem in his memoirs of Egypt; *she* had no means to represent herself. (Nor, I might add, has any one of us who lacks the power to roil history.)

But was it power alone, the power bequeathed to him by Napoleon, Champollion, and Jean-Baptiste-Joseph Fourier, that permitted Flaubert to "speak" Kuchuk Hanem? In 1846, Flaubert made this entry in another journal that Said does not quote:

> Among navigators there are some who discover worlds, who add new continents to the earth and new constellations to the heavens: they are the masters, eternally splendid. Others belch terror from their vessels' guns and wax rich and fat from their plunder. Still others leave home to seek gold and silk under foreign skies. And still others merely let down their nets to catch salmon for gourmets and cod for the poor. I am the obscure and patient pearl-fisher, who dives deep and comes up empty-handed and blue in the face. A fatal attraction draws me down into the abysses of thought, down to those innermost recesses that never lose their fascination for the strong.[26]

Here, I suggest, is the trace of an inner stance, of some willful personal attitude—the kind, incidentally, that Emerson would spontaneously understand—to which Flaubert's privileged discourse owes more than we admit. Here is an artistic version of the "ideology of adventure" we have already met, so crucial to the West.

The irksome point requires that I return to it by another way. No doubt the West has constituted, often controlled, its silent Others by the institutions of Orientalism. But such institutions are not unique to the West. Said ignores a tradition of Counter-Orientalism, a popular "Occidentalism," so to speak, rather contemptuous of "infidel and uncircumcised" Europeans. Coincidentally, another scholar, also named Said, Quadi of the Moslem city of Toledo, wrote in 1068 about northern (i.e., European) barbarians, "more like beasts than like men":

> For those of them who live furthest to the north . . . the excessive distance of the sun in relation to the zenith line makes the air cold and the sky cloudy. Their temperaments are therefore frigid, their humors raw, their bellies gross, their color pale, their hair long and lank. Thus they lack keenness of understanding and clarity of intelligence, and are overcome by ignorance and apathy. . . .[27]

Conceivably, Edward Said neglects this old tradition of reverse discrimination because it has proven, until quite recently, impotent, unable to translate—translation deals always with figures of power and foreignness—to carry itself over, in an effective ideological discourse of its own. But why? Why did the "infidel" and "barbarous" West possess that historical power? Why was it able, since the Age of Exploration, to impose its will on so many others? What induced those explorations in the first place, that urge for adventure and quest? And why did the Occident develop the discipline of Orientalism while the Orient lacked, until the mid-nineteenth century, any sustained scholarship about the Occident, even any grammar or lexicon of a European language?[28] To answer simply by invoking science, technology, or sea power is to beg one renitent question with another.

Such questions may seem indelicate — or perhaps merely delicate — yet they must be faced. Certainly I have no confident answers to offer, only meditated guesses. Let us suppose that a set of circumstances arose in Europe, by accident or design, by everything that still defies historical explanation. Among these circumstances I want to count diverse factors: geography, mercantilism, secularization, an idea of progress, scientific detachment, individual rights, some political freedoms, a certain fluidity in class structures. I want to count also personal qualities: will, consequence, self-reliance, a transgressive (or innovative) urge, a capacity for sustained self-criticism, that inner stance Flaubert revealed a moment ago. Could these begin to explain the ascendancy of the West, the projection of modernity, in the last three centuries? Could they provide the basis of some "a-causal explanation"?

But my task, finally, is not to second-guess the inequities of history, only to comprehend the motives of its seekers. Certainly the latter exhibit an independent attitude. Emerson put it more forcibly: "A man should learn to detect and watch that gleam of light which flashes across his mind from within, more than the lustre of the firmament of bards and sages. . . . I shun father and mother and wife and brother when my genius calls me. I would write on the lintels of the door-post, *Whim.* I hope it is somewhat better than whim at last, but we cannot spend the day in explanation. Expect me not to show cause why I seek. . . ."[29]

5

I will return to that Emersonian Whim. But the name of the sublime essayist reminds us that our subject — a self on quest — is after all American. Though he — increasingly she — may move alone in transhumanized space, the subject remains the unwilling emblem of American power, of an anguished, latter-day "manifest destiny." Once the frontier absorbed all his vision and fury; but the frontier closed, except in Alaska or outer space; now he is loosed upon the world, a brave, new "third world," a wanderer without innocence, abroad.

Yet that third world, a cauldron of contradictions, differs greatly from the old colonial order. Nor is the American adventurer heir to the grand illusions of European imperialism, even if democracy ("making the world safe for democracy") and empire (manifest and destined) remain aggressive in his politics. From Andrew Jackson to Teddy Roosevelt, of course, an exuberant jingoism rang in the United States, and still rings today. But

America lacked such men as Palmerston, Disraeli, Salisbury, Balfour, Cromer, Curzon, Kitchener, Lugard, architects of an empire on which the sun began to set only in 1945. Nor did America raise generation after generation of men and women "who went out to the tropics at the imperial high noon," says the English author of *Out in the Noonday Sun,* "unclouded by doubts about their mission to 'rule the earth,' or at least to sort out its dark untidy places into some kind of decent order."[30]

Discovered more than discovering in earlier centuries, America had no dubious romance with Africa or Asia, and despite its Rough Riders or marines, had no great military investment abroad.[31] This aloofness, of course, has drastically changed. But so has the world out there, no longer so alluring or strange. Where is Shangri-la now? Chinese troops have stormed Tibet, and Soviet tanks rumbled in the legendary mountain paths of the North-West Frontier. A new, often savage, nationalism sweeps the remotest lands, even as modern ideologies contend bloodily with the tribal myths of nations developing mainly in birth and death rates.[32] And as revolution after counterrevolution there fails, hunger and torture compete to hold the higher ground.

Once again, this is the geopolitical space of quest, the space of our planetization, retribalization. The paradox assaults developing nations from *within* even more than from without. For in these nations, as Clifford Geertz acutely sees, primordial ("indigenous") attachments and civic ("epochal") orders — say tribe and state — constantly clash:

> peoples of the new states are simultaneously animated by two powerful, thoroughly interdependent, yet distinct and often actually opposed motives — the desire to be recognized as responsible agents whose wishes, acts, hopes, and opinions "matter," and the desire to build an efficient, dynamic modern state. The one aim is to be noticed: it is a search for an identity, and a demand that the identity be publicly acknowledged as having import, a social assertion of the self as "being somebody in the world." The other aim is practical: it is a demand for progress, for a rising standard of living, more effective political order, greater social justice, and beyond that of "playing a part in the larger arena of world politics," of "exercising influence among the nations." The two motives are, again, most intimately related, because citizenship in a truly modern state has more and more become the most broadly negotiable claim to personal significance. . . .[33]

Meanwhile, an opposite trend, perhaps merely complementary, emerges in "truly modern states." This trend — call it international tourism — appears as the latest stage of colonialism and modernization. For several centuries, of course, Western discourse distinguished between "civilized" and "primitive" societies — euphemistically, we now say "developed" and "developing." And for several centuries, we have seen, the West enhanced its identity in negotiations with its others, leading Dean MacCannell to remark that self-discovery through encounters with an "Absolute Other" is a sign of our civilization.[34] But mass tourism and mass leisure redefine the world's geopolitical space: "the best indication," MacCannell claims, "of the final victory of modernity over other sociocultural arrangements is not the disappearance of the nonmodern world, but its artificial preservation and reconstruction in modern society" through a giant tourist industry.[35] The focus of this industry is "sightseeing":

> Sightseeing is a kind of collective striving for a transcendence of the modern totality, a way of attempting to overcome the discontinuity of modernity, of incorporating its fragments into unified experience. Of course, it is doomed to eventual failure: even as it tries to construct totalities, it celebrates differentiation.
>
> The locus of sightseeing in the middle class is understandable in other than merely economic terms. It is the middle class that systematically scavenges the earth for new experiences to be woven into a collective, touristic version of other peoples and other places. . . .
>
> The touristic integration of society resembles a catalogue of displaced forms. In this regard it is empirically accurate. The differentiations of the modern world have the same structure as tourist attractions: elements dislodged from their original natural, historical and cultural contexts fit together with other such displaced or modernized things and people. The differentiations *are* the attractions.[36]

Such is the irritable condition the Western seeker encounters in the world today. But if he is an American, the encounter is all the more grating. For America, both democracy and empire, now carries a titanic burden in the world, far heavier than any colonial White Man's Burden. America has become *itself the world's other,* a dangerous or ambiguous other to all nations, even in the West. This geopolitical sentiment, which no American tourist escapes, is also what we crassly call anti-Americanism, the latest version of "Occidentalism," a global discourse that constitutes America, interprets it systematically to its demerit. Whence its origins? Why does America currently attract so much mixed curiosity, admiration, aversion, and disdain? Here I can only adduce the sense of my own experience as a naturalized American, though I do recall a long tradition of deprecation, reverting to Columbus, rife with stereotypes about "naked savages," "shiftless emigrants," "cunning Yankees," "ruthless profiteers," and "ugly Americans." In our own moment, though, the provocations are more proximate:

1. Envy. America still "has it better," as Goethe said, despite all the afflictions of its recent history. Everyone, after all — everyone except certain intellectuals — can recognize the difference between nations that build walls

to prevent their inmates from breaking out, and others, like America, that build ineffectual barriers to prevent millions from rushing in.

2. Americanization has come to mean the very process of modernization, radical, interactive change. This brings future shock, current schlock, menaces to traditional values of every kind. For modernization also means dispersal, diffusion (mass society, mass media), an immanence of codes and products, "Dallas" everywhere. Countries suddenly catapulted into the twentieth century (Iran), and others with vast cultural pretensions (France), resent this threat to their primordial or national identities. Thus America becomes "The Great Satan" (Khomeini).

3. America also projects the threat of the "new colonialism," especially in nations that still resent the old. As synecdoche of the West, America has become the symbol of military and economic imperialism, whether actual, virtual, or imaginary. As one of the two superpowers, America inspires little affection, except where the other superpower reigns. (At Yalta, we recall, the superpowers carved up Europe as the old soi-disant "Great Powers" once carved up their colonies in Africa or Asia.)

4. Because of its wealth, because of its vested geopolitical interests — interests, incidentally, from which *every* American benefits, if unequally — America acts cautiously, too cautiously, toward liberation movements in the world. Hence it is perceived as conservative, even reactionary, a friend to oppressive regimes (in Iran and the Philippines formerly, in South Korea and South Africa now).

5. America's allies suffer from a Middle Power Complex. They can not abide an America too weak or an America too strong — too weak for their security, too strong for their self-esteem. Yet none there knows where to draw the magic line between fear and vainglory. Profoundly dependent on American power, they surrender easily to pique, cavil, defiance, that irascibility which marks Euro-Gaullism.

6. Around the world, a new generation has come of age, recalling little of America's role in World War II, little of its generosity and idealism. And since few in that generation ever heard boot steps on their own stairs, the terrible knock at three o'clock in the morning, they denigrate affluent democracy, using their freedoms to undermine the freedom of all.

7. Worst of all, anti-Americanism battens on America's own failures of itself. The dirge is familiar: Vietnam, Watergate, political assassination, perfidious or feeble presidents, a degree of poverty and illiteracy intolerable amid our riches. Some, like George Steiner, even add that American culture itself has become archival, its energy mainly "custodian" and "exhibitionist" rather than originary, a culture, finally, of pop and glitz.[37]

Cause enough for anti-Americanism, all these animadversions; and cause enough to mark any hero on his quest. But how many of these strictures are specious, or else inevitable in the historic course of things? In their ceaseless historical labor, power and error find pause in the lucidity of American self-criticism, our bequest from Puritans and revolutionaries. On July 3, 1776, John Adams wrote to Abigail: "The furnace of affliction produces refinement, in States as well as individuals. And the new governments we are assuming in every part will require a purification from our vices, and an augmentation of our virtues, or they will be no blessings. The people will have unbounded power, and the people are extremely addicted to venality, as well as the great."[38]

6

For us, however, the abiding questions concern the American quester, the motive, history, and space of his journey, how that space affects him, and the nature of his own self-apprehension as an other, an American, as he moves in the contemporary world. For Otherness is not merely *given,* an attribute of others; it can be an attribute of ourselves, either in self-alienation or in response to the relentless gaze of another—not only in colonies, prison camps, hostage cells, but sometimes even in the broad light of day, as I once experienced my own strangeness in Shanghai, alone in a sea of Sinic faces.

The seeker, then, is a traveler among realms of being, eternal mediator between our multiple selves and our multiple othernesses. This sustains, as Geertz says, "'the social history of the moral imagination,' meaning by that the tracing out of the way in which our sense of ourselves and others—ourselves amidst others—is affected not only by our traffic with our own cultural forms but to a significant extent by the characterization of forms not immediately ours. . . ."[39] Unlike the anthropologist, however, the seeker puts himself at larger risk, physical and spiritual, a risk not only of death but of derangement, ostracism, desperate failure.

In the end, some Emersonian Whim is at the bottom of all quest, I think. But something else, too, that Emerson neglects: a Wound. For the adventurer/seeker is mainly a Westerner, scion of the rich of the earth, drawn to the wretched by a need, a dis-ease, they may find ludicrous. Though he may be neither soldier nor colonizer, domination no less than quest is the motive of his history and its deep wound. But this is also the wound from which history, planetized history, flows, sometimes suppurates. His flight from modernity can not avail, nor his search for lost innocence, nor his nostalgia for otherness. His yearnings for desolations of sand and snow, in Arabia or Antarctica, lead him to an abandoned Coke bottle that rules space more than Stevens' jar ever ruled the hills of Tennessee. Yet his will, malaise, disequilibrium, some radical whim or wound or asymmetry in his being, has made our world knowable, made the world we know.[40] Edging cultures, hedging histories, acting riskily, most often alone, this seeker — man or woman — gives us an indefectible perception that, from our best selves, speaks to all.

Part 2
The Texts
of Quest

We are in search of quests, quests plural and in literature. But as we have seen, the genre is various, all blurred around the edges. We do better to look at particular works in the hope of discovering an "ideal text of quest" which, though imaginary, may illumine the field of our concern. This text will be germane to the forms of myth, romance, adventure, travel, and autobiography. In it, a self, wounded somehow yet acting willfully or whimsically upon its wound, puts itself at risk. In it, too, risk, physical and spiritual, calls for displacement, strain, a movement toward something other, unknown, numinous, something somehow redemptive. It is a teleological movement, albeit a movement full of diversions, disruptions, utter surprises. It is also a movement—personal on one level, sociopolitical on another—that entails encounters between cultures, values, histories, entails frictions between modes of human existence. Such encounters serve as critiques, implicit or explicit, of contemporary American society. Beyond such critiques, however, quests cry for openness of being, for atonement or cosmic reconciliation, a long desire rarely fully assuaged.

Can all these elements of an ideal, an imaginary text coincide in a given work? More probably one element or another will lack. But such lacks themselves help to limn the features, discern the faces, of quest. In the end, viewing these faces as we move from text to text may reward us more than defining an ideal text of quest. For thus only can we sense the prodigal diversity of private motives and public obsessions in America, the luxuriance in the forms of our want. Thus only can we perceive the formal cunning of desire in literature.

In Part 2, therefore, I examine some works of nonfiction and of fiction, moving gradually in each chapter to exemplary texts of quest. In no way, though, should this suggest that a work deficient in the attributes of quest is consequently deficient as a literary work; *merit derives from no preconceived ideal or mode. We should not wonder, though, if quest, ever companion to romance, finds a more genial home in novels than in factual narratives. In novels, imaginative freedom, a certain gaiety of reality, is more keenly felt; in them, too, interest in story, character, dialogue, style is generally more vivid. But these are matters of degree, of nuance. In fiction as in nonfiction, quest takes the language of the self to task and witness, and words walk in the shadow of death.*

Chapter Five
Faces of Quest: Fact

Women who travel as I travel are dreamers. Our lives seem to be lives of endless possibility. Like readers of romances we think that anything can happen to us at any time. We forget that this is not our real life—our life of domestic details, work pressures, attempts and failures at human relations. We keep moving. From anecdote to anecdote, from hope to hope. Around the next bend something new will befall us. Nostalgia has no place for the woman traveling alone. Our motion is forward, whether by train or daydream. Our sights are on the horizon, across strange terrain, vast desert, unfordable rivers, impenetrable ice peaks.

— Mary Morris

. . . wishing is a form of destiny. Making our wish, we make ourselves. We exist in the time between the wish and its fulfillment.

— Paul Zweig

1

EVERY NARRATIVE with a far gleam in the narrator's eye aspires to quest. If factual, the story may further claim the authority of the real: "I was there, I speak true!" But these veridical accounts, mingling memory and desire, differ greatly in form, differ even more in their assumptions about quest. Hence our need to move freely, glimpsing the faces of seekers and nonseekers, of quests and pseudo quests, alike.

Is, for instance, the most spectacular achievement of our century, perhaps of all centuries—I mean the voyage to the moon—a quest? Michael Collins' *Carrying the Fire* (1974) helps us to pose the question. Literate, precise, Collins' personal account of the *Gemini 10* and *Apollo 11* space journeys strikes in its very title the right (i.e., WASP) Promethean note. The training, the trials, the feats are staggering; it takes the drive of a test pilot, "mostly hyperthyroid, superachieving first sons of superachievers" (C, 1),[1] to make an astronaut. Indomitable will and physical fitness, though, are scarcely enough. Both technological and ecological know-how are necessary, both individual initiative and team effort. Above all, a certain need, urgency, spirit are required. Collins quotes Thoreau: "It is not worthwhile to go around the world to count the cats in Zanzibar," then remarks: "Oh no? Then for what purpose, to count the pulse of man?" (*C,* 135). Here is the motive, sufficient unto itself.

Though he is only the seventeenth man in space, and though he himself never leaves *Columbia* — Neil Armstrong and Buzz Aldrin shuttle in *Eagle* to the moon — Collins reveals, beneath his astronaut's cool, an epic sense of his mission. He experiences his solitude acutely as he awaits in orbit his companions' return from the moon, a crux in infinite space, a human hinge of fate. But he experiences, too, the exalted meaning, the symbolic import, of *Apollo 11,* as do the other two astronauts. "This is a small step for a man, but a great leap for mankind," Armstrong historically declares, while Aldrin quotes from the Psalms: "When I consider the heavens, the work of Thy fingers, the moon and the stars, which Thou has ordained; what is man that Thou art mindful of him?" and Collins quotes from Eliot's *Quartets:* "We shall not cease from exploration and the end of all our exploring will be to arrive where we started and know the place for the first time" (*C,* 453, 462).

At journey's end, Collins shares with us his insights. He has acquired a certain perspective on worldly things, a detachment bordering at times on "earthly ennui." He has observed the earth, a floating miracle in black space, and perceived its utter fragility. From one hundred thousand miles out, he has also intuited its unity. "The earth *must* become as it appears," he says: "blue and white, not capitalist or Communist; blue and white, not rich or poor; blue and white, not envious or envied" (*C,* 479f.). Meanwhile, in his speech to a joint session of Congress on September 16, 1969, he recommends that we look both ways: to the earth and the moon, the past and the future. For Collins, the human imperative is never in doubt: "Man has always gone where he has been able to go. It's that simple. He will continue pushing back his frontier, no matter how far it may carry him from his homeland" (*C,* 487).

This is the right stuff, the stuff of risk and long vision. This is what prompted President Kennedy to commit the resources of the United States to put a man on the moon before the end of his fatal decade. This is also what moved Charles Lindbergh, in his foreword to *Carrying the Fire,* to suggest that *Apollo 11* takes us "to the periphery of human evolution," and beyond that to "universal explorations" which may "have no need for vehicles or matter" (*C,* xiif.). Still, we must wonder: is Collins' journey truly a quest? He chooses to become an astronaut because he is eager, adventurous, a West Pointer born to a military family of generals. The space program simply allows him to *distinguish* himself; it does not project for him an inner necessity or sound a personal call. For Collins, who claims to be "lazy," reveals no particular urgency in himself, or wound, no tendency to brood on motives, metaphysics, or the dark intricacies of the heart. As he candidly admits, his eyes see more on his miraculous journeys than his "brain" (he does not say mind) can assimilate. He remains resolutely Apollonian in his sunny, transparent prose, a knight in shining space suit, a knight without reproach. What else could we wish him to be? It is fit that he should say about the crucial docking of *Eagle:* "If we were bullfighters, we would call it the moment of truth, but all I want is a moment of no surprise" (*C,* 400). Collins is of course right, though his aseptic comment kills the germs of quest. Between NASA's astronauts and Jason's Argonauts lie all the feats of bureaucracy and technocracy, and three millennia of Western history.

2

The seeker as technocrat: is this the sole choice of our century? Hardly.

Though Annie Dillard does not travel into outer space, her work comes nearer to rendering the feeling of quest. This is perhaps due to her ecstatic prose, full of wonder and love. Thus she starts *Holy the Firm* (1977): "Every day is a god, each day is a god, and holiness holds forth in time" (*H,* 11). Her language is as textured as her perception, an Orphic poetry with terrors small and near at hand; her path is that of the solitary wanderer, in the wilderness of the Cascades or Blue Ridge Mountains, living in a rough log cabin to "study hard things."

She admits: "Nothing is going to happen in this book. There is only a little violence here and there in the language, at the corner where eternity clips time" (*H,* 24). Actually Julia, the child of a neighbor, burns off her face in an airplane accident. (Seraphs also blaze with Divine Love.) This becomes an occasion for Dillard's Job-like quarrel with God. The quarrel, as always, is and is never resolved. The book becomes spiritual meditation, accusation, devotional song, becomes, above all, paean and elegy to Julie, now dissolved into the English mystic, Julia of Norwich, now torched in trees near an airstrip at Puget Sound — a little girl baptized "into the bladelike arms of God" (*H,* 73).

But where is quest in all this? Perhaps only in the pilgrim passion of Dillard, a passion somewhat more evident in *Pilgrim at Tinker Creek* (1974). There, the author appears as poet, naturalist, mystic, but also as devotee of sight, by the world and all its creatures possessed, a sojourner in a Heraclitean scheme of change. "The whole show has been on fire from the word go . . ." (*P,* 10), she cries. In this scheme, she thinks of herself as a stalker, a hunter, or the instrument of the hunt itself, an arrow shaft, "carved along my length by unexpected lights and gashes from the very sky, and this book is the straying trail of blood" (*P,* 13). She is, above all, a *seer,* trying to cognize the world, name it as Adam did in his original sight, trying to see it as saints see by hushing all useless interior babble.

Dillard's world is suffused with violence and grace. A giant water bug devours horribly a frog. "That it's rough out there and chancy is no surprise. Every live thing is a survivor on a kind of extended emergency bivouac" (*P,* 7). But if profligacy is the hallmark of creation, so is epiphany or grace. Everything preys in nature on its kin; still, self and other can suddenly fuse. "I am the skin the wind plays over; I am petal, feather, stone" (*P,* 205), Dillard, latter-day Transcendentalist, exclaims. The miracle is in reciprocities, immanent and invisible. The miracle, also, is in the jungle seething within a water drop, observed beneath a scope. And the miracle of both miracles is in the human drive to comprehend both grace and violence when the "tense hum of consciousness" pauses.

Antic, ecological, epiphanic, Annie Dillard's vision, so rich in natural lore, may allude fleetingly to Thoreau's far crustier mood. But her vision is distinctly her own. It is a sweet, quizzical vision, firm enough to face evil and death in the universe. It knows the spareness of winter, "northings" of the soul: "I seek a reduction, a shedding, a sloughing off" (*P,* 257). It will not blink before horror: the water bug devouring a live frog, a hag skinning her daughter to wrap herself in bloody beauty and lie with her son-in-law. The prose may sometimes veer to pretty; the vision returns us to the whole. Is it not the vision of a true seeker?

The author of *Pilgrim at Tinker Creek* thinks of herself as "a fugitive and a vagabond, a sojurner seeking signs" (*P,* 274f.). She wants to "make whoopee" in the world, not hay, raise Cain or Lazarus instead of tomatoes. She wants, like Ezekiel to "go up in the gaps," the "spirit's home," "the clifts in the rock where you cower to see the back parts of God" (*P,* 276). And like Emerson, she dreams of eating the world whole, an apple proffered by the angel. This is the quester's stance. If the book strains the concept of quest, it is only because it lacks inner development—Dillard is no different at the end from the start—lacks also physical peril, exotic journeys, the call of distant cultures, lacks action in threatening space. But is *Pilgrim at Tinker Creek* any the worse for that?

3

There is another kind of quest: a search for origins, for roots, for identity really. The search, traversing time and space, also crosses ethnic borders or barriers of race. That is, the "backward" journey traces lineage in a motley world of tangled tribes, memories, generations.

The quest for remembrance, or rather, remembrance as heroic quest, is the compelling motive of Alex Haley's *Roots: The Saga of an American*

Family (1976), published coincidentally on the Bicentennial of the United States, and dedicated "as a birthday offering to my country." In this massive, moving, exhaustively researched book, a work of obsessive curiosity animated by anger, love, and reconciliation, Haley traces his ancestry back to the birth of Kunta Kinte, named "the African" by his American descendants, in the village of Juffure, The Gambia, West Africa, in "the spring of 1750." The vital clues come from tales, key words, handed down through seven generations—Haley hears them from his "Grandma, Aunt Liz, Aunt Plus, and Cousin Georgie"—from some linguists at the University of Wisconsin, and most decisively, from the *griot*s of the Mandinka tribe, "walking archives of oral history" who hold the collective memory of West Africa in their keep. As the latter remind him: "every living person ancestrally goes back to some time and some place where no writing existed; and then human memories and mouths and ears" carried the burden of history without "the crutch of print" (*R,* 674f.).

Roots has some crucial elements of quest. It has the drive, urgency, vision of quest. It has its critical moments: "poking about" the British Museum one day, Haley finds the Rosetta Stone, and hears a click in his mind, a door unlocking on his own past. The book also has its "peak experiences": for example, Haley in his Gambian "native" village, surrounded by "jet black" faces, *every one* of them black, chanting *"Meester Kinte! Meester Kinte!"* making him sob and "bawl out" as he had never done before. Finally, Haley himself refers to his search for roots, for an authentic historical and personal identity, as "quest" (*R,* 674).[2] For all that, *Roots* does not project itself, nor is it received by the reader, mainly as a quest romance.

The reasons for this are primarily formal. One hundred and seventeen of its one hundred and twenty chapters simply read as a historical novel, written from an omniscient point of view. How else could Haley render the story of his ancestors from Gambia, through the horrendous sea passage on the *Lord Ligonier* (98 survive out of 140) and slavery on Virginia plantations, to Reconstruction days in Tennessee? Suddenly, at the end of chapter 117, Haley shifts to the first person: "Her heart pounding, and with Will gazing incredulously over her shoulder, Cynthia pulled back the blanket's top fold—revealing a round brown face. . . . The baby boy, six weeks old, was me" (*R,* 662). From this point on, Haley speaks in his own personal voice, recapitulating in brief the main events of six generations we have seen, and recounting the story of his own search for the story we have read. Thus the quest part of *Roots* comprises only the last three chapters, "leading" in imagined flashbacks to the first hundred and seventeen.

What, then, is *Roots,* this work so moving and sometimes sentimental in its evocation of the African and American black experience, this testimony to a man's extraordinary will to atone for—Haley sleeps for ten nights,

half naked, on a plank in the hold of a freighter bound from Africa to
New York, as small memorial to the passion of Kunta Kinte—atone for
and become at one with his heritage? Exile and return, quest and fulfillment, are in its pattern, though none of these defines its form; nor does
fiction really define its mode. Haley defines best the genre:

> To the best of my knowledge and of my effort, every lineage statement within
> *Roots* is from either my African or American families' carefully preserved oral
> history, much of which I have been able conventionally to corroborate with
> documents. . . . Since I wasn't yet around when most of the story occurred,
> by far most of the dialogue and most of the incidents are of necessity a novel-
> ized amalgam of what I *know* took place together with what my researching
> led me to plausibly *feel* took place. (*R,* 686)

Elsewhere, Haley adds:

> Each character portrayed within *Roots* is felt to symbolize many thousands
> of persons of similar, general personalities and circumstances . . . who once
> lived in West Africa . . . who were crew and cargo of slave ships . . . and who
> lived in plantations within the United States.[3]

We can leave it at that.

Other journeys, in search of roots, may come closer in form to the auto-
biographical mode of quest: for instance, Michael J. Arlen's *Exiles* and
Passage to Ararat (1970, 1975), in which the author explores his repressed
Armenian heritage, his place in a history of massacres and diaspora, his
patrimony. His father, born Dikran Kouyoumdjian, becomes known as
Michael Arlen, a patrician anglophile, an affluent, popular novelist on easy
terms with Hemingway, Maugham, Fitzgerald, Clark Gable, and Noël
Coward, and perhaps the prototype for Michaelis in *Lady Chatterley's
Lover*—Arlen also tells his son that he introduced Duff Twysden to Hem-
ingway, who put her, as Lady Brett, in *The Sun Also Rises*.

The theme of *Exiles,* a memoir, is indeed exile: the exile of father and
son, first in England then America, from their heritage, the "exile," too,
of the son from his father who preserves an urbane and impervious stance
toward everyone except his wife. Arlen himself—henceforth I mean the
son—maintains a certain irony, an elegant detachment, toward life. This
veils his smoldering anger at his father, his gnawing anxiety about his own
identity and name. For Arlen suffers from a deep ethnic wound he wants
to heal. "At a particular time in my life, I set out on a voyage to discover
for myself what it is to be Armenian" (*E,* 3), he writes at the start of *Passage to Ararat.*

We follow Arlen to Soviet Armenia, which lies across the Turkish border from Mount Ararat—on its peak, Noah's Ark came to rest after the flood. The mountain, inaccessible to him from Russia, becomes a symbol of origins, destinations, the healing power of home. Arlen seeks it because ever since his childhood, and later at St. Paul's and Harvard, he senses his homelessness, his difference, something vaguely "Eastern" about him. After the deaths of his parents, he feels finally free to face the turbid sources of pain in his psyche, face his aversions and fears. He lectures on Armenian topics, speaks to Armenians in New York restaurants, reads avidly Armenian history. Gradually, he conquers his distaste for all the tales about Armenian miseries and the "fiendish" Turk. His journey has begun.

The journey takes Arlen first to Fresno, California, where so many Armenians had settled. But most of them have now dispersed in cities, their old culture receding before shopping malls. Arlen talks with William Saroyan in the lobby of the Fresno Hilton, hears how the house in which he was born, the entire neighborhood, has vanished to make way for an expressway. If you want to know about Armenians, Saroyan tells him, then go to Erevan in Soviet Armenia. Arlen acts on Saroyan's advice; with his wife, he flies to the Soviet Socialist Republic:

> From the start, I knew that it would be a complex journey, a journey on many levels. At the least, it would be a voyage within an adventure, for what could a trip of six thousand miles be—even six thousand boring sky miles—but an adventure? A flight into the past as well as a flight into that even more startling region of the present—although which past I would find, and whose present, it was hard to tell. I was excited by the prospect of the trip, and also apprehensive about it. With a new anxiety, I realized that although for so many years I had gone without my Armenian background—had gone without it to the point of finally feeling deprived of it—at the same time its very vagueness in my life had been a form of protection: the remote familiarity of a dream. All my life, Armenia and Armenians had been part of a dream; it and they were *out there* somewhere, hazy, nearly invisible. Now I was traveling into the dream. I would see what I would see. I would find what I would find. (*E*, 55f.)

Arlen sees awesome Ararat from the air, less a massif than some stupendous god—though, as a Russian businessman reminds him, the Americans have radar on the back of it; he sees the Monument to Armenian Martyrs; he dreams repeatedly about his father vanishing in a blue plane. He also reads and reads Armenian history, becomes slowly a "chauvinist of misfortune." Above all, he tries to confront himself through clichés about Armenians—"rug merchants," "wily traders," etc.—realizing that he had really detested being an Armenian, and that he had later come to despise his father for suppressing their common heritage, for stepping back and "giving him over to the Europeans."

The journey, then, is interior more than exterior, a journey of expiation for shameful self-rejection, a journey also of atonement and reconciliation: atonement with the father, reconciliation to Armenian history. This is a history that inevitably recalls Jewish history, however different the two histories may be, and recalls all the genocides of the last centuries. Here Arlen writes as a seeker for personal as well as historical truth, not as partisan or apologist. He sees, for instance, that during the long Stalinist nightmare, kulaks starved and other Soviet Armenians suffered immeasurably "without that coloring of lamentation and self-pity which so many Armenians elsewhere seemed to employ when they talked about the Turks" (*E*, 156).[4] He senses that Armenians may have become "crazed" — witness the recent, random terrorism of a few young Armenians — not crazed in some charming, eccentric way, but crazed "deep where the deep-sea souls of human beings twist and turn" (*E*, 142). He suspects that a "particular poison" had entered their system since the first massacres in the nineteenth century, "a poison that one might up to a point live with but that caused the limbs suddenly to twitch, or the mouth — perhaps in mid-sentence — to grimace grotesquely" (*E*, 186). This is, of course, the poison of hatred *and* of self-hate: death takes the victims but the survivors remember having been "hated unto death."

Arlen's *Passage to Ararat,* then, clearly engages some very public issues of our time as well as some very personal ones. At the end, alone, standing beneath overhanging slabs of the Monument to Armenian Martyrs, he suddenly feels at home. "It was the flattest, simplest, lightest of feelings. I thought, So this is what it's all about" (*E*, 254). He knows now that though the texture of his life is American, his true kin are Armenians, those same people whose greatest feat has been to persist, to endure, and, more than that, to show how an "ancient, sturdy, minor race" can proceed "*beyond* nationhood" (*E*, 291). At the end, Arlen's quest for his true name, Kouyoumdjian, brings him full circle to his father, and to a dream of his father about *his* father: "He stood at the end of our road speaking to me, calling. But he was speaking in Armenian, and I couldn't understand a word" (*E*, 293). The dreams merge as the generations merge; the dreams at last cease as all the ghosts rest, appeased.

Indubitably *Passage to Ararat* is a quest, quest of a certain kind. It has the personal urgency and brooding intensity of quest, though it lacks any real adventure or risk. Arlen's jeopardy remains only spiritual; his autobiographical narrative is also a prolix meditation on history and human nature. Its manner is maieutic, asking questions, answering them with further questions. He teases us into geopolitical thought. Was the massacre of Armenians the first technological genocide? Was it a fable of otherness or a story of misconceived brotherhood between Armenian and Turk? What role did the European Powers play and how did they acquiesce in the massacres? Where else may hatred erupt? Haunting, crucial questions those, questions for our age and every age.

Still, the reader feels a certain resistance to Arlen's quest, feels a need to counter questions with questions of his own. For instance: how valid is this ethnic definition of the self in a moment of planetization, global "contamination"? Who surmounts alienation best: one who yearns continually for a tribe, or another at ease in the universe? What noxious prejudice did Arlen ever experience as an American to justify this retreat into ancestral memory? Whence this racial defensiveness, this feeling of interior colonization? Or is this ethnic malaise much more personal, the form his oedipal struggle takes, perhaps a kind of moody self-preoccupation masked as ethnic concern? Arlen's own struggle with these questions often assumes a pose of incomprehension, a pose that sometimes makes the incomprehension all too real. Still, *Passage to Ararat* remains a kind of quest, an interior quest without adventure, in some ways retrograde, fusing private and public history in clear, meditative prose.

4

Quests, we have seen, most often entail journeys, displacement; but not all travel is quest. Still, a journey, even tourism, hints at something beyond itself, a need or dissatisfaction barely perceived, a curiosity enacted mildly in romance. Eleanor Clark's *Tamrart: Thirteen Days in the Sahara* (1984) is an example. It is a small adventure that the author and her husband, Robert Penn Warren, undertake, an adventure perhaps not so small at their advanced age. The trek is through the Hoggar (Arabic for stone), a forbidding region, larger than France, in southern Algeria, a tawny immensity, more rock than sand, where the once-feared Tuaregs still range. It is a space, as Clark says, where a dialogue between Self and Eternity takes place.

Clark and Warren travel, with their adventurous son, Jeepers, in a party of nine — no *tout terrain* vehicles, only camels, no tents, only sleeping bags. They undertake the journey because their friend Jacqueline had done it a couple of times, thus *"comme tout le monde"*; because "all our speed and other technology have left us with a boredom problem"; because "speak of travel, ticket and passport appear and you're off, that's the devil's way, whether you can afford it or not, whether you give a damn or not about either the procedure or the destination" (*T,* 8). This is a mysterious impulse or call.

In Hoggar country, no one listens to the news, no one uses the formal *vous*. The French guides, good ecologists, leave no speck of grease or paper behind; they flatten tin cans and bury them deep. The tourists endure the torture of diurnal camel rides, their underpants caked with blood. They eat little, sleep little, hardly sweat at all. Is this a senseless ordeal, Clark wonders, or the last luxury of the idle rich? Ah, but the senses key up in an extravagance of perception; moods swing to beatitude or suicide; there is growing freedom from tension. Death appears familiar. Not that Clark gives herself to desert exaltation or spiritual windbaggery. Rather, she favors humble truths, small tendernesses, attachments to simple things, a cup or pestle.

Does *Tamrart*—the name Eleanor Clark bears as senior woman of the company—does it have a dramatic center, a spiritual event on which the action turns? The event proves to be surprisingly paltry: Clark gives up cigarettes after a lifetime of smoking. Incongruously, Clark punctuates a narrative about the awesome Sahara, its Christian martyrs and colonial wars, with comments on her smoking habits. Tactlessly, she associates a heroic Trappist monk, Father Charles de Foucauld, a true nineteenth-century desert saint, with her renunciation of tobacco in the sight of his hermitage of Assekrem, after a "nightlong mystical vision" beneath an acacia tree. The note is jarring against the stupendous landscape of sky, stone, and sand; nor will the self-centered act bear the weight of politics and metaphysics Clark puts upon it. Still, she can render a moment like this:

> You don't know what it is that is being stretched in your guts, in your vision. The word, the idea of *travel* would not even be a bad joke at this point, it could make you vomit. Nothing to do with danger of course, nobody's looking for trouble or really risking any on this trip, except Jeepers and he's just constituted that way and would be doing the same anywhere. But a cat's claws are sliding up over that mountain's crest and it's after you. You mean it's like those posters some of us can remember, about joining the marines? Or you mean what's happening to you is like True Love, the personal Big Bang that changes the nature, the very constituent materials of everything? Exactly. Only not the coup de foudre. I'd say this is more the slow sulphurous type of illumination, leading however to the same result.
>
> Naturally we fight it; scowl, curse, complain; immolation is not to be taken lying down especially when attended by bodily discomforts and massive blows to pride. (*T,* 34)

The style here, even in its best moments, betrays what is really wrong with *Tamrart:* a quality of alert, mindful perception continually undercut by a mannerist disposition, a style sometimes of unbearable affectation, more suited perhaps to the depiction of a decadent Roman villa than to a harshly sublime desert landscape.

Clark does bring back a sign of the desert with her, a certain change in her personal life. But the most persuasive parts of the work are her reflections as she traverses, in thirteen days on a camel, different cultures, ecologies, histories. Clark sees the truck routes that make camels, caravans, and the tribesmen who lead them all nearly obsolete. She worries that in our "hear-everything, go any-where world" we will achieve only "goodby to our differences" (*T,* 23). She notes that the Algerian government has forced the Tuaregs to abandon patronyms, thus Westernizing its subjects from within. She recapitulates meticulously the history of the region, noting that "colonial rule is bound to leave some soreheads and screwballs on both sides long after the jig is up. A lot of love-hate everywhere . . ." (*T,* 43). She intuits the covert imperialism of travelers long after *la mission civilatrice de la France* has vanished, and at the same time recognizes that native rights and inheritances have become "globally the most confused of human attributes, *vide* the story of the American Indian" (*T,* 55). Finally, she frets about American Civilization: "Everybody agrees we're off our collective rocker. Crime in the streets and deconstruction in the lecture hall. So who's the barbarian now?" (*T,* 100).

Two cardinal recognitions emerge from Tamrart's journey, even if that journey can only hint at personal quest. The first is geopolitical. In a world transhumanized, continually transactive, the walls of the city, any city, are crumbling, and no barbarians storm the gates—the barbarians are nowhere, everywhere. Even the fierce and spare Tuaregs begin to import the clutter, mental or material, of the West. The second recognition is ecological, that is, at bottom sacramental. In the great, god-haunted desolation of the Hoggar, the human creature experiences life and death in a different order of intensities. Eternity is at hand. To these powerful recognitions, Tamrart's narrative testifies, despite its stylish distractions.

From the Sahara to Alaska. Quest takes men and women in anger or wonder out of cities, takes them to other people, other places. This is the transport of a summer in John McPhee's *Coming into the Country* (1977). The country is Alaska in August; the journey is a journey through tundras and trees, an immense, once-virgin land, no longer pristine. (The sexual metaphor is apt: the true Alaskan settler prizes his priority, though penetration of nature evokes its own atavism, its particular kind of surrender.) But McPhee is no settler. He has joined four men, members of a state-federal team inspecting an area of some thirty-two million acres to determine if it should be declared a national preserve. He himself has joined them merely to observe, or so it seems. He has also done his homework, knows everything around him, every flower, shrub, tree, bird, by name. He has learned about caribou, grizzly, grayling, the way rivers run, the permafrost underfoot. His ecology is resonant and rich on this "last American frontier." Thus the book, though reportage, often reads like a fable or romance.

The romance is the harsh romance of nature; that's part of the story. The other part is human, the Alaskan settlers. The settlers, a rare breed — not the ones who go to make big bucks on the oil pipeline or a killing in real estate — all want space, independence, a chance to prove their worth. They seek a sense of life, to which money, power, possessions, and celebrity are irrelevant; gold, they say, loves only itself. They want to live off the land, under the most exigent conditions, survive like Indian or Eskimo. They want to learn something about the final truths which civilization, "the Lower Forty-eight," masks or distorts. Thus their character tends to the solitary, anarchic, anti-authoritarian: no state or federal interference, please! They are not socialists, not feminists, not joiners of any kind. But they obey the ecological ethic, without sentimentality or abstraction, like Cooper's Leatherstocking. Ecology? It "means who's eating whom, and when," a settler says, but eating out of need, without malice or waste; nor is nature "balanced" really — it's all the time "feast or famine" (*CC*, 397, 296). The voices of these hardy, cranky people deserve to be heard in their own timbre:

> I want to change myself thoroughly "from a professional into a bum" — to learn to trap, to handle dogs and sleds, to net fish. . . . It isn't easy to lower your income and raise your independence. . . . I've had to work twice as hard as most people. (*CC*, 177f.)

> I wanted to get away from paying taxes to support something I didn't believe in, to get away from big business, to get away from a place where you can't be sure of anything you hear or anything you read. (*CC*, 178)

> The czars exiled misfits to Siberia. The Soviets do that, too. . . . Alaskans are inheritors of determinative genes that took people out of Europe to the New World. [We're] doers. [We] don't destroy, we build. (*CC*, 302)

> The bush is so far beyond what anybody has been taught. The religious power is here beyond all training. There are forces here that a lot of people don't know exist. (*CC*, 225)

> Life and death are not a duality. They're just simply here — life, death — in the all-pervading mesh that holds things together. (*CC*, 397)

Does it all seem too literary? These pioneers, seekers more than refugees, many of them college graduates, are articulate. McPhee joins them, drawn by their intransigent vision. He knows that in their demesne, the grizzly stands as a symbol of power and freedom, the totem of all natural men who accept the rules of the wilderness, survival or death. (Like Faulkner's Ike McCaslin, or Mailer's D.J., McPhee doesn't carry a gun to see the grizzly.) But McPhee is also sufficiently sober to perceive their ineluctable contradictions. For the Alaskans end by reproducing the same conflicts they presume to leave behind them. Rebels in their marrowbone, they find themselves mutually dependent, as if in a bathysphere. They bring with them alcoholism, envy, wife stealing, class consciousness, even murder. And they dramatize the acute political dilemmas of our world in the four-way struggles between Federal Government, the State of Alaska, Corporate Enterprise, and the Individual, struggles that bushplanes and snowmobiles carry to them at the edge of the Arctic.

In short, *Coming into the Country* conveys tensions within both the Individual and American society—Freedom versus Equality, Progress versus Conservation, Libertarianism versus Liberalism, State versus Federal rights—tensions that even the immense Alaskan wilderness cannot relieve. But the book also captures another persistent motive of the American Dream, the spirit of quest, an anarchic, quasi-religious impulse, still vibrant, still unappeased, in the space of that Dream. It is a "high," this being wholly free, a high like "doing acid," one Charlie Edwards says.

But whose quest really is this? McPhee's vignettes about the settlers, deft as these vignettes may be, render a collective portrait. Is the quest then McPhee's? Though he speaks in the first person, he speaks reticently about himself; an exquisite precisian, he observes patiently, self-effacingly, the scene. But McPhee, after all, is no "transparent eyeball." He meditates, he intervenes; sometimes he finds himself caught up in the Alaskan predicament. His ruminative involvements thus make him part of the scene. Munching, for instance, on cold Pop-Tarts in the wilderness, he wonders: which would taste better to an impartial palate, say a Martian's, a pink-icinged Pop Tart with raspberry filling or the fat gob from behind a caribou's eye? (All of intercultural hermeneutics is here.) Glimpsing a grazing grizzly, he feels in its sheer presence "an affirmation to the rest of the earth that his kind of place was extant" (*CC,* 60). (The whole issue of conservation is here.) He perceives the "abiding paradox" of the wilderness, its power to attract and repel at the same time, indifferent to man yet seductive in its (in)difference. (This is also the fascination of otherness.) He can take a clear stand; thus, for example, he says about the Gelvins, a consummately self-reliant family: "Their kind is more endangered every year. . . . Only an easygoing extremist would preserve every bit of the country. And extremists alone would exploit it all. . . . For myself, I am closer to the preserving side—that is, the side that would preserve the Gelvins" (*CC,* 410).

Such interventions give density to McPhee's account; they do not make it quest, though motifs of quest therein abound. For one thing, the work lacks the plot and suspense, the passionate shapeliness, of quest—its cumulative details, endless minutiae, finally numb. For another, the author himself is moved by reportorial curiosity more than personal need. McPhee may eat bear in final communion with the "total wild," but his journey earns him no personal revelation, at least none that he shares with readers. Nor is he really an adventurer, but rather a "what-if type—an advanced, thousand-deaths coward with oakleaf clusters" (*CC,* 88), as he says in an access of self-deprecation.[5] Finally, his particular Alaska yields no sense of cultural strangeness, its Eskimos and Indians being only tokens of otherness in the book, shadowy figures of some aboriginal difference.

Coming into the Country is not a naive text. Its present tense gives it immediacy; its catenas of quotations, dialogues, diary excerpts counter its delirium of facts; its flashbacks create a certain narrative interest. But the reader finds no dramatic focus for quest, finds, instead, a panorama of iterative yearnings, dissatisfactions, failures, filtered through McPhee's ambiguously objective eye. In the end, the work, constrained perhaps by its own genre, balks at any deeper interpretation of its materials, reminding us of an Alaskan settler, Dick Cook, who says about a book he once read: "The author's mistake is that he tries to express the meaning of nature. When you are writing about nature, you are writing about God, and it cannot be put into words" (*CC,* 387).

Back to Africa. Edward Hoagland, in *African Calliope: A Journey to the Sudan* (1979), is only a shade less reticent about himself. For three winter months, Hoagland trekked throughout the Sudan, crisscrossing a region one-fourth the size of Europe, the largest nation in Africa and one of the poorest, a people modern and medieval cheek by jowl. Hoagland calls his work a travel book, neither history nor personal memoir, a story shaped by its observations. Still, as he mischievously says, "Life is a novel" (*A,* 5), a novel about realities in that "enormous tumbling chunk" which is the Sudan.

From the start, Hoagland admits the anxieties, the afflictions, of his task. Natives, Africans that is, feel only "exasperation" with his kind of book, as did Americans only a century ago with the supercilious reports of English travelers. But the afflictions inhere also in the Sudan: famine, disease, torpor, illiteracy, coups, "the Troubles" (a crippling civil war), atrocity and absurdity side by side, and above all, dearth of every kind. The list of diseases alone may shatter our (Western) complacencies, unless it numbs: bilharzia, typhoid, malaria, meningitis, yaws, hookworm, sleeping sickness, amoebic dysentery, leprosy, giardiasis, kala-azar, pneumonia, tuberculosis, blinding-worms, and, worst of all, the ghastly ebola or Green Monkey Disease.

In the Sudan—let us recall its diversity: tribal women naked to the waist, Moslem women veiled to the eyes; one hundred and fifteen languages; desert, swamp, mountain, and green valley landscapes—in this space, Hoagland encounters all the geopolitical vexations of our age. There are the ancestral feuds between the dominant Moslem north and the beleaguered animist or Christian south; the legacies of British and Egyptian colonialism; the rivalries of "Great Powers," more or less great—the Soviet Union, the United States, Britain, France, Israel, Libya, Egypt, Saudia Arabia—all vying for influence in the Sudan. There are also businessmen, technocrats, teachers, arms dealers, health officials, consultants from every organization in the world. And there are, of course, the Sudanese, all the different kinds of Sudanese, their most intimate relations mediated by a gallimaufry of interests, their very clothes a ragged medley of "suburbiana—a plaid sport jacket, a paisley vest—donated by a church group in America" (A, 65).

Vast and barren as it may be, the country becomes for Hoagland a field of struggling (mis)representations. For the Sudanese, his admiration of a beautiful mountain peak seems preposterous, even louche—does it conceal a helicopter landing pad? His white body, tribal children believe, is the work of a goblin who flayed Hoagland's outer skin. His relative affluence shocks the Sudanese into embarrassed silence—except when they are drunk. His ideas of a political left and right puzzle them since such categories are superfluous to their needs. On his side, Hoagland labors to understand all he perceives. Thus, for instance, about their faith in miracles:

> A healing, miracle-working savior who would be locked in a cage within an hour if he appeared in Los Angeles or London could resurrect himself in Juba and see the populace catch fire, believe the evidence of their eyes, and make the sand streets resound once again.
>
> Maybe for all this to happen, it is necessary that there be lepers sitting beside the road, lazy, high-horned, biblical kine, a blind albino girl with stumps for arms, a man bustling about on all fours with his thin buttocks canted as high as a baboon's because of a spinal injury that had never been treated when he was a child, and a hunter arriving on foot, carrying gazelle meat on a shoulder frame, with five spears in his hands, a brown bush hat, mud smeared on his neck and forehead to ward away the flies, and a calabash full of milk hanging from a thong around his neck. . . . Miracles that wouldn't happen in New York or Jerusalem might occur in a place where the Son of God, if he were arrested, might still be killed, not entrusted to the care of social workers and psychologists. (A, 189)

Is that why Hoagland journeys to the Sudan? The question finds answer in certain themes or presages. Not sure of his own motives, Hoagland wonders about white residents in this hard, menacing land. They are mostly eccentric Britons, he thinks, or European misfits. The former may still retain their sense of colonial superiority, chasing away with squared chest and bare hands a Sudanese soldier carrying a Bren gun. But back in the Midlands, they feel they are beating their "wings against a cage." Some "hunger for a recklessness that is absent from their own makeup, except as a longing, and . . . go out on assignment to desperately poor countries to try to fill the hole"; others find exhilaration in a raw life that distracts them from "old bugaboos"; others still seek "primitive imperatives" to "damp them down and superimpose a substitute for self-control" (*A*, 160f.). Hoagland understands these dotty types, finds them even "reassuring."

But there is more to all this than dottiness or maladjustment. At one point, Hoagland refers to Marlow's outburst, in Conrad's *Heart of Darkness,* an outburst directed against his cozy listeners on the deck of a moored yawl, each with "two good addresses," a butcher around one corner, a policeman around another. Hoagland then remarks: "It's the cry of a homeless adventurer, with his shabby intestinal ailments and threadbare bank account, meeting the condescension of homebodies who believe he is roaming the world only because he is maladjusted or professionally second-rate" (*A*, 220). At another point, Hoagland reflects on explorers, trekkers, "wilderness enthusiasts," concluding that their "lone compulsion" may have been an "attempt, itself, to start over," and that in their memoirs they reveal the need to "be born again," to reexperience their own "birth and thereby possibly straighten [themselves] out." Tellingly, he adds: "So here was I in Gilo [near the Ugandan border], not utterly untypical of all the white people who had roamed Africa before . . ." (*A*, 70f.).

These, of course, are the motives of personal quest, flattened here by the conventions of verism and dispassionate observation, by a presumed lack of self-concern. That concern, though, can never be wholly erased. Asked bluntly why he has come to Africa, Hoagland replies: "I said that I was forty-four, and was after experiences and writing matter I had not tried before" (*A*, 98). This, too, is a version of quest. Indeed, we sense in *African Calliope* a still more intimate motive, more intimate, that is, than the adventurer's instinct to test the unknown and to feel on his return that he has, once more, "*walked away from another one*" (*A*, 109). We sense in Hoagland's book a certain loneliness, loneliness even in America. He hints estrangement from his second wife; he misses his little daughter in New York; he looks for a different woman, but finds only Lilah, an Egyptian Copt, who leaves him for an ambassador's son.

Like McPhee, however, like any good reporter, Hoagland is wary, chary, of personal confession. The state of his soul glimmers but briefly beneath the opulence of African facts. The work, after all, pretends to be neither spiritual autobiography nor quest. It is a brave journey through the Sudan, crowded with the history, politics, geography, zoology of a forgotten region, alive with novelistic sketches of its people, white and black. (The panoramic character of the book itself prevents us from seeing its author clearly or deeply.) The work is also a tough-minded meditation on geopolitics, leavened here and there by rakish irony. But its episodic structure, a series of forays in various parts of the Sudan, denies both chronology and plot, denies dramatic purpose. Hoagland finally, simply, stops: "I was weary of the whole African calliope—that nagging, pulsing musical din that has been reverberating strongly without letup for thousands of years before you arrive and will be continuing without any respite for sickness or fatigue long after you have left the earth. There was pathos in it, and endless, repetitive joy, but I was too tired for poignance or joy" (*A,* 265f.). We can well believe it: he is even physically ill. And so the book simply ceases, without the sense of an ending, in the Dar Kabbabish desert, at Umm Sunta, as a thousand camels charge by in growling gangs to water at the salted corral well.

Journeys abound. Many are chock-full with adventure; many are resplendent in style. Some, like Michael Parfit's *South Light,* about Antarctica, and Barry Lopez's *Arctic Dreams,* reveal the explorer, the naturalist, and the poet of one imagination compact. These are literary works of a high order, paeans to Gaia, odes to the antipodes. They offer also occasional meditations on human destiny, on the ecology of mind in the universe. Wonder suffuses them. Thus, for instance, Parfit sees that even the dark of the moon shines in Antarctica, a magic image of its promise; and Lopez, awestruck, depicts a landscape where icebergs are the size of Cleveland and polar bears "fly down out of the stars," "a region, like the desert, rich with metaphor, with adumbration."[6]

Still, despite all their intimations of wonder, the journeys we have glimpsed in this section withhold themselves from quest. True, fact in them, enlivened by risk, becomes richer than simple fact. But the journeys still maintain a stubborn—because generic—reserve regarding the deeper intimacies of pain and desire. This reticence, however, is constructive: paradoxically, reserve helps us to identify the note of quest in the chorus of autobiography, travel, adventure, and romance.

5

There is no ideal text of quest, as I have repeatedly said. There are texts, though, that enable us to envisage such a text. Mary Morris's *Nothing to Declare: Memoirs of a Woman Traveling Alone* (1988), and Paul Zweig's *Three Journeys: An Automythology* (1976) may be such texts.

On the surface of it, *Nothing to Declare* seems simply a memoir and travelogue of a woman alone; but each of these facts is emblematic of another, more elusive fact, perhaps less fact than dream, perhaps less dream than unfulfillable quest. Memoir here serves remembrance, what Morris calls "ghosts," and travelogue, its forward motion, serves hope, what she calls "gods." Between these two motions of time and space, her spirit moves in its own domain. This is a magical domain, fantastic, sacramental, full of good and ill omens like the "witch" figure Mary Morris meets in the Mexican sierras, signaling to her cryptically from the mouth of a cave. This figure of good forebodings—oxymorons here are needed—a beautiful hag, both young and old, with jet black hair turning white in a certain slant of the sun, this figure of mystery, seems to hold the mystery of Morris's own identity, as do other women—grandmother, mother, friends—who share in her inner landscape.

I dwell on emblems and omens—there are others, a cat, a rooster, a quetzal, a bald eagle—because the narrative moves in the space between fiction and fact. The facts are simple. Mary Morris, born in Highland Park, Illinois, lately of New York City, travels south after some unhappy love affairs. For a time, she settles in the attractive town of San Miguel de Allende, on the dry plateau north of Mexico City. From there, she forays further south, into the Yucatan Peninsula, Guatemala, Honduras, Nicaragua. Without hysteria and with scarcely a hyperbole, without rhetorical flutter, she records the perils and epiphanies of her travels. But what makes these travels quest is the character of the traveler—and the imagination of the writer.

As a child Mary Morris knows the rapture of maps. (She might have delighted in Baudelaire's "Le Voyage": "Pour l'enfant, amoureux de cartes et d'estampes, / L'univers est égal à son vaste appétit.") As a child she also has a sure sense of direction, and also of romance—she spends an ecstatic hour contemplating a bald eagle that strays into a Chicago suburb. As she remarks: "somehow I am intended to be a journeywoman, a wanderer of the planet, and, I suppose, of the heart. . . . Sometimes it is difficult, but I try to read other maps. Maps of my own inner landscape, of dreams and of the outcome of the events of my life, of the warnings and signs of others" (*N,* 23).

Morris reveals her character and motives gradually, discreetly. Already as an adolescent she leads at least two lives, that of the conventional "good little girl," and another, that of a truant, a rebel who steals car keys, slides down drainpipes, slips off to the beach for a night of beer, boys, and bonfires:

> No one could fault me. No one knew that underneath my propriety I was boiling over. On the surface I gave my parents whatever they wanted. I was a demilitarized zone, the buffer between them. I let them try to love each other through me. But beneath it all, I was plotting my escape, and when the time came, I was gone. (*N,* 177)

But "escape" brings no enduring relief. The complexities of life, of "men," set in. Before escaping again to Central America, Morris feels desolate:

It was a decade ago that I lost my way. Somewhere between the Midwest and Manhattan, childhood and old age, between college and life, I arrived at a desert more vast than the Gobi, more empty than space. My purpose escaped me; the meaning was lost. For a long time I lived in an American city in an L-shaped room that looked onto an air shaft. I used to spend hours gazing down into that shaft, until one day the woman who lived across from me stood at her window and shook her head, as if scolding me. "No," she mouthed. With her hand, she shooed me away. I had had no thoughts of jumping, but only then did I realize how I'd been gazing into the abyss. (*N,* 242)

"Abyss" may be a rare instance of hyperbole. Mary Morris, at any rate, heads south of the border. Alone, she learns to endure solitude, to forget one man who gave her a shiner, and another, Daniel, seven years her junior, whom she loved. She travels for a time with an American woman, Catherine Wilde, with whom she has a comforting, perhaps lesbian, relation. She takes an Aztec lover, Alejandro, a mild, caring man. She sleeps on the road in Honduras with an intelligent drifter from Berkeley: "I liked Josh. What more can I say? I liked him" (*N,* 166). Above all, she rents a house in the poorest section of San Miguel and tries to write. There she befriends an illiterate neighbor, Lupe, with a brood of illegitimate children.

Lupe is key to Morris's experience in Mexico. She exemplifies courage, warmth, endurance, a cheerful fatalism in life's despite. Abandoned several times by men, as is Morris, Lupe sustains the anxious *gringa,* and is by her sustained. It is what some might call a "nurturing relation," though nurture here is also spiritual, even supernatural—Lupe jokingly identifies the cave "witch" as her mother. Indeed, the aura of the supernatural pervading the book—in myths, dreams, omens, visions, superstitions, magic— evokes another dimension in Morris's journey, a journey not entirely worldly.

This is not to say that the author ignores social or political realities— how could she with Lupe at her doorstep or Alejandro in her bed? Quite to the contrary, Morris reckons with the past and present of Central America, reckons tactfully, without ideological machismo or claptrap. The splendors of jungles and sierras, the feasts of colored Indian garbs, the still mystery of ancient ruins, the hard, blue brightness of sea and sky, exotic fish, birds, butterflies—all these speak through the book. But grimly eloquent, too, are deprivation, disease, deformity, cockroaches everywhere, heat and excrement, a history of ceaseless exploitation, even genocide, a sense of grievance, heavy and sullen like jungle air. We learn about the vastations of Cortez, and of his captain, Pedro de Alvarado, a psychopath who ordered massacres in temples, rapine in towns, the roasting of babies before their mothers' eyes. We see the work of the United Fruit Company in Honduras. We hear about Aztec priests who flayed live sacrificial victims and wrapped themselves in the steaming skins, and about *la Man-*

tanza, the slaughter of Indian males wearing native dress in 1932. And we observe Sandinista revolutionaries, their heroism, petulance, lusts. Politics is indeed pervasive. But in this landscape of indifferent violence and death, human concerns shrivel, and even civilizations—including the American way of life—become paltry gestures of eternity.

And that, of course, is the point of Mary Morris's journey. Unlike most of the American "artists" of San Miguel, who want only to stretch lazy dollars on short talents, she immerses herself in the alien, fatal environment. She quotes Camus on fear giving value to travel, and is herself smartly alert to risks—from barracudas to rapists—that attend a woman traveling alone. She rides to a remote jungle town, Zinacantán, transfigured like a pilgrim riding to Jerusalem. She puts herself on "Indian time," life in relation to destiny, steeping herself in the *Popol Vuh,* the Mayan book of creation. Thus she proves herself not merely a shrewd and intrepid traveler— say, like Helen Winternitz in *East along the Equator: A Journey up the Congo and into Zaire* (1987)—but a genuine seeker, one who can infuse her experiences of cultural difference with an erotic and sacramental power.

The erotic urgency is there even before the journey starts. It is an urgency Mary Morris maintains, from the moment a white rooster jumps on her balcony in San Miguel, through nude bathings in the Caribbean and orgasmic dreams, to her affair with Alejandro. But the erotic is richly textured in poetic, mythic, spiritual hues:

> I walked into the water. The sand beneath my toes was silken, the water warm. I walked into the water as if into a baptismal. My feet disappeared into the blackness, my toes dug deeper into the sand. My feet were gone, my legs to the knees. At the edge of the Caribbean, on an isolated strip of beach, everything came back to me. Everything that had ever happened to me and to my body. It all came back there. And when I could stand the infusion of memory no longer, I dove in. I swam in the warm salt water, under the light of the moon. Water held me.
>
> Women remember. Our bodies remember. Every part of us remembers everything that has ever happened. Every touch, every feel, everything is there in our skin, ready to be awakened, revived. I swam in the sea. Salt water cradled me, washing over all I had ever felt. I swam without fear in the line of moonlight radiating on the surface of the sea. The water entered me and I could not tell where my body stopped and the sea began. My body was gone, but all the remembering was there. (*N,* 101)

Only memory for Morris perdures? In fact, she never renounces hope. "Women who travel as I travel are dreamers," she says. "Our lives seem to be lives of endless possibility" (*N,* 164). Put in her earlier terms, she seeks to reconcile "ghosts" and "gods." Or as she puts it, still more simply: "With a terrible feeling of isolation and a growing belief that America had become a foreign land, I headed south. I went in search of a place where the land and the people and the time in which they lived were somehow connected – where life would *begin to make sense again* [italics mine]" (*N*, 4).

Does life really begin to make more sense for Mary Morris? Quests, alas, are always equivocal. On the one hand, Morris experiences moments of universal love: "Not for a man or a woman, but for a way of being" (*N*, 61). She also attains moments of acute self-knowledge. On the other hand, though, Mary Morris never outgrows her naiveté, her illusions about men. She realizes that, like some other women, she loves only men who can not love her (Daniel) and fails to love the men who do (Alejandro) – the latter kind tends to be docile, even subservient. Indeed, her whole relation to Alejandro, a man whose life she can so little share, remains dubious, betraying a strong strain of feminine insecurity in her character. How, then, could this quest for identity, for autonomy, for renewed purpose end?

It ends realistically, that is, nearly accidentally. As the life of Mary Morris in San Miguel and Mexico City becomes increasingly fuddled, her wanderings become more haphazard. Her affair with Alejandro fades. The *federales* warn her that her visa has expired. She becomes older, more *gordita* (chubby), as Lupe seriously jokes. Morris poignantly admits: "At night, I lay in bed, running my hands across my thighs, my belly, my breasts. I was blind to myself. I could not see what others saw. . . . I lost track of the days" (*N*, 230). Then, suddenly, she develops peritonitis. The decision to return to America grows upon her as she convalesces in Alejandro's windowless apartment in Mexico City. Indeed, the decision appears less choice than chance.

Up to a point, *Nothing to Declare* simulates the classic path of quest. But it is also a modern work, touched by modern ironies and confusions. Toward the close of the book, Mary Morris candidly says:

> I had thought to myself the whole time I had been away that there would be a moment when everything would come clear, when I would understand what I had not understood before. I had been waiting for a clear moment when I would know that I'd traded cruelty for kindness, passion for companionship, anger for love. But now I knew that it would not happen this way.
>
> As I sat out on that porch, I understood that growth comes over time. Change happens step by step. All along things had been changing inside of me, bit by bit, in small, imperceptible ways. It had been subtle, not sudden. It had been happening over time. (*N*, 211)

The very structure of the memoir – a narrative without final resolution, except in the artist's power to tell it – attests to this insight. So does the title in its coiled puns. Nothing to declare means the citizen's liberty to cross administered borders, the seeker's urge to pursue gods and ghosts across time and place, the artist's need to say without declaring. Nothing to declare: yes, precisely, finally, just that, both the failure of quest and the end of all seeking.

Paul Zweig's interest in the elements of quest was evident in his earlier critical works. In *The Heresy of Self-Love,* he defended the reflexive genius of the Western self. The spirit of "subversive individualism" pitted itself repeatedly against society, Zweig argued with learned panache, and in Narcissus found an image of its longing for inward autonomy, a longing expressed in a "poetry of sentiment and inner violence."[7] In *The Adventurer,* as we have seen, Zweig pushed deeper into the mysteries of quest, a perilous action mirrored in *both* self and world. Indeed, adventure, for him never far from quest, constituted culture and myth; adventure was itself a cultural myth, presenting the hero "as a darkly, antisocial character, an escape artist from the confinements of the human situation"—hence the damnation of Odysseus in Dante's Eighth Circle—who nonetheless returns to found a city or tell a story.[8]

These features are also features, reduced to our unheroic scale, of Zweig's own "automythology." *Three Journeys* is really a triptych, or perhaps a face refracted in three mirrors, alive in each. This is partly, Zweig admits, the face of unrest, dissatisfaction: having gotten much of what he wanted in life, he still yearns to remake himself, to find within himself another person in that solid sea of solitude which is the Sahara. The journal he keeps, the book he writes, is his lifeline to the ordinary world, a line never severed.

The first journey, "Against Emptiness," concerns us here most. In the spring of 1974, Zweig spent a month jolting about trackless, flinty roads of the Sahara in an old 2CV Citroën. He kept a journal, starting on April 3, noting precisely, poetically, the landscape, the people, the history— all skillfully integrated in a narrative—of this vast, prehuman space. But the place is not so archaic as to escape all vestiges of the contemporary world. Traces of the modern state, following the Algerian War of Independence, reach deep into the inviolate desert, affecting even the most intractable nomads, the bellicose Tuaregs and bandit Requibat. Peddlers of *roses des sables* (pink crystals of gypsum) sit listlessly by empty roads, as if in some dreadful enchantment, to sell their wares for a few pennies, an image of Saharan misery. Others invite photographers to take a picture of them in exchange for a cigarette. Politics invade even remotest Tamanrasset where a wheezy policeman calls Zweig a spy because he carries an American passport. Everywhere, dusty, forlorn towns exhibit the "secondhand vestments of civilization: a rusty gas pump; bistros called the Café des Amis, or the Gargotte du Sud, resembling disaffected outhouses" (*TJ,* 50). Man has even altered the ecology of the desert, thinning out or eliminating forms of life left over from a moister period.

Yet the Sahara remains in the book, for both author and reader, an overwhelming fact. It is foremost the fact of hardship, exceeding the physical and mental resources of all but the most indomitable tribes, like the Beni Hillal who swept out from the Empty Quarter in Arabia twelve centuries ago. But the desert is also a "permanent prayer," a spiritual fact, as Charles de Foucauld — this harks back to Eleanor Clark — and his successors in the Petits Frères de Jésus, taking their cue from the simple piety of Saharan Moslems, continually testify. For Zweig, alas, the Sahara is a more personal, more self-regarding, fact. It is less an ideal than a "place, impure and complex, eluding definition," a speculum of his all-too-human soul. "Even after the appearance of ordinary events had been stripped away," he candidly writes, "and I advanced inside a geological fantasy so gripping and ice-clear that it pulled me out through my eyes into its enormousness, all too often a struggle of anxious thoughts distracted me from my experience, and the desert blurred past my self-preoccupation" (*TJ,* 49).

This bares the key question before our eyes, the question concerning Zweig's motives. As usual, the question finds no ready answer, especially for an artist in literary masquerade. Though Zweig disciplines himself, in the earlier stages of the journey, to observe the desert without artful self-concern — he even pretends that the Sahara threatens to make *him* altogether mute — he ends "Against Emptiness" with a sustained reflection on his myth of the desert, that is, a reflection on himself:

> For almost twenty years I've spent my best hours thinking and talking about books. It seems, at times, that I have justified my existence because of the books and poems I myself would write. Having lived for a day in the world has given me plenty to think about. But I've been distracted lately. I've begun to hear an enormous whispering, as if the room had gotten smaller, as if something new and indispensable were taking place in the world beyond my reach. I want to find my way outside to spend a second day, maybe a third. I probably couldn't stand much more than that. (*TJ,* 48)

That is why Zweig must opt, at last, "against emptiness," against a claim too inexorable for him to meet. The myth of the Sahara disintegrates before its brutal fact. That little, sturdy car, that 2CV, remains his "Ariadne thread," his spiritual "clay foot." Though Zweig identifies himself with the great American isolatos, Natty Bumppo, Ishmael, Huck Finn, he can not sustain his solitude; at Ghardia, he tries to call his second wife, Francine, not knowing whether she is in Paris, Venice, or New York. (How many of these "seekers" seem estranged from spouses, lovers, friends!) And though he reproaches himself for not venturing far enough into the truly trackless Sahara, he recognizes that his "mess of needs" will not abandon him so easily:

> I don't know much about faith. It requires, I think, more trust and vulnerability than I can manage. If I were to assign a category to my life it would be the category of longing, along with its corollary, nostalgia. But the desert is a sheer presence. . . . I managed, in the Sahara, to long for the Sahara; to leap acrobatically into its presence, only to collapse into "the world," and then to leap again, and yet again. (*TJ*, 60f.)

This is honest. But is Zweig's quest, then, an unmitigated bust? Hardly. The very recognition of failure proves his desert journey a stage in self-discovery. There are also two other journeys.

The second journey takes us back to Zweig's youth in Paris where he spent ten years after his graduation from Columbia College. Entitled "Automythology," this Proustian journey is more acutely, more preciously, auto-biographical. It reveals much about his erotic and political entanglements — as usual, these meet when Michèle, his mistress and later his first wife, embroils him passionately with communism and the Algerian Revolutionary War. The journey, though, reveals even more about the character of Zweig himself: his deep core of blandness, his addiction to superficial self-awareness, his anxious solitude. He wants to write an autobiography without any people in it — except, of course, himself; yet he feels that he has not lived enough to write an autobiography. Hence the "automythology" — call it verbal self-invention, a mental journey full of whispers, visitations, emblems, epiphanies, full of fugitive ceremonies, mingling memory and desire.

The speaker in this section is an adult, forty-one years old, an "I" viewing the education of another, his younger self whom he calls "the boy." Between this "I" and "he" is the space of perception, not quite so rich as in *The Education of Henry Adams*, but wide enough for irony, insight, self-reproach. The gap also permits Zweig to *imagine* the pattern of his life: a Brooklyn boy impersonating too perfectly a Frenchman, an avoider playing revolutionary, an artist in search of his vocation, a complaisant Wandering Jew. Search, wandering, exile, the artist's *disponibilité* — Zweig refuses to "become a man" — are his axial lines of existence. As an eminent Polish novelist (probably Gombrowicz) tells him in the gardens of Royaumont: "But don't forget, God is a wanderer too. That is why He appears mainly to wanderers, because wanderers exist principally among abstractions. They have given up so much that they have become light and unstable, like winged seedlings never touching the earth" (*TJ*, 85).

As a temporal journey, this "Automythology," Zweig says, recounts the "boy's" *ascesis:* "Under its protective shadow, his life had been as active and complete as Saint Anthony's haunted nights. . . . Without knowing it, he had made his apprenticeship of the desert in Paris" (*TJ,* 88). Even the Algerian revolutionaries he helped conceal in Michèle's apartment point him to a different Algeria, without *pieds noirs* — and to the Sahara where God wanders among the nomads. Thus, after two journeys, the reader may expect in the third a synthesis of hope, the fruit of quest. This is an expectation that will be, at best, only partly, only edgily, satisfied.

The third journey, entitled "The Bright Yellow Circus," is neither spatial nor temporal but noetic. It records Zweig's "conversion," a year after his Saharan adventure, to yoga under the influence of Swami Muktananda, nicknamed Baba, a Sadguru of the highest order. Wishing, Zweig suspects, is a kind of destiny; the seeker lives in the interval between urgent hope and elusive realization. But that interval is nothing if not filled by acts. Zweig now wants to act upon himself, and this takes him on a psychic "journey to the east." At first, he is repelled by the personal melodrama of Baba's devotees; gradually, he surrenders to his guru's calm, a force both supernal and seemingly banal. The Buddhist void, Zweig discovers, is like the ashen emptiness within himself, but without fear. Sitting in the tranquil presence of his mentor, he believes — erroneously as we shall see — that he is cured of the nightmare which he had considered the main premise of his life. "Suddenly a bright yellow light filled my eyes," Zweig writes. "The light resembled an enormous surface, covered with the baroque line drawing of a circus: trapezes, animals, trainers, clowns. I heard my voice saying: 'It's all a play of the divine energy'" (*TJ,* 161).

But exaltation gives way to expectations of relapse, in fact to relapse. The "magic of unwithholding presentness" Baba possesses does not seem contagious. Zweig never overcomes completely his fearful self-absorption, his habit of "watching himself live." The third journey proves to be no synthesis of hope, only another journey, a different face or phase of quest. The book ends with a rather wordy, somewhat banausic, eulogy to Baba, a pedestrian statement really on the "higher reality." Behind that statement lurk all the moods, evasions, anxieties of Paul Zweig, a most accomplished writer, if not one of the illuminati of our time.

Here we touch an inherent, disabling paradox, that of the artist as saint, mystic, or perfect. Zweig himself acknowledges the tension if not the full contradiction: writing, he knows, can displace spiritual enlightenment. He senses the radical betrayal of language, *his* language: "Adam named the animals according to a technique which had, apparently, been lost to me, for his animals stayed named, while mine sank back again instantly, so that nothing was ever gained" (*TJ,* 153). And he admits that his eulogy to Baba remains mere eloquence, that admission itself eloquent. Thus the

last words of *Three Journeys:* "This was as far as words would take me.
I had been lifted as by a gust of wisdom, which had set me down beyond
the reach of eloquence. Words had carried me as far as the beginning. Now,
in a far different sense, it was up to me to begin" (*TJ,* 182).

Perhaps, then, the truest quest, the most achieved, remains entirely mute.
But our concern is articulate quest, quest in American literature. In the
case of *Three Journeys,* the quest reveals all it *can* about itself even in its
final failure, *because* of its final failure. A tragic irony follows the book:
two years after its publication, Zweig develops lymphatic cancer, com-
plicated by leukemia. He dies in 1984 at the age of forty-nine. The last
six years of his life, lived terribly, lived tenderly, in the intermittent shadow
of death, round off his quest. As his friend Morris Dickstein put it in his
introduction to Zweig's last and posthumous work, *Departures: Memoirs:*
"The personal metamorphosis which Paul had failed to achieve in the Sahara Desert or in his relation to Muktananda now took place over a six-
year period as a result of his illness."[9] Indeed, all the spiritual hesitations
of Zweig, all the dregs of feeling, still appear — how could they not? — in
his memoirs, gradually purified. With new severity, he concedes his fail-
ings and yearnings: his anxiety ("a wound in the dark that was like another self"), his vagueness ("a vacant, elsewhere sort of boy"), his "old dream
of an enchanted ordinariness"; above all, his commitment to his vocation
("I felt that writing was my best self").[10]

At last, Paul Zweig manages somehow to absolve himself from guilt
by his writing, art, and so conquer his death — for what is fear of death
but a kind of guilt? — and bring his quest to a good end.

6

The factual mode may constrain the forms, without inhibiting the motives,
of quest. Even a reporter may suffer from whimsy or wound. Still, there
is a jagged, asymptotic quality to the texts we have seen in this chapter:
they move toward a realized and risky action of the spirit, an engagement
with final realities, a discovery of personal voice. In doing so, they help
us to imagine what an ideal work of quest might be. More to the point,
perhaps, they reveal the trials of selfhood, the spectrum of social dissatisfactions, as the world presses on each errant American, in tundra or desert. Paradoxically, we learn from these wanderers more about our homemade world — its packaged delights, its tedium, its raw desperations — than
from shrill ideologies of a passing day.

These wanderers, so different their faces, also show that quest can be
accident, vision, compulsion, like the dice of destiny, chance and necessity
all in one. Quest can be unconscious of itself before it finds its moment,

and it can be more escape than quest until it finds its sign. It can also be the call of darkness, given some bright, articulate form while the form lasts. For these wanderers write well, very well, as if to redeem their rage, redeem perhaps the violence of existence itself, in a felicity of words brought back from the border of death.

In any case, quest, however undefined in factual narratives or, in the next chapter, fictional, defines a mode of being in the world, an alternative existence to lives that lead us precisely — where?

Chapter Six
Faces of Quest: Fiction

"Americans are supposed to be dumb but they are willing to go into this. It isn't just me. You have to think about white Protestantism and the Constitution and the Civil War and capitalism and winning the West. All the major tasks and the big conquests were done before my time. That left the biggest problem of all, which was to encounter death. We've just got to do something about it. It isn't just me. Millions of Americans have gone forth since the war to redeem the present and discover the future. I can swear to you, Romilayu, there are guys exactly like me in India and in China and South America and all over the place. Just before I left home I saw an interview in the paper with a piano teacher from Muncie who became a Buddhist monk in Burma. You see, that's what I mean. I am a high-spirited kind of guy. And it's the destiny of my generation of Americans to go out in the world and try to find the wisdom of life. It just is. Why the hell do you think I'm out here, anyway?"

— Saul Bellow

1

HE TERM QUEST is also applied to a medley of fictions, ranging from any novel with mythic intent, like Bernard Malamud's *The Natural* (1952) or John Updike's *The Centaur* (1963), to ribald neopicaresques, like Saul Bellow's *The Adventures of Augie March* (1953) and Jack Kerouac's *On the Road* (1957). It is imputed as well to powerful images of a character's search, as in Ralph Ellison's *Invisible Man* (1952) and Thomas Pynchon's *The Crying of Lot 49* (1966), which evoke both myth and picaresque. Indeed, quest is ascribed to every form of dramatic restlessness in life or letters.

No doubt quest inheres in the human condition, inspirits every effort in the labyrinth of existence. But the idea of quest I offer here, or rather pursue, is of a particular kind. It requires more physical peril, for instance, than Pynchon's Oedipa Mass encounters, more even than Ellison's Invisible Man endures. It also entails diremption, disjunction, cultural exile, more than Los Angeles and New York — which have their jungles — require.

The element of acute risk is present, say, in Robert Stone's *A Flag for*

Sunrise (1981) and Philip Caputo's *Horn of Africa* (1980). These probing fictions, set in Central America and East Africa respectively, expose personal and political violence, the clash and din of societies in a postcolonial world. Still, crowded, electric, dramatic as they may be, such novels eschew individual focus, avoid moral insistence on the destiny of a singular character. They center on no organizing passion, emergent fate.

In this chapter, I start with a prelusive discussion of novels by Harriet Doerr and Joan Didion, which give us a glimpse of quest in fiction. I then consider, in more detail, works by Eleanor Clark, James Dickey, Norman Mailer, and Saul Bellow. The sequence is not chronological; it is rather typological, moving toward clarification of a type, but not less historical for that. Each novel comes to us carrying the historical burden of its moment.

2

In Harriet Doerr's lapidary novel *Stones for Ibarra* (1984), Richard and Sara Everton suddenly decide, in midlife, to reclaim a copper mine abandoned by Richard's grandfather during the Mexican Revolution of 1910. The mine, flooded and derelict, lies beneath the hills of a small, barren village, Ibarra. But Richard Everton dies of leukemia within six years of his arrival in Mexico, leaving behind him a thriving mine. The Evertons transform the village, the village transforms them. In *Ibarra,* Harriet Doerr renders the dramatic encounter between cultures with feeling, humor, poise.

What prompts the Evertons to leave a secure career in America, heedless of risk, oblivious to criticisms and entreaties alike? There is always an element of chance: some faded, sepia-colored pictures of the mine and adobe house come accidentally to light. Doerr, however, gives us more than chance:

> Five days ago the Evertons left San Francisco and their house with a narrow view of the bay in order to extend the family's Mexican history and patch the present onto the past. To find out if there was still copper underground and how much of the rest of it was true, the width of sky, the depth of stars, the air like new wine, the harsh noons and long, slow dusks. To weave chance and hope into a fabric that would clothe them as long as they lived. (*S,* 2f.)[1]

There is wonder here, desire, will — and a tacit judgment on American life. Can we surmise, then, that the Evertons are questers? Or are they merely settlers, pioneers of the old American kind?

The Evertons do seek a larger access to reality, though Ibarra offers only limited perils in scorpions, snakes, mining accidents. The reality they seek and the challenges they overcome find a focus not in physical dangers but in cultural misapprehensions. These are voiced by sundry villagers, most notably Remedios Acosta who serves as a kind of chorus in the novel. Her summary of the *norteamericanos* is succinct: "They are kind and friendly, but they are strangers to the exigencies of life" (*S,* 23). That is, unlike her people, the Evertons do not go out daily to meet their individual dooms without surprise. Nor do they resort to charms, talismans, and amulets to placate their fate. Nor, again, do they live with cold, hunger, fear, in a "thin borderline of existence, no wider than a ray of late sun penetrating a slit in the shutter . . ." (*S,* 26). To the Ibarrans, their benefactors seem spoiled, a little absurd, always *mediodesorientado* (half-disoriented).

There is some truth, envy, and misperception in all this. In fact, death, that ultimate exigency, casts a long, thickening shadow on the Evertons. If the Mexicans give constant evidence of courage, stoicism, simplicity, the Americans give equal evidence of spirit, awareness, ingenuity, and, in Sara's case, a vital sympathy crucial to any moral life. Sara does emerge as the moral center of the book, a custodian of consciousness and pain, of responsibility to things living and dead. Thus Doerr's narrative, though omniscient, tends to restrict its purview to Sara's concerns.

Still, *Stones for Ibarra* finally reveals more about life and death—piles of jagged stones commemorate the latter—in a Mexican village than about the motives of quest. Tacitly, of course, the novel alludes to the soft, factitious qualities of American life. But these, ironically, are the very qualities that the capable Evertons belie. A quester only in the large, human sense, intrepid and independent, "Don Ricardo Everton," as the assistant curate of Ibarra says, "has left footprints in this soil that neither rain nor wind can sweep away" (*S,* 212); for he was a good man, and like Sara, he could cross languages, nationalities, faiths without losing his purpose. But quest demands more than benevolence, more even than purpose.

Charlotte Douglas, in Joan Didion's *A Book of Common Prayer* (1977), also travels south, crossing cultures and languages, neither as settler nor pioneer in Boca Grande, nor really as seeker, only as "sojourner." She arrives in that equatorial republic of "flat bush and lifeless sea" with many visas in her passport, all stamped *Turista,* her profession *Madre.* This is Charlotte: "she left one man, she left a second man, she traveled again with the first; she let him die alone. She lost one child to 'history' and another to 'complications' . . . she imagined herself capable of shedding that baggage and came to Boca Grande, a tourist" (*B,* 3). There she is shot in one of the periodic coups of the "republic" after finally taking a stand at the end of a fugitive life. What, then, is her quest? And who, really, is this rich and seductive woman, this virtuoso of the unexamined life?

The Charlotte who comes to Boca Grande, the narrator tells us, is not the same who finds—courts?—her death there. She comes, first, because she does not want to be elsewhere; because Boca Grande seems to demand no "attentiveness" from her; because, in some dim way, it represents "the very cervix of the world, the place through which a child lost to history must eventually pass" (*B,* 199). Thus Charlotte haunts the local airport until they close it, waiting for her daughter, Marin, a revolutionary terrorist on the run, to appear suddenly on the tarmac, radiant in a subtropical sun; or waiting, perhaps, for *her own* plane to transport her to a special destiny. In the end, this poignant American heroine of delusions, always afraid of the dark, finally refuses to "walk away." From what? Her past failures, her vagueness—herself.

There is a self here put in considerable risk. But it is not a seeker's active self. In fact, Didion consciously avoids any ultimate clarification of character. Her intrusive narrator—it is her story as much as Charlotte's—is Grace Strasser-Mendana, an American anthropologist who studied with Kroeber and Lévi-Strauss, and has married into the wealthiest family in Boca Grande. She, a "prudent traveler from Denver," is everything Charlotte is not: tough, realistic, lucid, and a little prim. Grace is also dying of pancreatic cancer while serving as Charlotte's witness. But how can she witness? "I am an anthropologist who lost faith in her own method," she wryly admits, "who stopped believing that observable activity defined anthropos. . . . I did not know why I did or did not do anything at all" (*B,* 4). What, then, can Grace see of Charlotte?

Grace can, by the end of the narrative, attest to a change in her own view of Charlotte whom she initially considers a decent creature, rather in disrepair. At the close of the novel, Grace declares:

> All I know now is that when I think of Charlotte Douglas . . . I am less and less certain that this story has been one of delusion.
> Unless the delusion was mine.
> . . . The wind is up and I will die and rather soon and all I know empirically is *I am* told.
> I am told, as so she said. . . .
> Apparently.
> I have not been the witness I wanted to be. (*B,* 280)

Even Didion's stylized, indeed mannered, sentences maintain our epistemological uncertainty: "strike that," Grace Strasser-Mendana-Didion will say to revise the preceding sentence and begin anew. Still, ambiguities notwithstanding, we close the novel with sympathy, even admiration, for Didion's neurotic heroine, a woman who talks and acts as if "she had no specific history of her own" (*B,* 41), a woman who believes the world is peopled with others exactly like herself—a woman, too, who can slit a trachea to save a choking man and administer cholera vaccines for thirty-four hours at a stretch.

However we judge Charlotte Douglas, we sense that her last redemptive stand resists the name of quest; her moral regeneration culminates a lifetime of erasures, evasions, deferrals. The search is rather Didion's. Like the Anglican Book of Common Prayer, Didion's novel addresses a fallen world, a world without grace (the narrator's name). This is North America in the sixties, with all its hopes and claptrap; this is Central America, now as then, with all its violence and venality. This is life where death holds dominion over Charlotte—they throw her body on the American Embassy lawn—as over Grace. Yet in Didion's book, the spare, liturgical ring of the prose seems to suspend death for an instant as it exorcises the mournful frolics of the human condition. It does so by creating not a paradigm of quest but a moral and artistic order of human responsibility, the responsibility of Grace to Charlotte, of Charlotte to her children, of Didion to her characters—and, it is hoped, of readers to all concerned.

Crossings and displacements, then, though mythic, do not define quest; nor does the presence of peril to an identifiable self; nor yet the grating of cultures—"You smell American," says one character to Charlotte Douglas, while another calls her the "*norteamericana* cunt." Quest enacts will, a long desire, and in this enactment unforeseen changes occur. The encounter with otherness becomes deeply metamorphic, a passage into new knowledge, a different mode of being.

3

We come closer to the motive of quest in Eleanor Clark's intricate novel *Camping Out* (1986). The work centers on two women, Dennie Hensley, a diplomat's wife who lives in Rome, and her distant friend, Marilyn Grove, a lesbian poet. An accidental meeting of the two women—Dennie is back in the States to attend her mother's funeral—results in a joint canoe trip in some remote region of Vermont. There they meet "Fred," an escaped convict, a literate, handsome, homicidal psychopath, virtuoso on a penny whistle, who rips open Marilyn's terrier, Corky, sodomizes Marilyn herself, and devastates the lives of the two women before vanishing suddenly into the night.

The story is really Dennie's, her unconsicous search for her self, and it unfolds with both artful and fussy complexity. A Radcliffe graduate and *poète manqué* of good Yankee stock, she succumbs to a delicate nausea in her late thirties; in everything, she seems a dilettante. Alienated from

her mother, incestuous with her twin brother, Rick—to give her husband
a child—feeling fit neither as mother nor as wife, she still discovers within
herself shattering passions in the woods of Vermont. These are the inad-
missible passions of a night journey, passions for *both* Marilyn and Fred.
It is a different woman who returns to her family in Rome. But Dennie
does not survive to enjoy her new life. She and her husband, recently ap-
pointed ambassador to an African nation, perish in a helicopter crash for
which rival terrorist factions claim credit.

Was Dennie a seeker? She envies Rick's work with refugees in Cam-
bodia, which makes "her own life look so selfish and meaningless" (*C,* 19).
On an impulse, she goes camping out with Marilyn because "it's fun to
be crazy." But the more we know about Dennie, know about all the imbrications of her family relations, the more we realize that she is a time
traveler seeking a clue to reality in her past. This past is suddenly illumed
by violence: Dennie's most piercing insights come to her, an incandescence
of expectation and recall, as she waits for her turn to be raped. Roped
tightly to a tree, she sees the unappeased scenes of her life return, flashing
in the chiaroscuro of memory. Her grandmother, her father and mother,
her first husband, her second husband, and her brother's son, all crowd
in her search for forgiveness. Or is the impulse closer to fantasy than quest?
Still bound to that tree, she imagines she could redeem the rapist and be,
through him, redeemed:

> Dennie felt her own will ripening toward irresistible contagion, a better weapon
> than any hatchet or pointed ember; the man would forgive her life of privi-
> lege, would whisper his true name to her; overcome with desire for her alone,
> would dump his sorrows and struggles in her arms, then kill her if need be,
> but five minutes of that union would be worth an eternity of what she had been
> playing at for so long in the name of life. (*C,* 177)

The languages of memory and atonement are indeed key to Eleanor
Clark's work. Here truth comes always in recall, integrity in the acknowl-
edgment of sin; the worst betrayals spring from desire, desire reckless of
its past. Thus Dennie reflects: "Without the thought of perdition I see no
way to clarity and couldn't respect it if I did. . . . There's too much gabble
in the world, too much how-to; knowledge must be sacred to be any good"
(*C,* 215). Hence her various modes of confession throughout the work, including a long, rambling, unfinished letter she writes Marilyn after the event.
But is Dennie's final confession sincere? At the end, she feels an altered
person, more self-knowledgeable, and even "lifted to a certainty of sur-
prising love for her husband, Carter, of all people" (*C,* 209). Yet a month
after the savage episode, she confesses to a priest in Rome that she has

loved only one man in her life, her brother Rick; and she "tries out" the same "idea" on Carter who suggests "for therapy a mouthwash and three somersaults" (*C,* 214).

If Dennie Hensley's adventure is quest, it is haphazard quest. Clark conveys this sense of drift through her point of view which alternates between a third-person narrative (over Dennie's shoulder) and a first-person, pseudo-epistolary voice (Dennie's nattering letter, never sent, found in the Hensley papers after their death). The device fractures mimetic reality, undermines our certainties, and makes even shadier the shady revelations in which the novel abounds: the occult consent of both women to Fred, "artist of the abyss"; Dennie's jealousy of Marilyn because Fred chooses her first (he never gets around to Dennie); Carter's attempted rape of Marilyn, which she divulges to Dennie only after the encounter with Fred; Carter's marital rape of Dennie after she admits to him her attraction to Fred—ironically, it results in her only pregnancy by her spouse; Dennie's fleeting infatuation with Marilyn, her "goddess of a moment"; and Fred's own feline game with the two women, a deadly game of cat and mouse played out to an inconclusive end.

Dennie drifts into knowledge through violence and recall. Her journey brings her to no exotic land, except the strangeness within us all. She encounters the destructive element in reverse exile, not in some far, barbaric place but on native ground. This element lives in Fred as in an entire subclass that society hides behind euphemisms, stereotypes, prison bars. Dennie may step on a rusted nail and Corky tangle with a porcupine; but those are minor mishaps compared with Fred's malevolence. This is primal malevolence, shading into the more rational questions of deprivation and justice. As Dennie thinks: "Probably some such latent image of the enemy forces proliferating in society, the ignorant and unmoored, the drug-destroyed, the politically and/or sexually lunatic, had figured the night before too, in the dream that made her mistake an owl for that unknowable human threat" (*C,* 26).

To this "unknowable human threat," Clark makes clear, no current ideology and no liberal goodwill suffice. Indeed, the novel presents less quest than satire, projects rather a kind of moral despair at the fads, hype, and illusions of the Western world. In that world, literary theoreticians practice "nihilogatries," children of diplomats sniff coke, Roman princes affect Maoism, and the anal rape of a lesbian author becomes advertisement for her forthcoming work. But illusions shrivel in moments of terror. Here is Fred terrorizing the two women in one of his arias of hate:

> You dumb bourgeois broads, with your fancy foreign accents and your L. L. Bean whatsits and your fucking mommas and grampas and college degrees and your shitty little poems as you call them—yeah, po-ems like in po-

insettia — and your still shittier little ideas about how to clean up society. . . . We didn't get around to much of that, did we? but I know your type, give us another meal to sit through and you'd have the schmeer all over it. Wanted a peek into the lower depths, didn't you? just an itty bitty peek to see what it's like down there and why all those terrible people do all those terrible things, woof woof, welfare schmelfare, nothing like that where *you* come from, oh no, everybody's clean as a whistle and honest as the day is long up there, nez pah?" (*C,* 181)

But terror may also dissolve, and ideology wash off like so much dross, in mythic moments of the novel. Here is Dennie singing a very different aria, as she sees Marilyn come naked out of the lake:

I saw you without patrimony, without antecedents, sublime in your courage and total self-creation, believe me I did, as Venus rising from the sea and as beautiful, only without that twining garland of hair she holds with one hand across her pubic part — you know the Botticelli; and I was one of those honored handmaidens, made lovely too by your presence . . . those androgynous Greeks are a far cry from the pruderies we grew up on.

And a farther one, if that's possible, from all the women's lib jabber about the new woman that we hear even here in Italy but not as much as I did in my few days in the U.S. How pathetic, how piddling those programmatic rantings sound, compared to that vision on a cockleshell, of spume and ecstasy and perfect power and grace, with the knowledge of an immortality of happy amours wafting her to shore. So in my sudden blast of freedom, or dementia if you like, I saw you. (*C,* 58f.)

The "sudden blast of freedom" may sweep the landscape of quest. But *Camping Out* ends by retreating from its horizons. Whatever brief knowledge Dennie achieves, and whatever moral self-assurance, she can not put them to any vital test before her premature death. Life simply closes in on her, as it does on Raggedy Ann, her childhood doll riddled by fascist bullets, as it does on Corky, Marilyn's dog. Dauntless, involuted, at times highly mannered or cute, yet consummately intelligent, Eleanor Clark's fiction delimits a boundary of quest in an age of systems, unfriendly to the human referent. The novel's center is the past, its burden this: "cruelty multiplies and societies die from loss of memory" (*C,* 164). Call it, then, a quest for right, for answerable recall.

So far, our unwitting seekers perish; death reaches out for them in the three preceding novels. By contrast, James Dickey's *Deliverance* (1970) is a brutal tale of survival, though three men die in it, and an interesting foil to *Camping Out.* But the reader may want to know: deliverance from what? From moral complacencies, social pieties, perhaps from civilization itself? The clues are scattered, and in one place they become nearly explicit. Making love to his wife on the morning of his fateful adventure, the narrator, Ed Gentry, imagines—he is on the whole steady, unimaginative—the golden eye of a girl, a studio model: "The gold eye shone, not with the practicality of sex, so necessary to its survival, but the promise of it that promised other things, another life, deliverance" (D, 28). Another life, deliverance: there lies the book's knot which links its two heroes, Ed Gentry and Lewis Medlock, doubles.

Ed—all four are called by their first names—is practical and forthright, given to the task at hand, as Lewis is visionary, ever the restless seeker, a little like Bellow's Henderson. Ed says:

> Lewis wanted to be immortal. He had everything that life could give, and he couldn't make it work. And he couldn't bear to give it up or see age take it away from him, either, because in the meantime he might be able to find what it was he wanted, the thing that must be there, and that must be subject to the will. He was the kind of man who tries by any means—weight lifting, diet, exercise, self-help manuals from taxidermy to modern art—to hold on to his body and mind and improve them, to rise above them. And yet he was also the first to take a chance, as though the burden of his own laborious immortality were too heavy to bear, and he wanted to get out of it by means of an accident, or what would appear to others to be an accident. (D, 9)

Meantime, Lewis trains himself implacably, trains his instincts, will, and powerful body, to survive an atomic holocaust in the Georgia woods. He insists on turning the canoe trip of four urban businessmen into a Moral, a Life Principle, a Way, a Provocation to everything Western civilization has achieved in three thousand years. He wants to recover something absolutely essential, and in doing so perform some superhuman feat that beggars eternity. But Lewis breaks his leg early on the trip—again the seeker's wound—and it is Ed who pulls the survivors through, after three murders.

The scene is perfectly set for the encounter between nature and civilization, instinct and law, *within* America itself. An entire region of the north Georgia wilderness is about to drown, turned into a holiday resort and lake. The Cahulawassee River, with its horrendously beautiful whitewater rapids, must vanish. Ageless cemeteries of hillbillies must be moved to higher ground. Marinas and real estate developments sprout around the dammed lake. On the eve of their departure, the four white, married, middle-class men pore over a colored map of the region, intuiting the secret harmonies of the land, thinking that, henceforth, a fragment of the American wilderness will survive only in archives and the failing memories of old woodsmen.

Excepting Lewis, though, these businessmen are unfit to venture; they have learned to meet existence mainly on legal, domestic, or social terms;

they are not particularly successful in their careers. Still, they sense obscurely an alternative to their humdrum lives. "Up yonder," as Lewis tells them, life *demands* to be taken on other terms. This they discover in scene after harrowing scene, in encounters with the stupendous force of nature (the rapids) and malevolence of man (two hillbilly outlaws). Yet they also experience a strange happiness at the heart of violence. Three of them survive, irrevocably altered, one with a broken leg, another homosexually raped by a hillbilly. As for the outlaws, Lewis kills one, Ed the other — with bow and broadhead arrows.

Dickey's novel is a masterpiece in the poetry of action and menace. Relentlessly, it renders, in a prose at once tight, elusive, and earthy, the atavism and terror of three autumn days in the Georgia woods. The book spares us no detail in the struggle of life for itself. But the book also reveals instants of subtle intimacy, moments of pure being. Having climbed, with bare hands, the sheer face of a gorge to kill an outlaw who wants to ambush him at daybreak, Ed suddenly exclaims:

> What a view. *What* a view. But I had my eyes closed. The river was running in my mind, and I raised my lids and saw exactly what had been the image of my thought. For a second I did not know what I was seeing and what I was imagining; there was such an utter sameness that it didn't matter; both were the river. It spread there eternally, the moon so huge on it that it hurt the eyes, and the mind, too, flinched like an eye. What? I said. Where? There was nowhere but here. Who, though? Unknown. Where can I start? . . . What a view, I said again. The river was blank and mindless with beauty. It was the most glorious thing I had ever seen. But it was not seeing, really. For once it was not just seeing. It was beholding. I *beheld* the river in its icy pit of brightness, in its far-below sound and indifference, in its large coil and tiny points and flashes of the moon, in its long sinuous form, in its uncomprehending consequence. What was there? (*D,* 170f.)

The sentiment, which strikingly recalls Chris Bonington's (see pp. 49–50), adverts to a kind of "selflessness" that every mountaineer, every seeker or adventurer, comes intimately to know. In a moment "mindless with beauty," all insufficiencies vanish, all lacks.

Dickey prefixes to his novel an epigraph from Georges Bataille, which proposes a "principle of insufficiency" at the base of human existence, Freud's Ananke. This radical lack may underlie all life *as perceived by human beings,* the perception itself implying a missing term. Something is always buried, hidden, lost to us: murdered bodies lying under forest leaves; the forest itself flooded beneath a lake; invisible hillbillies colonized within their own state; some part of our own nature, concealed and irreclaimable. Ed and Lewis — Ed *becomes* Lewis — manage to discover this perilous part of existence, and manage through great pain to reclaim it.

But they must also face the ordinary world again, which Ed sees, at the end, in the image of a policeman: "When we reached town he [the policeman] went into a cafe and made a couple of calls. It frightened me some to watch him talk through the tripled glass — windshield, plate glass, and phone booth — for it made me feel caught in the whole vast, inexorable web of modern communication" (*D*, 252). The feeling passes, for Ed possesses the river permanently: "Now it ran nowhere but in my head, but there it ran as though immortally" (*D*, 275).

Deliverance has all the marks of adventure and some of quest. An adventurer by instinct, Lewis Medlock is constrained in his quest by an archaic vision of survival in a postatomic world. Indeed, his prophecy of Armageddon is itself a measure of his grievance against tawdriness and debility in the civilization we all know. But though he changes at the end, becomes almost Zen — "He can die now; he knows that dying is better than immortality" (*D*, 277) — the story is not really Lewis's. It is Ed's, the narrator's, precisely because change in him is more crucial.

Is Ed, then, a seeker? Married to an ex-nurse, Martha, and father to a healthy child, Dean, Ed nonetheless suffers from pangs of "inconsequence," that "old, helpless, time-terrified human feeling" (*D*, 277). By nature a "slider," living, as he says, by "antifriction," not in the least mad or macho, he still yearns powerfully for some omen of wonder in the world, some sign of significance. Hence his latent need for adventure. The river, the gorge, the impenetrable woods without Clabber Girl ads or country Jesus posters, without shopping malls or tourist motels, mean to him freedom, freedom in some vanishing terrain, a place altogether different. Ed even identifies with a huge owl perched atop his tent at night: "I hunted with him as well as I could, there in my weightlessness. The woods burned in my head. Toward morning I could reach up and touch the claw without turning on the light" (*D*, 89).

The ordeal of quest is an ordeal by otherness, and here, as in *Camping Out,* man proves more alien, certainly more vicious, than nature. Ed "dies" several times: first, as he feels a shotgun jammed into his belly; next as he capsizes in the rapids; then as he crawls up the sheer cliff; and finally, having shot a hillbilly dead from the branches of a tree, when he tumbles to the ground, a spare broadhead arrow stuck between his own ribs. It is a story of killing and dying, of pure will against rock, of surrender to rushing waters, of omnipotence and panic. Yet all this awakens Ed to an intense new sensation of things within and without him, a stabbing insight into reality. It is deliverance by danger, self-mastery, violent survival — an answer of sorts to Ed's feeling of "inconsequence." It is deliverance also by comradeship and conspiracy; for the survivors must hide their own crimes. It is deliverance by nature or instinct, as Ed drinks for the last

time from the river that had borne him through death to—exactly what?
The answer is not self-evident. At the end, the three survivors return
to their towns, their jobs, their families. The narrator himself tells us: "The
main thing was to get back into my life as quickly and as deeply as I could;
as if I had never left it. I went into my office and opened the door wide . . ."
(*D,* 274). Even the girl with the golden eye becomes for Ed "imaginary."
Her "gold-halved eye" loses its fascination for him: "Its place was in the
night river, in the land of impossibility" (*D,* 277). Still, the river runs within
him, underlies everything he does, finds always some way to serve him.
Is this vanished river, then, the attained goal, or at least the vital residue,
of his quest? Everything in the novel would want us to answer yes, yes.
Yet we must wonder: can a quest be won once and for all? Is this novel
quest at all?

Here a quick comparison with Clark's *Camping Out* may prove useful.
In that novel, Dennie stumbles into violence, self-knowledge, liberating
recall, even if she does not live long enough to profit from her adventure.
By contrast, Ed's quest in *Deliverance* seems a shade more self-conscious;
certainly the force of intention is more palpable in the latter work as a
whole. This may be due in part to its narrative voice. The voice is Ed's,
purposeful and direct, rendering rapid actions in a glaring present, without sustained, meditative flashbacks. Thus what *Deliverance* loses to *Camping Out* in subtlety, it gains in suspense, immediacy, sustained, even brutal, power. The difference between the two works thus springs from their
informing themes: salvation by right memory in Clark's case, salvation
by right action in Dickey's.

The difference may or may not confirm ascriptions of gender—too much
on this topic is fancy, at best politics. But masculine as is the enterprise
of *Deliverance,* Dickey himself wants to give women their share in it, their
critical, qualifying vision. Ed himself detests the cheap use of sex in ads,
even more in pornography, the violation of woman's privacy and body.
He describes the gold-eyed model in the studio with warmth, delicacy, feeling, without trace of misogyny or leering. Still, he is aware of an inevitable
tension between man's and woman's world, the latter more social, somehow more constraining. Martha asks him on the eve of his adventure: "Is
it my fault?" "'Lord, no,' I said, but it partly was, just as it's any woman's
fault who represents normalcy" (*D,* 27). He also associates all the secre-
taries swarming about him on the street, their hair piled and shellacked
and horned, with a sense of social desolation. And he renders the incongruity between the *idea* of the Cahulawassee River and the *reality* of quotidian life in a bar thus: "Waitresses in sheer net tights and corsages kept
staring down into the map [of the river]. It was time to go. Lewis took
off the weight of two steins and the map leapt shut" (*D,* 12). Nevertheless,

when the widow of Drew Ballinger says, on hearing of her husband's death on the trip, "So useless. . . . So useless. . . . Such a goddamned useless way to die," Ed can only answer: "Yes, it was useless. . ." (*D*, 271).

Is this a comforting, Conradian lie, like Marlow's to Kurtz's intended in *Heart of Darkness?* Or does Ed really believe it was useless, or only that every death is useless, or that some deaths are worth risking in order to live and die well? The atavism of *Deliverance,* the rush of its action, its thematic closure at the end, all suggest the last. But the narrator's voice, mostly stoical, devoid of bravado or presumption, inflected sometimes with fear and self-doubt — that voice gives nuance to the action, an action, finally, closer to edifying and poetic adventure than to fully motivated quest.

4

The tang of adventure in the great American wilderness, a wilderness still fraught with magic and menace in the twentieth century, emanates from Norman Mailer's *Why Are We in Vietnam?* (1967). Heroic despite all its mockeries, the book restores to quest its magnitude of spirit. Ostensibly a rousing hunt for grizzly in the Brooks Range of Alaska, the novel also renders the initiation of a sixteen-year-old Texan, called D.J., into the violence within him and around him, a quest for manhood and identity which will permit him to meet "the Wizard" (Death) and confront the war in Vietnam two years later — that is, to understand contemporary American reality.

D.J. is, of course, in the tradition of questing, adolescent heroes — Huck Finn (Twain), Henry Fleming (Crane), Nick Adams (Hemingway), Ike Mc-Caslin (Faulkner), Holden Caulfield (Salinger) — whose initiation into reality also provides a critique of American society. Thus, in the remote wilderness of Alaska, under the aurora borealis, D.J. learns something about the betrayals of his father, the corruptions of America, the merciless laws of nature, the love and fear he harbors toward his friend, Tex — learns, above all, something about the intractable mystery of existence and himself. Love, Power, Knowledge, Magic, Nature, and Death are all intimately bound; when their vital relations decay, we enter the universe of waste: cancer, excrement, money, Vietnam.

As in many works of adventure, social criticism blends easily into the metaphysics of quest. Indeed, Mailer's satire of America — that "sad deep sweet beauteous mystery land" (*W*, 205) which has allowed plastic to enter its soul (materialism), corporate cancer and bureaucratic violence to shape its policy (Vietnam) — can be savage as well as obscene. No one, nothing, is spared in the "United Greedies of America," as its messages collect nightly in the E.M.F. of the North Pole, and an "hour before sunrise" begin "to smog the predawning air with their psychic glug, glut and exudations, not

to mention all the funeral parlors cooling out in the premature morn . . ."
(*W,* 206). Even Rusty Jethroe, D.J.'s father, all killer instinct, Texas will,
and executive panache mixed in his funk, thinks "it's a secret crime that
America, which is the greatest nation ever lived, better read a lot of history to see how shit-and-sure a proposition that is, is nonetheless represented, indeed even symbolized by an eagle, the most miserable of the
scavengers, worse than crow" (*W,* 132f.).

Mailer's obscene critique of America, however, is a poetic labor of love.
What turned America into a scavenger in Vietnam? What ravaged the
psychic ecology of the Republic? What made the animals, all the way to
the Arctic, crazier, meaner than napalmed Vietcong? His answers delineate
a politics of Primal Being (God and the Devil), which bring acute discomfort to liberal readers. Yet Mailer is also preternaturally attuned to historical change; he knows all the fools, knaves, and villains of the age. Thus
Rusty's ugly bemusement has its poignant, even truthful side, a *cri de mau-
vais coeur* from the sixties:

> Yeah, sighs Rusty, the twentieth century is breaking up the ball game, and
> Rusty thinks large common thoughts such as these: (1) The women are free.
> They fuck too many to believe one man can do the job. (2) The Niggers are
> free, and the dues they got to be paid is no Texas virgin's delight. (3) The Nig-
> gers and the women are fucking each other. (4) The Yellow races are break-
> ing loose. (5) Africa is breaking loose. (6) The adolescents are breaking loose
> including his own son. (7) The European nations hate America's guts. (8) The
> products are no fucking good anymore. (9) Communism is a system guaran-
> teed to collect dues from all losers. (9a) More losers than winners. (9b) and
> out: Communism is going to defeat capitalism, unless promptly destroyed.
> (10) a. Fucking is king. b. Jerk-off dances are the royal road to the fuck. c.
> Rusty no great jerk-off dancer. d. Rusty disqualified from playing King Fuck.
> (11) The white men are no longer champions in boxing. (12) The great white
> athlete is being superseded by the great black athlete. (13) The Jews run the
> Eastern wing of the Democratic party. (14) Karate, a Jap sport, is now pre-
> requisite to good street fighting. (15) The sons of the working class are run-
> ning around America on motorcycles. (16) Church is out, LSD is in. (17) He,
> Rusty, is fucked unless he gets that bear, for if he don't, white men are fucked
> more and they can take no more. Rusty's secret is that he sees himself as one
> of the pillars of the firmament, yeah, man—he reads the world's doom in his
> own fuckup. If he is less great than God intended him to be, then America is
> in Trouble. They don't breed Texans for nothing. (*W,* 110f.)

That, too, is why we were in Vietnam.

As in most quest and adventure stories, however, the critique of Western society relies on certain contrasts between nature and civilization
("syphilization"). Here the contrast is between the Brooks Range and Dal-

las, and by extension, between the Alaskan hunter-guides Big Luke and Big Ollie, on one side, and their Texas clients, Rusty and M.A.'s ("Middle Assholes") Pete and Bill, on the other — while D.J. and Tex stand aloof on their own initiatory ground. More subtly, the contrast is between rooted and rootless values generally, between ecological and alienated tempers — that is, between men who can "execute" an animal cleanly with a bullet to a vital part and others who destroy game with howitzers from helicopters. More subtly still, the contrast itself blurs at the fringe of violence which both nature and civilization share. Thus Mailer about Big Luke: "You could hang him, and he'd weigh just as much as Charley Wilson or Robert Bonehead McNamara, I mean you'd get the same intensity of death ray off his dying . . ." (*W,* 47). In precisely this region of *force,* of energy, which can become cancerous, lies the motive of war: why we were in Vietnam.

Yet in that very same region also lie the motives of love, courage, identity, an achieved selfhood. This last is D.J.'s quest, a quest that enables him, through narrative memory, through the story we read, to face Vietnam. The quest is not abstract. It demands that D.J. confront his father, Rusty, his friend, Tex, and his own death, a charging, howling grizzly bear. The confrontation takes place in a part of America so remote that it may as well have been Venus or Mars — indeed, both Venus and Mars — a zone buzzing with all the electric mysteries of the universe.

The confrontation with the father has a history of wishful murder on both parts: beatings, pickaxe fights, rump bitings which leave a permanent scar on D.J.'s butt, and leave wounds deeper than any scar. As he sees it: "Rusty bit his ass so bad because he was too chicken to bite Hallelujah's [Hallie, D.J.'s mother, Rusty's wife] beautiful butt — she'd have made him pay a half million dollars for each separate hole in her marble palace" (*W,* 41). The climax, however, takes the form not of murder but betrayal: Rusty claims for himself a bear that D.J. has actually mortally wounded. D.J., like Huck or Holden, possesses "one great American virtue," which is to "see right through shit"; and so Rusty's vain and abject claim brings "final end of love of one son for one father" (*W,* 49, 147). D.J. has started to become his own man.

This manhood must clash with his friend's. Tex is "redskin and Nazi in one paternal blood" (*W,* 17); and in Mailer's metaphysics, the virility of the two boys demands that they love, bugger, or kill one another. On a side trip alone in the Endicott Range, freed from corrupt authority, their weapons wrapped up and lashed to a tree (a gesture toward Faulkner's *The Bear*), they repel a big white wolf at one hundred yards with "the voltage of their resolve," climb a tree to escape a grizzly, and generally indulge in "pederastic palaver." There, under the aurora borealis, beneath dancing sunspots and rippling red and green lights, God talks to them in the voice of some Huge Beast:

> yeah, now it was there, murder between them under all friendship, for God was a beast, not a man, and God said, "Go out and kill — fulfill my will, go and kill," and they hung there each of them on the knife of the divide in all conflict . . . and the lights shifted, something in the radiance of the North went into them, and owned their fear . . . and they were twins, never to be near as brothers again, but killer brothers, owned by something, prince of darkness, lord of light, they did not know . . . and each bit a drop of blood from his own finger and touched them across and met, blood to blood . . . and the deep beast whispering Fulfill my will, go forth and kill. . . . (*W,* 204)

Hence Vietnam? Or should we rather say, *thence* to Vietnam? From this moment on, the two men can face the world as it is, a world of death, including Vietnam.

This moment of knowledge and achieved manhood rests, for Mailer as for D.J., on a prior experience of ultimate jeopardy. D.J. tempts death at several points in the narrative, but never more starkly than when he faces down the charging grizzly:

> At twenty feet away, D.J.'s little cool began to evaporate. Yeah, that beast was huge and then huge again, and he was still alive — his eyes looked right at D.J.'s like wise old gorilla eyes, and then they turned gold brown and red like the sky seen through a ruby crystal ball, eyes were transparent, and D.J. looked . . . and something in that grizzer's eyes locked into his, a message, fellow, an intelligence of something very fine and very far away, just about as intelligent and wicked and merry as any sharp light D.J. had ever seen in any Texan's eyes any time (or overseas around the world) those eyes were telling him something, singeing him, branding some part of D.J.'s future, and then the reflection of a shattering message from the shattered internal organs of that bear came twisting through his eyes in a gale of pain, and the head went up, and the bear now too weak to stand up, the jaws worked the pain. (*W,* 146)

It may be argued that D.J.'s story is more initiation than quest. This proves only the confluence of two ambiguous motives, adolescent self-discovery and adult search. The two meet in some irrecusable demand of the heart, meet also in mythic encounters — between Son and Father, Man and Beast, Self and Other, Dr. Jekyll (D.J.) and Mr. (Tex) Hyde, etc. — leading to a higher perception of reality. But a deeper, more deliberate ambiguity resides in *Why Are We in Vietnam?* This ambiguity, sustained by the narrative itself, concerns the identity of the speaker. Here two facts are key.

First, we note that the narrator, presumably D.J., relates events two years past: the hunt took place when he was sixteen, "now" he is eighteen.

As someone reminds us in parenthesis: "(this is D.J. being pontiferous, for we are contemplating emotion recollected in tranquillity back at the Dallas ass manse, RTPY—Remembrance of Things Past, Yeah, you remember?)" (*W,* 186f.). Mailer waves to Wordsworth and Proust. Thus the narrative, insisting on the gap between word and deed, is the process of understanding, the experience of maturing—call it the fruit of quest, which the speaker wants to offer his readers, knowing, as Mailer knows, that memory is always "more narrative than the tohu-bohu of the present" (*W,* 60).

We note, next, that the speaker is elusive. Who comments on "D.J. being pontiferous"? It could be D.J. himself, or Mailer, or simply "the speaker" in the "Intro Beep" sections which Mailer distinguishes from his narrative chapters, as a dramatist might distinguish between chorus and action. The question, however, blends into another: who speaks in the first person, in the first place? Is it really D.J. (Ranald Jethroe Jellico Jethroe), the white, athletic son of Dallas millionaires, or some "mad genius spade" up in Harlem, a hip, crippled disk jockey (D.J.)? Who is America's "own wandering troubadour . . . here to sell America its new handbook on how to live" (*W,* 8)? One may answer that the text speaks, or simply "Mailer," even though Mailer himself plays sly: "The fact of the matter is that you're up tight with a mystery, me, and this mystery can't be solved because I'm the center of it and I don't comprehend, not necessarily, I could be traducing myself" (*W,* 23).

Some may wonder: why these games? Are they merely ludic and self-conscious postures of a postmodern age? By its very nature, *Why Are We in Vietnam?* can not eschew a certain trendiness. But the narrative is also timeless, crafty in the traditional arts of telling—foreshadowing, suspense, iteration, divagation. The mystery of the speaker is rather the mystery of quest itself, of the oedipal self asking: who am I? More publicly, it is the dilemma of national representation after Vietnam: who can speak for America, a fractious, divided land? Mailer will not explicitly answer, though his prose persuades us that the novel is less a critique of America than a paean to it.

The prose is astonishing, unique in American letters, the hip creation of a demiurge. The language hops and bops and jives, a new, scurrilous, vituperative, metaphysical language, crackling with wit, conceit, learning, obscenity, and nonsense, a language of mimicry and misery, insight and self-delight, hallelujah and hallucination, a riot of rhyme, pun, assonance, and alliteration, full of smells, alive to the touch. Mailer understands the uses of obscenity as protest, release, comedy, sacrament, remembrance of human mortality in its house of flesh, as procreative force in its genital inflections and as dead waste in its scatological flow, as a power that clutches the roots of language, exploding in symbols and stars. Mailer also knows that the hierarchy of senses tumbles from sight to hearing to smell to taste to touch, the more primitive the sense, the more ineluctable. Hence his intuition that "blood smell like cunt and ass all mix in one, but rotten, man, the flesh all rotten like meat and fish is biting each other to death" (*W,* 9), an intuition of obscene entropy, blood turning into excrement, life reduced to death. Hence, too, the synaesthetic turn of the prose, its continual play on the senses, its continual transposition of realms: art and politics, myth and science, magic and money, sex and electronics. For all that, and for all its psychedelic obscenities and obscurities, the style works its wonders upon us.

Nor does the zany humor of the novel diminish its life. Humor here, like parody, criticizes everything without destroying the possibilities of heroism; bravery and truth remain untouched. Somewhat professorially, Mailer writes: "Comedy is the study of the unsound actions of the cowardly under stress, just as tragedy is equal study time of the brave under heroic but enigmatic, reverberating, resonant conditions of loss . . ." (*W,* 81). If so, *Why Are We in Vietnam?* is neither comedy nor tragedy, but a heroic parody, a novel of self-initiation, a quest for reality, and possibly Mailer's best work, despite its Manichean bombast. The novel, in any case, endures as a *positive* quest, promising individual fulfillment on a landscape of defeat, a quest also, on Mailer's part, of the true original idiom of an epoch.[2] This double achievement remains rare in contemporary American fiction.

Is there an ideal text of quest? Ideals, of course, inhabit only the mind, though they help us to recognize the palpable shapes of this world. In that sense, Saul Bellow's *Henderson the Rain King* (1959) comes close to an ideal conception of quest. The novel—like Norman Mailer, I consider it Bellow's best—is anomalous in the corpus of its author. For in the fabulous story of Henderson, Bellow goes farther than he has ever done in freeing the individual's quest from the entrapments of society. "Africa" here is the setting. This is a land of parodic romance—Bellow had never traveled to Africa when he wrote *Henderson,* no more than Defoe had visited the Americas when he wrote *Robinson Crusoe*—a neverland of quests, ordeals, rituals, a place of meditations, initiations, illuminations, the happy hunting ground of archetypes and myths.

Henderson enjoys certain advantages of birth and power which the heroes of romance traditionally enjoy. Unlike Bellow's other protagonists, Henderson is no outsider or Jew; he is the scion of an old American family distinguished for scholarship, military prowess, and public service. He is not poor, but many times a millionaire. And he is not defined by any particular urban role. Quite to the contrary, his roles and travels take him in the fifty-five years of his life over many strange grounds. Freed externally from necessity, he is thus forced to pursue the inner promptings of his being, to answer that unappeasable voice in him which constantly cries "I want, I want, I want," to burst his spirit's sleep and carry his life to a certain depth, to discover that service which, performed, may be the human retort to death. His travels are also mental journeys, and the great turbulence of his spirit attests to the measure of his involvement with reality.

A man of gigantic size and enormous strength, at once brutal and tender, "an exceptional amalgam of vehement forces," Henderson hauls his passionate bulk across the African wilderness like some wrathful clown or outlandish healer — his guiding image is that of men like Albert Schweitzer and Sir Wilfred Grenfell — seeking salvation and reflecting in his big suffering face, "like an unfinished church," all "the human passions at the point of doubt — I mean the humanity of them lying in doubt" (*H,* 271, 76, 131). His search, first and foremost, is for reality, that same vibrant medley of fiction and fact which Eliot's nightingale pretended humankind could not bear too much of. But how much unreality can men bear, Henderson retorts? And though he claims to be on better terms with reality than most people — than his second wife, Lily, for instance — it is in keeping with his spiritual progress, his comic humility and humiliation before life, that he discovers: "The physical is all there, and it belongs to science. But then there is the noumenal department, and there we create and create and create" (*H,* 167).

Despite the archaic haze of fertility rituals, ceremonial hunts, and totemic cults through which the action of the novel flashes, the motive of Henderson's search and the stages of his progress remain clear. When Henderson leaves Lily behind, he leaves the only person with whom he has a struggling and irreplaceable relation. But in leaving her he also turns his back on the passive morality she represents, dampened by social pieties and noble hypocrisies — she wants, for instance, her portrait to hang in the gallery of Henderson's ancestors. For society is precisely what Henderson cannot fathom; all his deeds, heroic or clownish, transcend their social reference; his political judgments remain mute, or else mere mutterings about an "age of madness." These are the fifties, the Eisenhower years.

The true starting point of Henderson's quest is a quotation he discovers in his father's library: "The forgiveness of sins is perpetual and righteousness first is not required" (*H,* 3). Because his disorderly life is so full of errors and remissions — a father he cannot reach though he takes up playing the violin with great hairy paws to do so, his own son alienated from him, a first wife, remote and neurotic, who can only laugh at his quixotic idealism, a career of false starts and frantic assertions — because of all this

Henderson is compelled to seek redemption in an act of charity, knowledge, and depth. The compulsion is as strong as death itself, the death of spirit and of organic matter too, that same death his hurtling soul both seeks and wholly defies — the dead, his heart cries, have not utterly died.

Bellow renders this fundamental antithesis of Henderson's character in a pattern of recurrent images: the octopus whose cold eyes and slow tentacles communicate to him a feeling of cosmic coldness, the dead man he has to carry on his back among the Wariri. In contrast to these intimations of death, the terrible fear of a traceless calm, there are the images of life to which Henderson responds with a singing soul: the wonder of a child in a world death has not yet touched, the rapture that an African sunrise produces, "some powerful magnificence not human," pink light on a white wall with prickles and the whole physical universe wrinkling, heaving. Between life and death, tumult and tranquillity, reality beckons to Henderson, and the light of wisdom erratically gleams. His teeth itch in aesthetic as in sacramental pleasure.

It is while Henderson is chopping wood at home — a log hits his face — that it first occurs to him truth must come in blows. Later, while he is wrestling with Prince Itelo, in a ritual gesture of acquaintance, he realizes once again that nothing but the *blows* of truth can burst the spirit's sleep. Yearning, he learns, is suffering, and suffering a kind of unhappy strength. But the latter is only a preamble to the wisdom that we already contain in pieces. With his unusual capacity to relate one fragment of experience to another — Bellow communicates this through a deft use of numerous flashbacks — Henderson, unlike Augie March say, gives the impression of creating the destiny he seeks.

Henderson's quest, though fully justified, takes him at *whim* to the Dark Continent. This is not only an exotic and distant place; not only the land we exploit or colonize (a fact elided in the novel); but also the space where we meet our darker self or double. Thus, soon after his arrival in Africa, Henderson strikes out into the bush, accompanied only by Romilayu, his wrinkled and inseparable guide. Henderson claims to have no geographical sense whatever, but he quickly responds to the essential quality of the Arnewi's land: "it was all simplified and splendid, and I felt I was entering the past — the real past, no history or junk like that. The prehuman past. And I believed that there was something between the stones and me" (*H*, 46). In this arid landscape, he begins to experience his purification, his dispossession, his release from the world's sorrows and his own.

But Henderson's ordeals, ordeals physical and spiritual, have just started. He will wrestle Prince Itelo; sing Handel's *Messiah* — "He was despised and rejected, a man of sorrows and acquainted with grief" — to Queen Willatale; absorb her primordial vitality, her *"Bittahness,"* through her enormous belly and navel; dynamite the Arnewi cistern to rid it of frogs and polliwogs. And though he typically bungles the job of "lifting the curse" on the Arnewi cattle, he takes away with his failure the friendship of Itelo and the wisdom of Queen Willatale who teaches him that a frenzied lust for living, *"grun-tu-molani,"* not only affirms the basic value of human existence but further incarnates the desire to redeem its griefs.

This wisdom, however, is partial, a stage in his quest. Henderson travels next to Wariri land where he participates in darker rituals. There he meets King Dahfu, who went to school with Prince Itelo in Beirut, and thinks to himself: "What a person to meet at this distance from home. Yes, travel is advisable. And believe me, the world is mind. Travel is mental travel" (*H,* 167). There, too, he spends the night with a corpse in his hut; then lifts colossal Mummah, whom no one can budge, to bring rain to the Wariris. Thus he redeems his failure with the Arnewi, and hopes to redeem all the errors of his past. He assumes the "errand of mercy" that promises salvation.

That promise, however, waits upon still a further stage in his quest. Under the hypnotic influence of King Dahfu (daffy?), Henderson comes to realize that a rage for living is not enough. Man must also put an end to his *becoming* and enter the realm of *being,* the only realm in which love is possible. Between human beings, Henderson understands, there can be either brotherhood or crime, love or aggression. To attain the state of being man owes to his fellow man, humankind must turn to the beasts. This explains why the prophecy of Daniel — "They shall drive you from among men, and thy dwelling shall be with the beasts of the field" — is so constantly in Henderson's mind, and explains also why, in the past, Henderson raised pigs with such lavish care and performed with a bear in a roller coaster. The prophecy is actually consummated in a lion's den, under Dahfu's castle, where the king teaches Henderson in the dark, wordless presence of a lioness how to capture the emanations of a vital creature, how to consummate friendship, how to be still and active, sufficient and attuned. It is not merely by journeying to Africa, with its strange kings and primitive rituals, nor is it merely by performing a serviceable act of extermination or rain-giving strength that Henderson begins to attain his depth. It is, rather, by learning how to absorb the pure, unavoidable moment of being, an animal *presence,* that he seeps into reality. The extraordinary scene merits quotation at length:

> The odor was blinding, for here, near the door where the air was trapped, it stank radiantly. From this darkness came the face of the lioness, wrinkling, with her whiskers like the thinnest spindles scratched with a diamond on the surface of a glass. She allowed the king to fondle her, but passed by him to examine me, coming round with those clear circles of inhuman wrath, con-

vex, brown, and pure, rings of black light within them. Between her mouth
and nostrils a line divided her lip, like the waist of the hourglass, expanding
into the muzzle. She sniffed my feet, working her way to the crotch once more
and causing my parts to hide in my belly as best they could. She next put her
head into my armpit and purred with such tremendous vibration it made my
head buzz like a kettle.

    Dahfu whispered, "She likes you. Oh, I am glad. I am enthusiastic. I am
so proud of both of you. Are you afraid?" (*H,* 261)

Here Henderson's wound — not literal though deep enough — begins to
heal. At least, so Henderson tells us in a fiction no less open or whimsical
than life. The clamorous voice that used to cry, "I want, I want, I want,"
can now listen to other, equally authentic voices: "*she* wants, *he* wants,
they want" (*H,* 286). Identity is found in communion, and communion
reached not only in our own society but also out of it, not only with men
but also with beasts, not only for the sake of the living but also for the
dead. The grip of the self, however, will not relax. Henderson must still
confront his ravenous desires and fears, and must struggle against death
ceaselessly. He writes his beloved Lily to announce that he will take up
medicine on his return. When King Dahfu dies in an ancestral lion hunt,
and Henderson replaces him as a Scapegoat King, the exotic part of the
quest comes suddenly to an end. He escapes with Romilayu and a lion
cub to Harar (where Rimbaud died) and thence back to "civilization." In
the last moving scene of the book, Henderson, on his way back to Lily,
clasps an orphan child to his chest and runs about the homebound plane
with him, "leaping, leaping, pounding, and tingling over the pure white
lining of the gray Arctic silence," knowing that though "for creatures there
is nothing that ever runs unmingled," chaos does not run the whole human show, and ours is not "a sick and hasty ride, helpless, through a dream
into oblivion" (*H,* 341, 175).

Henderson the Rain King, paradigm of modern, ironic quests, is also —
like *Why Are We in Vietnam?* — a signal American novel of the postwar
era. But it is not immune to criticism for all that. Bellow's Africa is not
Conrad's or Fanon's. It rather shares the eerie, spiritual space of Cooper's
prairie, Poe's Antarctica, Melville's Pacific. Nor are Henderson's African
tutors — Prince Itelo, Queen Willatale, King Dahfu — other than idealized
foils or constructions. Nor, again, is Henderson's guide, Romilayu, other
than a device for the seeker's own gargantuan, sometimes maudlin, and
often capricious needs. Nor, finally, does Henderson himself escape the
role of an obsequious straight man in a Socratic dialogue with African
sages, echoing like a great, shuddering reverberator thoughts that are con-
spicuously Bellow's own.

    Henderson, of course, is the speaker, and as in most first-person narratives — this is the artistic dilemma of the genre — he must both present and judge himself, mixing authorial truths with a (fictive) character's illusions. Henderson attempts to do precisely this without entirely succeeding. This is really to say that Bellow himself fails to make Henderson an agent of our knowledge and at the same time an object of our critical sympathy. This is also to say that Henderson's garrulous sincerity assumes more pain — he constantly threatens to blow out his brains — than the novel reveals; that his gestures place a higher spiritual valuation on events than the events warrant; and that his admixture of bravado and lamentation becomes at times too easy a substitute for the full range of human emotions. The effect, in the novel's worst moments, is that of a pantomime coauthored by Rider Haggard and Fyodor Dostoyevsky.

This effect, however, is happily mediated by the virtuosity of Bellow's style. Precipitate, colorful, candid as it is immensely vital, the style leaps with the contortions of its hero's soul and sheds itself again on earth in a poetry of acceptance. Though it often rambles and digresses with the errant human spirit, though it conjures with fantasy, myth, and romance, the style also conveys both an insistent mindfulness and a cosmic apprehension of reality. In this cosmic scheme, imagination is key. Thus King Dahfu:

> Imagination is a force of nature. Is this not enough to make a person full of ecstasy? Imagination, imagination, imagination! It converts to actual. It sustains, it alters, it redeems. . . . What Homo sapiens imagines, he may slowly convert himself to. (H, 271)

And thus Henderson, more homespun:

> We're supposed to think that nobility is unreal. But that's just it. The illusion is on the other foot. They make us think we crave more and more illusions. Why, I don't crave illusions at all. They say, Think big. Well, that's boloney of course, another business slogan. But greatness! That's another thing altogether. Oh, greatness! Oh, God! Romilayu, I don't mean inflated, swollen, false greatness. I don't mean pride or throwing your weight around. But the universe itself being put into us, it calls out for scope. The eternal is bonded onto us. It calls out for its share. (H, 318)

Henderson the Rain King remains, in a genuine way, the most affirmative of Bellow's works. Starting with the familiar figure of the solitary American hero, unattached to father, wife, or son, fleeing civilization and in search of love, prodigal in his services to all, Bellow leads Henderson through reality's dark dream to a vision of light, and a commitment that can only bind man back again to life. For once, the American hero can go back home again. Having learned acceptance, having slain the mythic monsters within him and overcome his death, the seeker goes back to society, to Lily. Thus Bellow encompasses both "Africa" and "America," nature and civilization, though he leaves us in no doubt which is wiser: the former colony now becomes moral colonizer of the West.

5

The faces of quest may be as infinitely various as human faces, but the conventions of literature impose certain common features on this ancient form. The form, as we have seen, is mythic, predicated on elements of adventure, autobiography, and, above all, romance. These elements endure through postmodern dislocations, through parody and pastiche, transformed by the act of poiesis, as in the narrative cunning of Clark, the stylistic exuberance of Bellow or Mailer. Still, the tales of quest testify to the human consistency of self and other, of search sometimes indistinguishable from flight, of mortality overcome in a rare moment of peril or transgression. These tales also tell us the story of our times: the forties, the fifties, the sixties and after in America. And in telling us that story, they show what in our existence has and has not changed. Thus history itself, in the guise of fiction, generates transhistorical insights.

But how do such strange tales, often rife with fustian and machismo — not all machismo, after all, is vain — how do such exotic novels possess our lives? Asked which of his characters resembled him most, Bellow answered: "Henderson — the absurd seeker of high qualities."[3] There is, of course, something of that seeker in us all. But when the search attains a certain degree of risk, exaltation, or even absurdity, something in these seekers compels our assent. Perhaps it is the quality of their whim or depth of their wound. Perhaps it is the insistence that a realized life can be personal, political, sacramental, all within a single arc of the will. Perhaps it is simply that these seekers are figures of a powerful authorial imagination — Bellow's, say, or Mailer's — which can bring order and vision to the derelictions of our age. Out of ruin, roughage, gaudiness, bane, come marvels of prose, an art that proves nothing human is ever won once for all.

Part 3
Three
Exemplary
Cases

In this final section, Part 3, I address three errant writers who exemplify, both in their life and in their art, the main issues of quest. In fact, they "exemplify" less than they amplify, qualify, rectify these issues; or else they remake them in new figures of their own imagination. In these writers, the concept of quest ceases to be abstract; it loses purity even as it gains texture; it becomes practical, actual, in the experience of men who have devoted much of their time to wandering in Asia, Africa, South America.

"Exemplary" here, then, implies no literary judgment or perfection: Bowles, Theroux, Matthiessen are not necessarily "greater" writers than, say, Bellow or Mailer. Rather, the act of exemplification rests on a pragmatic intuition: that quest, adventure, autobiography, interactive, require the impurity of lived experience to become truly exemplary. Thus quest may take the form of exile (Bowles), travel (Theroux), or naturalist and anthropological curiosity (Matthiessen), but it remains quest nonetheless, as I hope to show. I mean quest as lived and felt and rendered into language, in the second half of our century.

Chapter Seven
Paul Bowles:
The Imagination of Exile

I'm always happy leaving the United States, and the farther away I
go the happier I am generally.

— Paul Bowles

A

1

RT, TRAVEL, and exile possess Bowles's life, shape his
fiction as well, deriving from one another eerie power, a sense of fatality
and dread. The dread, in his best work, is real, elsewhere simulated, wafted
like some dark incense. What lives in that dread? What makes Bowles run?
What cunning transmutes his exile into art? And why do his pilgrims, lost
seekers in North Africa or Central America, become preys? Given Bowles's
compulsive travels, the questions seem personal; they turn us quizzically
toward his autobiography, aptly titled *Without Stopping* (1972).

At first, the work appears to yield no clues. The memoirs are reticent,
like much of Bowles's fiction, but without the latter's resonances. One thing
seems to happen after another, like entries in an international Who's Who
of the Arts; name after glamorous name simply drops. Ships sail, trains
and caravans depart — Bowles detests planes. We follow him — his mood
usually one of deadpan restlessness — from house to rented house, through
endless hotel rooms, across oceans, mountains, islands, deserts. We follow
his movements, hear him name people and places, without traces of acrimony or plaint. And occasionally, as if by oversight, we come upon a magic
scene, a secretive insight.

Bowles, in fact, is more self-aware in his autobiography than its flat
surface betrays. At the end of *Without Stopping,* as he reflects on the fragments of his life now pieced in a "sequential skeleton," he notes his reticence and says:

> As I see it, this precaution implies making the effort to reserve judgment and
> the resolve to give a minimum of importance to personal attitudes. Writing
> an autobiography is an ungratifying occupation at best. It is a sort of jour-
> nalism, in which the report, rather than being an eyewitness account of the

135

event, is instead only a memory of the last time it was recalled. . . . In my tale . . . there are no dramatic victories because there was no struggle. I hung on and waited. It seems to me that this must be what most people do. . . . (*WS,* 366f.)[1]

In another sense, though, Bowles has done more than hang on and wait: he has run. Less seeker or adventurer than refugee from Western, particularly American, civilization, he seems always a man in flight. His memoirs reveal an accomplished artist (composer, writer), a compulsive expatriate, an international bohemian caught between the Lost and the Beat Generations, a gregarious outsider who travels always with companions and eighteen or more valises. Why?

The story, up to a point, is familiar. A stubborn, imaginative only child, alienated from both parents, especially the father, becomes inwardly a kind of outlaw. Later, reading Arthur Waley's translations from the Chinese, the boy learns to become a precise "registering consciousness," putting his "nonexistence" in the service of "the invented cosmos" (*WS,* 52f.). The outlaw becomes an artist, always looking up other artists, always intact. "Relationships with other people are at best nebulous," Bowles writes; "their presence keeps us from being aware of the problem of giving form to our life" (*WS,* 69). But one day, at the University of Virginia, the youth undergoes his "first compulsive experience," sensing that he must "do something explosive and irrevocable" (*WS,* 77): he must either commit suicide or escape abroad. This is the start of exile, an exile that began in the child long ago, exile itself being only a trope for memories, miseries, and desires that no autobiographer, no adult really, knows how to convey.

In France, a virgin still, Bowles is first seduced by a Hungarian woman then by an adopted relative, Uncle Hubert. Thereafter, Bowles will remain hermetically discreet about his sexual experiences. But he is talkative enough about all the people he meets, notably Gertrude Stein who immediately sees in him a "sociological exhibit . . . of a species then rare, now the commonest of contemporary phenomena, the American suburban child with its unrelenting spleen" (*WS,* 119). Could Stein foresee Abbie Hoffman, Bernardine Dohrn? Bowles's "spleen," in any case, finds no balm in politics, though he will casually join the Communist party for two years in the thirties. The balm is in art, magic, dream, and in everything "other," deviating from the American norm. When Gertrude Stein sends Bowles to Tangier with Aaron Copland, the future novelist, not yet twenty-one, feels a peculiar excitement:

it was as if some interior mechanism had been set in motion by the sight of the approaching land. Always without formulating the concept, I had based my sense of being in the world partly on an unreasoned conviction that cer-

tain areas of the earth's surface contained more magic than others. Had anyone asked me what I meant by magic, I should probably have defined the word
by calling it a secret connection between the world of nature and the consciousness of man, a hidden but direct passage which bypassed the mind. (The op-
erative word here is "direct," because in this case it was equivalent to "visceral.")
Like any Romantic, I had always been vaguely certain that sometime during
my life I should come into a magic place which in disclosing its secrets would
give me wisdom and ecstasy—perhaps even death. And now, as I stood in the
wind looking at the mountains ahead, I felt the stirring of the engine within,
and it was as if I were drawing close to the solution of an as-yet-unposed problem. I was incredibly happy as I watched the wall of mountains slowly take
on substance, but I let the happiness wash over me and asked no questions.
(*WS,* 125)

There it is, at once answer—why travel? what seek?—and conundrum.
When he returns to the United States, as he will periodically return, Bowles
feels in a prison house, each day abroad a day in freedom. He is aware
of the paranoia in his attitude, its ebbs and flows and mysteries; but travel,
compose, and write he must, travel to Guatemala, Ceylon, the Sahara. His
marriage to a brilliant, willful girl, Jane Auer—she will be known as Jane
Bowles, novelist and playwright—inhibits nothing; they both continue to
wander, separately or together. The wanderings have their peril: disease,
short funds, acute discomfort, alien violence, severe mishaps of every kind.
But the wanderings remain sanative, a necessity. Asked by nonplussed FBI
agents why her husband travels so much, Jane Bowles helplessly shrugs:
"*I* don't know. He's nervous, I guess" (*WS,* 243).

This intuition may be nearer the mark than any political explanation;
for Bowles's politics are elementary, perhaps elemental. He joins the Communist party largely because it helps him go on relief and bring back a
"suitcaseful of sugar, butter, prunes, and flour. The idea of getting something for nothing is always exciting . . ." (*WS,* 214). Both Jane and Paul
Bowles compensate for their "lack of devotion to Marxism-Leninism by
seeing every Russian film that came to New York" (*WS,* 215). Later, when
the Hitler-Stalin pact is announced, Paul Bowles justifies it as "a Soviet
ploy to crush the Nazis" (*WS,* 216). Later still, when the United States and
the Soviet Union become allies in the war, he reasons: "If we were going
to be partners of the Russians, I must get out of the party" (*WS,* 230).
The thing, then, is to align oneself always *against* one's native land—or,
as a Freudian might say, against one's parents. This is elemental politics.

We are scarcely shocked, therefore, when Bowles registers, in a perfunc-
tory paragraph, his outrage at the Hiroshima bomb, only to start the next
paragraph, without any transition whatever, thus: "Schuyler Watts, who
had directed the dramatic action in *The Wind Remains,* has now trans-

lated Giraudoux's *Ondine* and, although he had no producer in view, came to me to commission a score for it" (*WS,* 265). We rather believe him when, in his preface to the second edition of *The Spider's House* (1955, 1982), he states: "Fiction should always stay clear of political considerations" (*SH,* i). If so, what is the source of Bowles's aversion to colonialism, a feeling both real and pervasive in his work?

More than anything else, the feeling is an aversion to the taint of Western civilization. That is why Bowles disapproves of postcolonial nationalists who want to rush their countries into the abominations of technology. If Morocco had remained, until recently, a medieval land, it was because *the French* had kept it so. Nationalists had no interest "in ridding Morocco of all traces of European civilization and restoring it to its precolonial state; on the contrary, their aim was to make it even more 'European' than the French had made it" (*SH,* i)—exactly the point we saw Fanon make. As for Fez, once marvelous Fez, it has ceased to serve as "the intellectual and cultural center of North Africa," becoming "merely one more city beset by the insoluble problems of the Third World" (*SH,* ii).

Is this realism, *passéisme,* or colonialism with a nostalgic face? If the latter, there may be no escape from the colonialist trace. In fact, realism and romantic primitivism mingle in Bowles's attitude toward poorer nations. In any case, Bowles's euphoria in strange lands remains a central fact of his life. In New York, he dreams of a Tangier he visited sixteen years earlier, in 1931, and the dream leaves behind "a state of enameled precision: a residue of ineffable sweetness and calm" (*WS,* 274). Bowles then sails to Tangier where he begins writing his first novel, *The Sheltering Sky* (1949). Once there, the exhilaration returns: dream and reality seem to have become one. Later still, on the way to Ceylon, he reflects:

> I had the illusion of being about to add another country, another culture, to my total experience, and the further illusion that to do so would in itself be of value. My curiosity about alien cultures was avid and obsessive. I had a placid belief that it was good for me to live in the midst of people whose motives I did not understand; this unreasoned conviction was clearly an attempt to legitimize my curiosity. I tried to get as many pages [of *Let It Come Down* (1952)] written as I could before arriving, in order not to be sidetracked by the initial contact with an unknown land. (*WS,* 297)

As the century wanes—colonialism recedes, Bowles himself ages—these "other countries" also become less other, less exotic and strange; the history of planetization, of contamination, sets in. Even life in America changes, becoming unrecognizable to Bowles: "I felt that I was in the middle of a truly exotic culture, and perhaps one of the strangest of all time" (*WS,* 341). This is an otherness, however, he had not expected, an America still more alien than the one from which he had fled. Once again, he can only escape to Tangier, itself altered, though less so than New York. He no longer wishes to travel. But there, in the African night, he can at least sense that sorcery is still alive. "Spells are being cast, poison is running its course; souls are being dispossessed of parasitic pseudo-consciousnesses that lurk in the unguarded recesses of the mind" (*WS,* 366).

2

At best, autobiography reveals only a facet of an author, a face among other faces; it reveals even less his work. Bowles's essays and novels take us to the same distant worlds — jungles, saharas — but they tell us a richer story.

Yallah! (1957) speaks largely in images, magnificent photographs that a young Swiss adventurer, Peter Häberlin, took on a trans-Saharan journey before dying in an accident in the Andes. Bowles collated the pictures, wrote an introduction, provided terse notes. The pictures, precise in black and white, awe the eye with images of one of "the last great terrae incognitae left on this shrinking planet — a vast, mysterious, lunar land which seems almost to possess natural laws of its own" (*Y,* 5). The landscape, though crystalline on each page, defies comprehension, especially in the Hoggar, home of the indigo-faced Tuaregs. The people take on the qualities of the Sahara: simplicity, hardness, the human hues of permanence. Their indigence begets nobility, style; their isolation, solidarity. Nothing here suggests urban blight or cushy American lives. And though some maim their bodies with ritual violence or weird ornaments, they all possess the highest *seriousness,* a knowledge of life and death, deeper than flesh.

These are the qualities Bowles can not find in his native New York, nor find in Europe. He fears their obliteration by colonial rule "which of course shatters all social, moral, and economic patterns, leaving in their place only inner chaos . . ." (*Y,* 9). But he does not confront the tragic impasse of modernity, preferring always to opt for a vanished past. He can tell us exactly how many francs a slave fetched a few decades ago, without conveying any sense of uneasiness about slavery. He can pass lightly over the perpetual wars, raids, rapine of Saharan tribes, then inveigh against the "hypocrisy, cynicism, and opportunism" of the white colonists. Still, he can speak eloquently about Arab and African cultures:

> And how greatly the West needs to study the religions, the music, and the dances of the doomed African cultures! How much, if we wished, we could learn from them about man's relationship to the cosmos, about his conscious connection with his own soul. Instead of which, we talk about raising their

standard of living! Where we could learn *why,* we try to teach them our all-important *how,* so that they may become as rootless and futile and materialistic as we are. Perhaps this, at least, is not wholly inevitable. I cannot help interpreting the title of this book (which in Arabic means: Let us be off!) as an exhortation to those of us who are able, to salvage what is still intact and valuable in a part of the world which, more than any other at this point in history, needs our understanding and sympathetic guidance, if we wish to avoid seeing a world-shaking catastrophe take place before our eyes. (*Y,* 19)

Bowles is here accurate, in some ways prophetic. Still, he implies no sense of what the historical process might mean to developing nations, what viable future *they* can contemplate. Nor does he reckon with the possibility, already latent in his time, that such nations might choke not on a surfeit of "Europeanization" but on an excess of xenophobia or Islamic fundamentalism. All the same, Bowles reminds us of a crucial mission; he calls for an existential anthropology with redemptive intent.

The intent is manifest in the essays of *Their Heads Are Green and Their Hands Are Blue* (1963).[2] In these essays — more nuanced than *Yallah!* — Bowles admits that change is hourly, inevitable; the status quo, however attractive to the romantic exile, dissolves before our eyes. Though travel remains a search for differences, differences in people rather than landscapes, such differences are becoming elusive. The seekers of exotica, adventurers in alterity — call them "Jumblie hunters" — "are having to increase the radius of their searches and lower their standards," Bowles says. "For a man to qualify as a Jumblie today he need not practice anthropophagy or infibulation; it is enough for him to sacrifice a coconut or bury a packet of curses in his neighbor's garden" (*THA,* ix). But then, Bowles warns, we may wake up one day to find that *we* have become the Jumblies to denizens of another planet.

The interface of cultures, the interplay of epochs, ideologies, tempers, gives these essays their interest. The irony or pathos of incongruity is everywhere. A clanking generator drowns out a Buddhist *pirith,* or ceremony of purification. An old Berber, his finger accidentally severed by a truck door, thanks Allah — things could be worse. A Moslem ascetic uses a short-wave radio neither for entertainment nor for information but as a "sort of metaphysical umbilical cord," connecting him to a larger life. *Moussems,* religious festivals, and cultic trances occur even in the most sophisticated urban setting. "Statistical truth" and "truth of the heart" collide. An anecdote tells it all:

> Not long ago I wrote on the character of the North Africa Moslem. An illiterate Moroccan friend wanted to know what was in it, and so, in a running translation into Moghrebi, I read him certain passages. His comment was terse: "That's shameful."

"Why?" I demanded.
"Because you've written about people just as they are."
"For us that's not shameful."
"For us it is. You've made us like animals. You've said that only a few of us can read or write."
"Isn't that true?"
"Of course not! We can all read and write, just like you. And we would, if only we'd had lessons." (*THA*, 32)

Bowles is not dismissive here or elsewhere; he is rather quizzical, even self-doubting, about assumptions he once thought self-evident. He wishes to observe, to preserve. He responds to his environment, particularly its sensuous and musical qualities. The irritations of travel, its real dangers, leave him equable; the pervasive smell of urine and excrement in some towns provokes no hygienic outrage. But the mummeries of modernization exasperate him—and sometimes amuse him, as in the "synthetic orthography" of Turkish script which renders toilet as "Tualet" and sexology as "Seksoloji." Above all, Bowles likes to immerse himself into the alien element, less destructive than salvific. "In order to be really present," he remarks, "you must have your feet in the dust, and be aware of the hot, dusty smell of mud walls beside your face" (*THA*, 162). This is the bias of Bowles's existential anthropology, its curative and custodial intent.

Cure and custody coexist. With a grant from the Rockefeller Foundation, Bowles travels some twenty-five thousand miles in North Africa, recording native music for the Library of Congress. He visits far, unfamiliar places—Lunawa, Kaduwela, Essaouira, Taghit, Barrebi—and brings back notes, pictures, memories, to convert into articles for glossy magazines like *Holiday*. And he edits, transcribes, translates works of such Moroccan writers as Mohammed Mrabet, Ahmed Yacoubi, Driss ben Hamed Charhabi. These are the tasks, perhaps the passions, of preservation.

We may indeed ask: what motive lies behind this anthropological project, what quest within the geographic quest? Why undergo or simulate adventure—Bowles prefers not to reserve hotel rooms ahead in order to keep his sense of "adventure" alive—and why undergo exile, again and again? Why, for that matter, smoke *kif* or *majoun?* In other words, what inaudible story do these essays tell mixing memory and desire, travel, autobiography, and fiction? Or in other words still: what "I" pretends here to speak and what voice the reader really hears?

Bowles's persona is watchful, fastidious, laconic. His desire for the other, his feeling for female or (mostly) male companions, remains unstated; his eroticism is mute. Yet the observer's voice, flat as it may seem, hints continually at some unity of being, a presence not found but sought. The hints are also in his descriptions of fellow Americans when asked about the object of their quest: "Almost without exception, regardless of the way they express it, the answer, reduced to its simplest terms, is: a sense of mystery" (*THA,* 24).

The mystery is greatest in the Sahara, under its tremendous sky. There men endure the "baptism of solitude": a dissolution of the Western ego. "Perhaps the logical question to ask at this point is: Why go?" "The answer," Bowles writes, "is that when a man has been there and undergone the baptism of solitude he can't help himself. Once under the spell of the vast, luminous, silent country, no other place is quite strong enough for him, no other surrounding can provide the supremely satisfying sensation of existing in the midst of something that absolute. He will go back, whatever the cost in comfort and money, for the absolute has no price" (*THA,* 143f.). Saharan sand and sky and the absolute as wholly other: these are elements of the *mysterium tremendum* to which the fictional characters of Paul Bowles, as we shall see, become unwitting pilgrims and preys.

3

If Bowles's essays engage us more than his autobiography, his fictions compel us still more. At their finest, the novels and stories attain the high intensity of art, suggesting, like Poe, a poetics of delirium and dread.

This is certainly true of Bowles's first novel, *The Sheltering Sky* (1949), perhaps his best. The work finds its germ in an earlier story, "A Distant Episode," and no doubt in autobiographical elements of Paul and Jane Bowles's lives—including their countless valises. The work also echoes some existential notes, from Camus's *The Stranger,* and earlier, from Hemingway's "A Clean Well-Lighted Place" or "Hills like White Elephants." In the end, though, Bowles's characters are fated, bored, and blighted in their own distinctive ways; in quest or escape, they are destined to nothingness, as if private omens or recollections defined for each a singular kismet. Collectively, though, they exemplify the predicament of Western civilization—its nihilism, acedia, hysteria, its "spiritual paralysis," as Bowles would say—when its codes collide with other codes under the pitiless Saharan sky.

But why are these Americans there? Their story answers for itself, a story hard and clear like desert quartz. Port and Kit Moresby, and Tunner, have with various motives turned their backs on New York; they plunge into the desolations of North Africa soon after the last world war. Port is the driving force of this excursion into the void, which remains for Tunner, an "ugly American," an exotic slumming expedition and an opportunity to seduce Kit. Port himself is driven by a despair he can sometimes theorize but never name; as he tells Kit, his sickness is caused by something he "ate" decades ago. But the "certitude of an infinite sadness at the core of his consciousness" (*SS,* 8) also affords him a certain consolation: nothing really needs to be said or done further in the world. Thus he feels "unaccustomed exaltation" when he sniffs the fragments of mystery in North Africa.

Port's predestined path to death leads him, through a maze of broken experiences, ever farther from civilization: a violent nocturnal affair with an Arab prostitute; solitary rambles that bring an inkling of self-knowledge; moments in which he alternately seeks and rebuffs Kit's love; and finally, when the two of them succeed in giving Tunner the slip, when they find themselves alone in a remote sand-locked settlement, the delirium of typhoid, senseless death. It is a death that confirms the dismal, single conclusion of Port's life: "For in order to avoid having to deal with relative values, he had long since come to deny all purpose to the phenomenon of existence—it was more expedient and comforting" (*SS,* 51). Still, Port cannot cease to yearn for something sacral, a greater mystery.

And Kit? Atavisms, augurs, and terrors rule her existence; hysteria gnaws ever on the rim of her mind. She wakes most mornings with "doom hanging over her head like a low rain cloud" (*SS,* 29). Yet she will accompany Port anywhere, into the abyss itself, while "waiting for some unlikely caprice on his part, something which might in some unforeseen manner bring him back" (*SS,* 31). But Kit has her own love of the abyss, a love darker than any love. Hours before Port's death, driven by her own stunned despair, she locks him in a dark, airless room, then walks out. There is a stark and terrible scene in which she bathes naked by moonlight and then walks like a somnambulist into the desert to be found by two nomads, raped, made the willing concubine of Belquassim, the younger of the two Arabs. He takes her to his home, far, far to the south, where she lives disguised as a boy until his wives find her out, find and lash her in a frenzy of jealousy. Her life in the tiny mud-walled cubicle, and later as the privileged mate of Belquassim, is one of lurid regression: she surrenders to nymphomania, the last affirmation of the senses, then drifts into madness, the ultimate negation of values. And when she is at last rescued and taken back to Oran, through Tunner's efforts with officialdom, it is only to vanish quietly again into the Casbah, eyes staring wide. This is the end of the line.

Lurid as it may have once seemed to readers in the fifties, the action is inevitable, fitting each fate to the character's motive: the terrors of Kit, the deadness at the core of Port's being. Still, husband and wife experience moments of shared tenderness, perhaps of something more than tenderness:

> Kit took Port's hand. They climbed in silence, happy to be together. . . .
> It was such places as this, such moments that he loved above all else in life;
> she knew that, and she also knew that he loved them more if she could be there
> to experience them with him. . . . It was as if always he held the fresh hope
> that she too would be touched in the same way as he by solitude and the prox-
> imity of infinite things. (*SS,* 68)

But her radical anxiety is always imminent, even in the face of love:

> "You know," said Port, and his voice sounded unreal, as voices are likely
> to do after a long pause in an utterly silent spot, "the sky here's very strange.
> I often have the sensation when I look at it that it's a solid thing up there, pro-
> tecting us from what's behind."
> Kit shuddered slightly as she said: "From what's behind?"
> "Yes."
> "But what *is* behind?" Her voice was very small.
> "Nothing, I suppose. Just darkness. Absolute night."
> "Please don't talk about it now." There was agony in her entreaty. (*SS,* 69)

The last passage gives the novel its title just as it characterizes the
Moresbys perfectly. But the moment is circumscribed by ironies. On the
top of the hill from which the Moresbys view the desert sunset, an old
Arab sits a few yards away, immobile, nearly invisible; his lips move in
silent prayer. The venerable man seems ravaged by neither dread nor deadness in the soul; his faith matches their disbelief. The ironies continue.
Port himself returns to the site later in the evening, *without* Kit, to reexperience the place alone: "He sat on the rock and let the wind chill him.
Riding down to Boussif he realized he never could tell Kit that he had been
back there" (*SS,* 70). Then, too, the reader recalls that Kit, a day earlier,
had given herself to Tunner on a ghastly train ride, in a moment of revul-
sion and fear. The act, of course, does not negate her love for Port; it merely
reflects upon the nature of their love, its broken reciprocities. For on his
side, too, Port waits as Kit waits for the "distant light of a possible miracle":
renewed love. On his deathbed, in the full heat of delirium — or is it of
lucidity? — he babbles: "Kit, Kit. I'm afraid, but it's not only that. Kit! All
these years I've been living for you. I didn't know it, and now I do"; but
then, "as he lay still for a while, breathing violently, she began to think:
'He says it's more than just being afraid. But it isn't. He's never lived for
me. Never. Never'" (*SS,* 151).

Love will not save under this sheltering sky; it leaves the protagonists —
who sleep always in separate rooms — in horrible solitude, diseased or de-
bauched, subject only to physical processes of decay, the "meaningless
hegemony of the involuntary" (*SS,* 149). On this point, Bowles's vision will
not hedge. What, after all, is there to which Westerners can aspire, besides

the bumptious jollities of Tunner, the unspeakable vulgarities of the Lyles, the rigid, colonial condescensions of Capitaine Broussard, what except the brilliant hysteria of Kit and Port's ascetic nihilism, a state of consciousness symbolized by the vast, reciprocal blankness of desert and sky? Nothing returns to nothing: without passport, profession, or identity, Port dies alone in a desolate outpost, and Kit vanishes, insane, in the Casbah.

Not that Bowles romanticizes North Africa. The mongrels are mangy and mean; children run naked in the sun, covered with sores and flies; a woman throws her unwanted baby in a ditch, to be eaten by dogs; lepers move freely about, noseless, with dried white lips; the stench of cloaca fills the air and insects float in the soup; men crunch locusts in their mouths and large beetles under their feet. Nor are his Arabs really anything but shadowy, except for an old Jew at Sbâ, who gives shelter to Kit. Still, such is the torque on Bowles's moral temper that he must show his Western characters as vulgar, venal, complacent, pusillanimous, hypocritical; or, at very best, scorched deep in their spirit, and capable only of some desperate splendor in their moment of total self-dispossession. There is no Arab so parched as Port, none so pathetic as Kit surrounded by her cosmetics and gewgaws, fondling each fetish of Western civilization to ward off her primal fear.

In the end, the novel may portray exile, exposure, expropriation of the self, more than quest. For the true seeker, unlike the tourist, Bowles says, puts his own society in question—indeed, puts his own self in ultimate jeopardy. Port travels in order to see life with greater clarity, but he can not act on what he sees. Self and society suffer from an irreversible drought; or as Nietzsche cries, "the desert grows!"; nor is there any mythic grail to redeem this wasteland. The deadly routine of the quotidian becomes ritual without sense. Alterity in the desert remains total, something no American can apprehend or mediate. Is it a wonder that Port yearns sometimes for a world without people? Or if not exactly an empty world, then a different one, without illusion of justice, in which the "unit of exchange" is the human tear. Such a world, though, would be indeed different from the world Bowles has created for us in *The Sheltering Sky,* a world of words, bringing blighted characters to violent life in a disciplined phantasmagoria that leaves Kafka's terrible dictum in ironic doubt: "From a certain point onward there is no longer any turning back. That is the point that must be reached" (*SS,* 185).

Did Port reach that point? Did Kit reach it more decisively than Port? Did neither, impelled as they are by a fatality they do not choose? Or does Bowles himself, like his readers, reach that point vicariously, reach it but for an instant before relapsing into the ordinary world? And is this also the point Western civilization must reach? The novel urges these questions upon us, urges them implacably, without answering them except as art answers our needs.

4

Bowles's second novel, *Let It Come Down* (1952, 1980), is a willed work, somewhat lurid and contrived, lacking the tautness, necessity, and stern clarity of *The Sheltering Sky*. Yet both novels reveal similar dramatic structures: a seeker, more somnambulist than seeker, disintegrates on alien ground before our eyes.

Nelson Dyar—the pun is obvious—seems dead before he starts: it is not so much meaning he seeks as some knowledge, some proof, that he is alive. A New York bank teller, he suddenly, or finally, becomes sated with his own inertia, with the squalid routine and patterned void of his existence. He decides to take advantage of a vague job offer that a former acquaintance, Wilcox, extends to him from the International Zone in Tangier. There, without passion or self-awareness, he dabbles in smuggling, fornication, narcotics, espionage, and murder. He seems like a man sealed within a dark bottle. The emotional demands he makes on the beautiful Arab courtesan Hadija are piteously beyond what that spirited young animal can satisfy. He can turn to no one: in Eunice Good he finds a jealous and implacable enemy determined to gain possession of Hadija for her own sexual ends; in Wilcox he discovers a treacherous friend intent on using him as a dupe in a black-market and smuggling scheme; and in Thami, the native, he meets a prurient, resentful, and greedy parasite. Only Daisy de Valverde, tough, astute, and unexpectedly wholesome, might have been capable of forestalling Dyar's crackup, but the two come no closer to each other than a futile and farcical lovemaking scene.

The retort of Dyar—as of Kit and many of the characters of Bowles's short stories—to a fundamental inadequacy is one of arbitrary actions, happenings, rejecting all ideas of order and value. For him there is no chance of self-apprehension, nor even the infinitesimal promise of a possible change. The debacle is certain, certain as is the feeling of the retired professor in "Pages from Cold Point": "Each wave at my feet, each bird-call in the forest at my back, does *not* carry me one step nearer the final disaster. The disaster is certain, but it will suddenly have happened, that is all. Until then, time stays still" (*CS,* 89). Thus Dyar, for ten years a staid bank teller, terminates his career by stealing black-market money he can never use and fleeing to the Spanish Zone. There, in a bare native dwelling, isolated from all but sand and sky, he drives a nail, under the influence of hashish, into the ear of his sleeping Arab companion, Thami.

This hallucinatory deed is not the "gratuitous act" of Lafcadio in Gide's

Lafcadio's Adventures, nor Meursault's "absurd act" in Camus's *The Stranger,* though it recalls both. In Bowles's work, hashish, *majoun,* and *kif,* together with cultic religious trances, introduce the "existential" element, subverting the common world, exposing its arbitrariness. But these altered states, hinting at some beyond, some region of transcendence, achieve their task chemically or behaviorally, achieve it, that is, with a determinism that French existentialism repudiates. Still, the practice of fatidic violence in Bowles's fiction broaches a cardinal question: what constitutes reality or being? Dyar approaches the question in terms of his own experience, his own sense of unreality:

> The feeling of unreality was too strong in him, all around him, sharp as a toothache, definite as the smell of ammonia, yet impalpable, unlocatable, a great smear across the lens of his consciousness. . . .
> He was not thinking, but words came into his mind, they all formed questions: "What am I doing here? Where am I getting? What's it all about? Why am I doing this? What good is it? What's going to happen?" (*LCD,* 128f.)

But Dyar can live the ironic answer to his own implicit questions only by ceding the initiative to circumstances. These, evil as they may appear in the context of traditional Western values, appear to Dyar wholly stripped of any moral implication. To him, they are merely dim occasions for self-definition, or rather, *accidents* of self-discovery. Thus Dyar muses at the end of the novel, after discovering the murder he has committed in a drugged delirium: "A place in the world, a definite status, a precise relationship with the rest of men. Even if it had to be one of open hostility, it was his, created by him" (*LCD,* 256).

Unfortunately, Dyar remains unconvincing as a character. He suffers from a certain rigidity in portraiture as in spirit; after his moment of grotesque intimacy with Daisy, she reflects upon the act: "It doesn't exist because he doesn't exist" (*LCD,* 190). Worse, Dyar, unlike Kit or Port Moresby, is finally uninteresting. His philosophical musings seem, therefore, authorial impositions: "The sudden sight of a human being deprived of its dignity [Wilcox slips on some dog offal] did not strike him [Dyar] as basically any more ludicrous and absurd than the constant effort required for the maintenance of that dignity, or than the state itself of being human in what seemed an undeniably nonhuman world" (*LCD,* 153). Nor can Dyar sustain the weight of geopolitical implication placed upon him.

The implications are palpable. For Bowles does much to present the International Zone in Tangier — with all its fools, scoundrels, degenerates, and plain criminals — as a microcosm of the world, mingling the worst elements of East and West. This mutual contamination is flagrant in the Bedaoui evening party, where all nationalities mix in mutual incomprehen-

sion, eager to exchange the currencies of lust, greed, and vanity, in a babel
of unctuous or venomous tongues. Even Dyar suddenly feels himself —
note the irony of the dead speaking of the dead — "surrounded by dead
people — or perhaps figures in a film that had been made a long time before" (*LCD*, 105f.). Call it *La Dolce Vita*, in bastard Tangier and American
style.

America is indeed present at the party as it is a dubious immanence
in the world. Daisy, the Marquesa de Valverde, may love Coca-Cola — she
also keeps cuttlefish in her living room tank — but she ascribes to America
a great emptiness, a blankness like Dyar's unlined hand. "My mother was
from Boston, you know," she tells Dyar, "so I'm part American. I know
what it's like. Oh, God, only too well" (*LCD*, 97). But is Tangier any different really from New York? At the party, a man comments on the two cities
thus: "you must see how alike the two places are. The life revolves wholly
about the making of money. Practically everyone is dishonest" (*LCD*, 100).
To what, then, has Dyar escaped? In an interactive world, nothing, not
even the Sahara, avoids contamination.

Certainly the Arabs of Tangier do not. The wealthy Bedaoui brothers
may try to preserve part of their lives, or wives, from the cosmopolitan
rot, but Thami, the youngest, can not. In him all the contradictions, all
the miseries, of colonialism meet. Thami marries Kinza, an illiterate Rif
girl, to flout his own educated class and somehow flout "Europe." But he
can not overcome his complex rancors: "He had no patience with their
[Moroccans'] ignorance and backwardness; if he damned the Europeans
with one breath, he was bound to damn the Moroccans with the next. No
one escaped but him, and that was because he hated himself most of all"
(*LCD*, 32). It is ironic, and also strangely apt, that Thami and Dyar, aliens
in their own lands, outsiders of history, should end as unconscious victim
and victimizer, brutalized by their own lives.

Nothing is salubrious in this novel, except perhaps certain natural scenes
at the beach, certain moods of subliminal wonder or deep repose, which
technology disrupts — a blaring transistor radio, the horn of an American
convertible. Nullity and dissolution prevail, both within and without the
characters, among both Arabs and Westerners. When cultures meet, they
do so as in this typical interchange between Thami and Eunice:

> "You want us all to be snake-charmers and scorpion-eaters," he raged, at
> one point in their conversation, which he had inevitably maneuvered in such
> a direction as to permit him to make his favorite accusations.
> "Naturally," Eunice replied in her most provoking manner. "It would be
> far preferable to being a nation of tenth-rate pseudo-civilized rug-sellers." She
> smiled poisonously and then belched in his face. (*TCD*, 110)

Nor is there any true meeting in eroticism, or even in mutual distress; for as Kinza's father declares: "only bad things happen when Nazarenes and Moslems come together" (*LCD*, 228). It is no wonder that Daisy believes we live in an "age of monsters," or that Dyar's father, more clipped than Daisy, thinks his son belongs to an "unhealthy generation."

We never quite know what preordains the fate of the characters in this as in the earlier novel — biology, biography, culture, the world, or artistic necessity? But there are also differences between the two fictions. Whereas, in the first, Port Moresby wants to lose his consciousness, Nelson Dyar, in the second, hopes to find it. Furthermore, *Let It Come Down,* though less realized as a novel, renders Moroccans with a certain roundness of history and character. Otherwise the work hardly enhances the scope of Bowles's sensibility. A larger cast of characters, of course, adds to the dramatic complexity of the book; but the complexity remains mechanical, a skill in plotting rather than a real interaction of characters who retain the power to affect each other's lives. Indeed, Bowles conveys no impression of dramatic resilience, as if people were so many cue balls, still or moving in their incidental order, impinging randomly on one another. Hence the semblance of eventuation, without internal development, without genuine self-recognition, without even surprise in the disclosure of character — except, perhaps, Daisy's.

5

Bowles's next novel, *The Spider's House,* hardly concerns quest. A quasi-political novel, it centers, as I have noted, on Fez between two worlds, one dying, the other muddling to be born. Its hero, Amar, unlike Dyar or Moresby, is a Moroccan, in touch with the spontaneous source of sympathy in human beings, fully alive to his cultural moment. Less seeker than mediator, he refuses to yield to either fatalism or nihilism, Orient or Occident, taking upon himself, in a kind of holy innocence, the mysteries of history. The Westerners on the scene, a diverse lot, seem finally irrelevant to it.

Up Above the World (1966, 1982), however, returns to quest, exile, dissolution, in an absentminded sort of way. Two Americans, Doctor and Mrs. Slade — he could be his wife's father or even grandfather, he says — wander about Central America, and find themselves embroiled in a sequence of events leading to their murder. This is the matter of thrillers, as Bowles admits, intending to write the novel as "a purely pleasurable pastime," and thereby to "recapture the state of mind that had produced the thrillers" he had "read to the seventh grade in primary school . . ." (*WS*, 355). That state of mind, alas, proves difficult for the mature reader to recover, so rambling and distraught the action seems.

Again, the plot recalls *The Sheltering Sky,* though this setting is jungly and humid. Here, again, is the curious couple, sleeping in different rooms — or, if in the same room, with a "no-mans-land between the beds" (*UAW,* 26) — the remote husband, the latently hysterical wife, the obscure motive of travel, the predestined blight. In this displaced, gothic world of deferred terrors, no human bond sustains. Grover Soto arranges the murder of his mother to inherit her fortune, and then murders his two guests, the Slades, because he *suspects* they may have witnessed the crime; his own mistress, Luchita, escapes to Paris at the first opportunity; and Doctor and Mrs. Slade, while still alive, deny any possibility of love, even of intimacy. In this closed yet arbitrary world, freedom becomes mere motion: "Not to have to make reservations ahead of time" (*UAW,* 101).

Deracination, in any case, no longer seems a uniquely American phenomenon; Arabs and Latinos, the late novels of Bowles show, find no firm roots in their own hybrid or frayed traditions. Luchita, in effect, sells herself to escape the nameless provincial capital, "up above the world"; all the native characters smoke *grifas* or marijuana, or drink double martinis, waiting for something to happen. Grover Soto himself, Canadian on his mother's side and Spanish on his father's, embodies the clash of cultures in his baleful, pathological character. He lives in a timeless space, cultivating repetition without history: "using an empirical system of autohypnosis he obliged himself to believe that the present was already past, that what he felt himself to be doing he had already done before, so that present action became merely a kind of playback of the experience" (*UAW,* 83). And his factotum, Thornby, a parasite and derelict, drifts in a drugged, homicidal state in which two murders seem to him less consequential than running over a stray dog with his car.

Moving at the interface of cultures, the Slades expose dire differences of assumptions. The Sotos, father and son, believe "that the only way to be free in life was to adhere so strictly to an orthodoxy [like the Catholic church] that everything save the spirit became a matter of reflex" (*UAW,* 91); to the Canadian mother, divorced and now called Mrs. Rainmantle, this is incomprehensible fanaticism. On the other hand, when Doctor Slade speaks up against exploitative labor on Soto's ranch, citing human rights, the latter coldly replies: "Yes, but what does the term 'human rights' mean? The American idea is based completely on the fact that Americans have always had more than their share. . . . Put them in the same position as the rest of the world, and they'll understand soon enough that what they've had so far have been only privileges, not rights" (*UAW,* 152). Indeed, to

Grover Soto, life is essentially about "who's going to clean up the shit";
as he explains to the liberal American, Mrs. Slade, "The work's got to be
done. If *you* don't want to do it, you've got to be able to make somebody
else do it. . . . Or isn't that the way you like to hear about it?" (*UAW,* 180).
This, of course, she finds wholly "repulsive."

In their alien settings, full of erotic menace, all the novels of Bowles
subvert the pieties of progress, modernity, liberal democracy. And they do
so without offering us an alternative except a willed, primeval vision, gravid
with mythic ecstasies and horrors. In that vision, victim and victimizer,
prey and pilgrim, meet. That is why Mrs. Slade feels that she knows Grover
Soto—who will murder her in a few days—so extraordinarily well: "His
voice particularly—it was like a sound she had known all her life. There
was something abnormal in the terrible familiarity she felt with its cadence
and inflections" (*UAW,* 152). It is as if Bowles were saying that in the great
emptiness of the American soul, atavistic death waits, waits to break out
in some far and forlorn place.

Bowles's style, his voice, the tenor of his fictions convey the same point.
In *Up Above the World,* the narrative voice, always controlled, always in
the third person, subtly shifts as it associates itself coldly with one character or another. Even the names shift as we observe the person from one
point of view or another. Thus Grover Soto becomes Grove, Vero, or Soto,
depending on the perspective Bowles wishes to adopt on him. The omens
of evil, the imminence of peril, heighten the alienation of characters from
their selves, their milieus, and from one another. Hallucinatory scenes, induced by various drugs and dreads, also heighten that pervasive alienation
of characters, even from their own bodies. Yet the same scenes, exercises
in surrealism, end also by betraying Bowles to his readers: the threat of
existence seems finally stylistic, not some radical evil but a poetic form
of it, a gothic threat.

6

More than the novels, perhaps, the quartzlike stories of Bowles reflect
sharply his imagination of exile. The stories do recall Poe, filtered sometimes through French Surrealism, colored often by the primary hues of
Mexican or Moroccan folklore; at their baneful best, they excel the gothic
fictions of Tennessee Williams or Carson McCullers, which they evoke.
From the start, though, Bowles wanted to invent his own myths, adopting
the insights of a "primitive mind." He did so—the claim finds no proof
in the finely wrought stories—by emulating the Surrealists, "abandoning
conscious control," and writing first animal legends, "then tales of ani-

mals disguised as 'basic human' beings" (*WS,* 261). From this came his earliest published story, "The Scorpion" (1945), and his commencement as a fiction writer:

> When *View* published it, I received compliments and went on inventing myths. The subject matter of the myths soon turned from "primitive" to contemporary, but the objectives and behavior of the protagonists remained the same as in the beast legends. It was through this unexpected little gate that I crept back into the land of fiction writing. Long ago I had decided that the world was too complex for me ever to be able to write fiction; since I failed to understand life, I would not be able to find points of reference which the hypothetical reader might have in common with me. When *Partisan Review* accepted "A Distant Episode," even though I had already sold two or three other tales to *Harper's Bazaar,* I was triumphant: it meant that I would be able to go on writing fiction. (*WS,* 262)

The short fiction is indeed various, spanning four decades. But it achieves its greatest effect, as Gore Vidal has noted in his preface to the *Collected Stories,* when Bowles attends minutely to surfaces: the harsh face of nature, the set visage of violence, dissolution, flight. Beneath the surface, of course, beneath the floor of a ramshackle civilization, lie the horrors of existence, just as beyond the "sheltering sky" lies a horrible absence. Still, despite their fidelity to terror—terror, as I have suggested, made poetic—the stories explore the assorted errors, travesties, and miseries of human as of cultural encounters. Regarding the latter, Bowles's own sense of local mores and colonial complexities deepens—increasingly, his later stories concern native themes and characters. He had never really romanticized alien settings, despite all his dramas of deracination. About his favorite, Arabic culture, he could be painfully candid. In an early interview, he observed: "I don't think we're likely to get to know the Moslems very well, and I suspect that if we should we'd find them less sympathetic than we do at present. . . . Their culture is essentially barbarous, their mentality that of a purely predatory people."[3] Yet as his stories show, the "barbarous" element becomes increasingly qualified, sometimes reversed, as in "Here to Learn" (1981) where a Moroccan girl, Malika, wanders dazed and uncomprehending through Los Angeles. "The fact that Malika's heart of darkness lies in the opposite direction," Richard Patteson perceives, "unmistakably establishes that the alien, at least in Bowles, cannot be seen in purely political, cultural, or historical terms."[4]

The alien element, of course, is what the American protagonists of the stories seek, even as they are repelled or violated by it. Often, as in the novels, that element is disturbingly, even grimly, erotic. The American writer in "Tea on the Mountain" (written in 1939) responds to an Arab schoolboy, Mjid, precisely because she could never know him. Though no sexual intercourse takes place between them, her thoughts linger wistfully on sex. When Mjid tells her that on his days away from school he makes love all day long, she responds, "'Really? You mean all day?' She was thoughtful" (*CS*, 23). And a little earlier, in Mjid's room, she reflects:

> "There is nothing wrong. It should have been a man, not a boy, that's all." It did not occur to her to ask herself: "But would I have come if it had been a man?" She looked at him tenderly, and decided that his face was probably the most intense and beautiful she had ever seen. She murmured a word without quite knowing what it was.
> "What?" he said.
> She repeated it: "Incredible."
> He smiled inscrutably. (*CS*, 22)

What is incredible? His beauty? His otherness? Her desire? What she has missed in life? Or is it rather the fact that, though she is a writer, she barely knows herself?

Similarly, the blonde tourist in "Under the Sky" (written 1946) has no self-knowledge; she is "raped" — the act is ambiguous — in the cemetery of a dismal Latin American town. An Indian villager, Jacinto, who had been smoking *grifas,* stares at her and her two companions in the marketplace. She "noticed him and smiled faintly as she went by" (*CS*, 79). Later in the night, she comes out of the hotel alone. Jacinto has been sitting on the bench patiently, waiting. He orders her to sit by him, and she obeys laughingly. Then:

> "And you, what are you looking for?"
> "Nothing."
> "Yes. You are looking for something," he said solemnly.
> "I was not sleeping. It is very hot."
> "No. It is not hot," said Jacinto. . . . "What are you doing in this town?" he asked her after a moment. (*CS*, 81)

Later, he drags her through the town streets to the cemetery. Then, a year after, he returns to the cemetery, recalls "the yellow-haired" woman. "After a time he began to weep and rolled over onto the earth, clutching the pebbles as he sobbed" (*CS*, 82). No less than the errant Westerner, the Indian, it seems, can not find the lineaments of gratified desire.

Once again, we see, Bowles's characters, neither tourists nor seekers, answer some obscure call. They leave behind civilization, false shelter — for Bowles, all security is false — taking with them a lack or hurt they can not name. But their desire, in deprivation or fulfillment, is not simply sexual. "They are all," as Bowles says, "the professor [in "A Distant Episode" (written 1945)]. . . . The desert is the protagonist."[5] This professor, a lin-

guist, becomes a raging clown or "holy maniac," swathed in belts made
of tin cans, his tongue cut out by the ruthless Reguibat tribe. We see him,
at the end, run out into the desert, gesticulating wildly toward the setting
sun. But what did this professor want in the hinterlands of North Africa?
Presumably, variant dialects of Moghrebi, which he collects. Or is the need
stranger, as he innocently walks, among snarling dogs, into the Reguibat
camp? "It occurred to him that he ought to ask himself why he was doing
this irrational thing," the professor thinks just before his ghastly captivity,
"but he was intelligent enough to know that since he was doing it, it was
not so important to probe for explanations at that moment" (*CS,* 43f.).

This "irrational thing" is key to the wanderers of Bowles, to their motive
and act. For they are, in some part of their being, seekers without realizing
why or what they seek. Therefore, chance and fatality, freedom and necessity, appear to them a single fact. Thus the American photographer in
"Tapiama" (written 1957) meditates on his midnight stroll in some desolate coastal region of Latin America:

> Perhaps he was enjoying it simply because the fabric here was of pure free-
> dom. He was not looking for anything. . . . The question of freedom was
> governed by the law of diminishing returns, he said to himself, walking faster.
> If you went beyond a certain point of intensity in your consciousness of de-
> siring it, you furnished yourself with a guarantee of not achieving it. In any
> case, he thought, what is freedom in the last analysis, other than the state of
> being totally, instead of only partially, subject to the tyranny of chance? (*CS,* 279)

As it turns out, the photographer "chooses" to surrender to events that
bring him to the edge of delirium, as he drifts along in a punt on some
marshy river. Is this man, then, quester, adventurer, drifter, simply a pro-
fessional on holiday? Or is he like the inquiline bird of the story, an
Idigaraga, crying: "*Iri garagua, nadie me quiere,* nobody likes me" (*CS,*
290)? Or again, is he a man weary of awareness, seeking in drugs or
drinks—a foul, potent *cumbiamba* concoction, in this case—an alternative to himself, "someone who was not he" (*CS,* 284), seeking *otherness*
like so many characters of Bowles?

Questions about the nameless characters of Bowles's stories—a "writer,"
a "tourist," a "professor," a "journalist"—will yield no clear or happy answer; they can only suggest the lineaments of a cold and distant doom.

7

What, then, may we conclude about quest in Bowles? As we have seen,
his most notable characters, in both novels and stories, suffer grisly mishaps, a sinister fatality that they themselves seem to contain. Their com-

pulsive quest, if quest at all, is a prior destiny with silence, savagery, annihilation. Like the "professor," they find in language only the intolerable burden of consciousness, hence a renewal of pain. This is the pain of existence itself, a radical senselessness and solitude. Crossing cultures, wandering in the wastes of nature or in the drug-altered states of their minds, they encounter the truth according to Bowles: a violence at the core of existence, more indifferent than the sun.[6] Fictive subjects, they never attest to their lives personally, never speak autobiographically, in the first person, so alienated they seem from their own selves, so dwarfed they appear in the "desert." Their risk, nonetheless, is real, the very air they breathe charged with threat. Mythic voyagers, epic seekers of a kind, they evoke only, as Northrop Frye would say, the ironic mythos of winter, ruled by the demonic imagery of constriction and dismemberment. They whisper the end of things, without hint of regeneration.

This rude fatality is no artistic flaw; it is integral to Bowles's vision. He admits to a grudge against existence: "the only way I could satisfy my grudge," he says in an interview, "was by writing words, attacking in words. . . . I want to *help* society go to pieces, make it easy."[7] In this romantic fantasy of hastening the end, of regaining a state of innocence through self-negation, Bowles is complicit with his most haunting characters. Quite like Bowles, these characters, Americans all, do not reveal much about the conditions of American society, that same society they so strenuously flee, so desperately condemn. But neither do they, like Bowles again, indulge in political cant, the jargon of colonialism or countercolonialism. In this Bowles shows himself to be a writer of the fifties, mainly, with equal distaste for noisy ideologies and (postmodern) technical experiments, for the dogmas of power and the "purely literary magma" of words. "I have no ego," he once said, and also, "I'm happiest when I'm moving," and again, "the future will be infinitely 'worse' than the present": these are the small, poignant hints of Bowles's imagination of exile, making for itself a home in art.[8]

Chapter Eight
Paul Theroux:
The Traveler as Seeker

> From a very early age, I read very intensively. I had very intense imaginary experiences, and wanted both metaphorically and actually to be transported. . . . Why it's there I don't know, but I think it comes from both a very strong sense of security, coming from a large happy family, and also a desire to be an individual, to stake some sort of claim and to assert my own individuality. . . . I was looking for a way of making life interesting. I also thought by leaving my community, by leaving Medford, Mass., that I would somehow find something about myself, something that would be hidden if I stayed at home.
> — Paul Theroux

1

IT MAY SEEM ODD to include Paul Theroux in a book about quest. Is he not mainly the sardonic traveler, a self-confessed "coward" — more of this later — a wry, dry observer, averse to spiritual pretensions of every kind? There is some truth in these and kindred epithets, though the truth of Theroux's work leaves such epithets behind. The energy of his obsessions, the gritty wit and precision of his prose, the gimlet-eyed view of nations both rich and poor, the sheer, cranky life of his insights into alien landscapes that reveal inscapes of the Western mind — all these prove him a more compelling, more complex writer than academic critics have allowed.

The situation of Theroux recalls a little V. S. Naipaul's: in both, we find wandering, exile, grudging acclaim. The two writers did meet in Uganda in 1966, a serendipitous meeting from which came, among other things, Theroux's only critical book to date, *V. S. Naipaul: An Introduction to His Work* (1972). This early book is of particular interest because it serves as a reflection on Theroux's own sensibility, his emergent work. Beyond "introducing" his subject with due homage, Theroux shows a writerly affinity with his senior, and an intimate appreciation of Naipaul's clear mind, exact style, firm perception. "Creation in Naipaul's terms," Theroux notes, "involves perception. The ability to assess oneself in one's setting is nec-

essary . . . details must be seen, judgments questioned. With these perceptions . . . arrives a specific calmness which is resolution" (*N,* 15).[1]

This calmness of resolution, though, is not always conspicuous in Theroux. The need for rebellion — "a vital attitude of mind, a writer's best impulse . . . missing in non-literate societies" (*N,* 114) — is acute, particularly
in his earlier work, and skews sometimes his view. Recollecting his youth
after a high school reunion, Theroux says: "I saw that it was not education
that made me a writer, but perhaps its opposite — my sense of incomplete-
ness, of being outside the currents of society and powerless and unprivileged and anxious to prove myself; that, and my membership in a large
family, with childhood fantasies of travel and, in general, being if not a
rebel then an isolated and hot-eyed punk" (*SS,* 3). There is candor in this
recognition, and probity too; there is clarity and a touch of whimsy; but
there is no assurance that Theroux has completely overcome the "hot-eyed
punk" in himself.

2

Theroux's confessional tendency, an American tendency foreign to the prim
reserve of Naipaul, prompts us to touch briefly on his biography.

Born in Medford, Massachusetts, in 1941, Theroux grows up in a large
family of mixed French Canadian and Italian ancestry. The family is
talented, theatrical, tightly knit — the seven children successful as lawyers,
writers, nurses. But Medford is drab, a working-class town of rust-colored
shingles and sagging houses, though once it sent proud clippers to trade
on the seven seas. Nothing in Medford really pleases, especially its high
school which Alexander Theroux — Paul's older brother, an erudite and
arcane novelist — calls a "sink of mediocrity" and Paul, ever more tangy,
calls "crummy."[2] The town is that archetypal place, muddy pool of the
heart, from which the hero must escape, and to which he returns only after
"making life interesting," proving himself, and discovering his concealed
fate.[3] For cooperative, supportive as it may be, Theroux's family contains
all those primal conflicts that fuel daring, rebellion, even rage, in the human enterprise.

At Medford High, Theroux joins no team, wins no prize, excels in no
subject; he even copies some of his English essays from the *Reader's Di-
gest.*[4] He makes bombs and lights fires. Bookish and bespectacled, he finds
sex "a harrowing bargain," does not sleep with a girl until he is nineteen —
nor do most of his classmates in the good, gray fifties. Above all, he broods.
Twenty years later, he would write: "What shocked me there at the Hilton
Inn, among the class of '59, was the fact that I had kept my secrets so
well they had become practically undiscoverable to me, and if I had not

gone to the reunion I would never have known how I made my childhood and high school days into a fiction" (*SS,* 188). But why did Theroux, wanderer without nostalgia, attend the reunion at all? Was it return, symbolic renunciation, a sense of impending death—I will return to this last—or a touch of vanity in his success?

In any case, the fitful arc of Theroux's life takes him first to the University of Maine, then to the University of Massachusetts, traversing all the protests, all the churning movements of the sixties. But the traveler soon declares himself: Theroux joins the Peace Corps in 1963, and goes to the Protectorate of Nyasaland, later called Malawi. In 1965, both the American and Malawi authorities expel him for his "political activities"; he moves to Uganda where he teaches at Makerere University. In Kampala, he meets Anne Castle, an Englishwoman; they marry at the local Registry Office. But Uganda is brewing with colonial hatreds too; Theroux's own students assault him as a "white man." He moves to Singapore in 1968, teaches Jacobean drama at the university. Teaching, though, becomes for him drudgery. He moves again with his family to England in 1971, settling first in South Bowood, Dorset, then in London. By that time, five of his books have appeared: *Waldo* (1967), *Fong and the Indians* (1968), *Murder at Mount Holly* (1969), *Girls at Play* (1969), and *Jungle Lovers* (1971). Popular success comes with *The Great Railway Bazaar* (1975), a Book-of-the-Month Club main selection, and *The Old Patagonian Express* (1979), that club's alternate selection. *The Consul's File* (1977) receives an award from the American Academy and Institute of Arts and Letters. *The Mosquito Coast* (1982) and *Half Moon Street* (1984) become films, starring Harrison Ford and Michael Caine respectively. In 1984, the American Academy elects Theroux. The election is timely; his publications accrue. To date, twenty-seven books of fiction and nonfiction carry his name, though Theroux never received a fellowship, a fact he cannily exploits in "Easy Money—Patronage" (*SS,* 259-77).

But where, in all this, is the pattern of quest? And quest for what?

3

A first answer emerges from the essays of *Sunrise with Seamonsters: Travels and Discoveries, 1964-1984* (1985), a title borrowed from Turner's painting, awash with light, spume, and vague terror. The essays are *interesting*—the book doesn't drop from the hand like so many books of "critical theory"—and also remarkable for their range of interests: travel, autobiography, geopolitics, photography, subways, older women, literary men as diverse as Hemingway, Kazantzakis, V. S. Pritchett, Henry James, Henry Miller, and V. S. Naipaul, sundry personalities, from Nixon to John McEnroe. Yet all this journalism, "writing for money" over two decades, results in "something more than a rag-bag anthology" (*SS*, 1); the work spins out a kind of narrative, the story of an inquisitive and vagrant imagination.

But this is not, as Bowles's is, an imagination of exile. Theroux does not flee America or repudiate it. Quite the contrary, like many of his compatriots, he never feels more American than abroad. After nearly two decades in England, he does not aspire to become English—they are too insular for his taste, he, no doubt, too abrasive for theirs. In any case, he lives in London only part of the year—his wife works as a BBC producer—and returns every summer with his family to Cape Cod. "I do think that it's helpful to distinguish between trying to get away from your family . . . which wasn't the case with me," Theroux says in an interview, "and a more positive impulse of actually wanting to go somewhere, pursuing something rather than fleeing something."[5] Still, reading Theroux on Medford, we sense that though exile may be extraneous to his purpose, flight is part of his pursuit.

The question remains: what shapes Theroux's vision, what quest, if quest at all, lies behind his peregrinations, full of perils and pains? "Vision" is not a word Theroux willingly employs; he calls his best books an "indulgence": "I mean a 'vision' but the word sounds too pompous and spiritual" (*SS*, 2). Romantic, like all travelers, he prefers to strike a hard-bitten stance, skeptical of religions, ideologies, myths. For him, man's fate is bound not to God but to "a belief in man"; and shrewdly he adds, "I sometimes think there is a horror of death in my fiction, and that grows out of an absence of religion."[6] That horror may also sustain his "cowardice." As he admits: "I am unable to understand what could make me risk death: neither patriotism, a desire to preserve anything, nor a hatred of anyone could rouse me to fight" (*SS*, 43).

Yet risk and romance do enter Theroux's work. Thus, for instance, his essay "Mapping the World," a paean to both explorers and cartographers, opens on this note:

> Cartography, the most aesthetically pleasing of the sciences, draws its power from the greatest of man's gifts—courage, the spirit of inquiry, artistic skill, man's sense of order and design, his understanding of natural laws, and his capacity for singular journeys to the most distant places. They are the brightest attributes and they have made maps one of the most luminous of man's creations. . . .
>
> Most novelists are map conscious, and all great novelists are cartographers. So are all true explorers, and the most intrepid travelers and traders. The real explorer is not the man who is following the map, but the man who is making one. (*SS*, 278, 282)

Exploration, we see, is a writer's habit, both literally and metaphorically, physically and mentally—this was also Butor's point. Could we then infer that behind Theroux's traveling urge is the need to map out reality in words and deeds? Theroux himself might demur — and I would demur at his demurral — claiming that he does not travel to write, and would travel even if he were never to write again.

To inquire about quest in Theroux is to inquire into his crowded notions of travel. "Travel is everything," he avows, "and my way of travelling is completely personal. This is not a category — it is more like a whole way of life" (*SS,* 3). Travel is challenge, to body and mind, to spirit, since an alien landscape can engulf a traveler, overwhelm him like the Sublime. But travel is also confidence, competence, optimism, a mode of self-definition in the world. Travel is perception, too, a knowledge of differences, a kind of lucidity. Travel, in any case, is the condition of our planetized earth, the way we live and the way we will live, a geopolitical condition experienced in every stomach cramp, feverish brow, aching bone. Inevitably, too, travel for Theroux is in the American grain: it carries the promise of self-renewal. It is not born of the colonial will to domination, or of postcolonial condescensions toward "primitive" peoples. It recalls, rather, the old Puritan dream of salvation, tainted now by the Americanization of the world. Thus Theroux, though born a Catholic, may find in travel "a precise task . . . a puritanical proof of meaning."[7]

We should note, however, that Theroux favors in his travels developing nations, societies in the throes of difficult change. This is not because he considers them "exotic"; like Naipaul, he senses the doom hanging over many of them since decolonization.[8] He favors them, of course, because they challenge him personally, but also because they signal a historical warning. How can the West, Theroux seems to ask, anticipate an impending global catastrophe whose signs are writ in these societies, writ so frighteningly large?

The answer is not cheery. In an early, acerbic essay, entitled "Tarzan Is an Expatriate," Theroux proposes Edgar Rice Burroughs' arboreal hero as prototype of the white settler in former colonies. "The last thing I want to be is the King of the Jungle," Theroux writes, "any jungle, and that includes Boston as much as it does Bujumbura"; then, unable to resist hectoring the new nations, he adds: "Someone must convince the African governments that fascism is not the special property of the Italians and Germans, and ask why independent African rule has made it infinitely easier for Tarzan, complete with *fasces,* to exist undisturbed and unchallenged" (*SS,* 39). Someone? As Theroux admits, the enlightened liberal view changes nothing in Africa; he himself simply leaves. A decade later, he calmly remarks: "I would like my children to understand that they can expect little from the state; that they will be swindled by politics and shortchanged by every authority except the family" (*SS,* 163f.). Quite possibly so. Yet the remark also intimates despair that so much knowledge gained in travel must remain powerless. Proleptic as it may be, travel can not remedy hunger or disease, nor can it relieve oppression in the world.

This nascent pessimism — or is it just realism? — may explain why, in his later work, Theroux stresses the private values of travel. The personal accent, however, betrays no urge to self-dramatization, none, as Theroux thinks, of the histrionic machismo of Hemingway or Mailer.[9] The accent indicates, rather, a shift in Theroux's own outlook, a new balance of tensions between private and public values. Thus in "Stranger on a Train," for instance, Theroux rejects the "ridiculous conceit" — held by Paul Fussell, among others — that the great age of travel has gone, that "this enormous world has been exhausted of interest." "The train," he says, "is the answer; for the bold and even the not-so-bold . . . the going is still good" (SS, 130). The train, then, can still offer the truth of travel, which "has less to do with distance than with insight" (SS, 131). On the surface of it, the insight refers to the prodigal diversity of the earth; at bottom, it concerns the self. Hence Theroux's relish of solitude on trains; there, huddled in his corner for days, he encounters that most intriguing of strangers, himself. "Mine is the purest form of travel," he boasts, "a combination of flight and suspended animation. I enjoy getting on trains; I loathe getting off" (SS, 126). One wants to ask: is the whole world, then, crammed in a train?

This might be the case for an introspective mind, and introspection constitutes one element in Theroux's quest for self-knowledge. But another element, curiosity or experience, also constitutes his quest. The two elements join in the titular essay, "Sunrise with Seamonsters," which depicts in marvelously realized detail Theroux's hazardous sea journeys in a light rowing skiff. Cannily, ironically, the piece renders symbolic contrasts in Theroux's life: between land and sea, home and adventure, past and present, a sushi invitation from the Styrons and the "seamonsters" (vicious currents and waves) out on Nantucket Sound. Theroux tries to mediate these antinomies, and endures his brother, Alexander, who calls him an Ishmael eating homemade spaghetti in his mother's kitchen. "The absurdity of it all!" Theroux exclaims. "I was self-sufficient and private in the boat, but from this protection at sea I had gone ashore and been half-drowned by the clamor and old jokes and nakedness at home" (SS, 352). And so he rows farther and farther out, till one day, with his son Marcel, he nearly drowns, rowing to Martha's Vineyard. It is an experience of both exaltation and dread.

Is this man the avowed "coward" of a confessional essay written seventeen years earlier? Are we closer here to discerning the motives of Theroux's compulsive travels, his covert quest? The motives, I think, are knowledge, curiosity, experience; also autonomy, mapping out a world in words; above all, an ontological motive, call it self-affirmation or being. Such motives may inspire in others, including Theroux's readers, admiration laced, alas, with envy. It takes little, it seems, to arouse envy. "This pretty skiff," Theroux laments, "aroused a harassing instinct among bystanders. They shouted at me, they yodeled, they threw stones" (*SS,* 356). Seamonsters on land as well as in the sea. Or is it rather that all travel, that motion itself, fascinates, and in fascination lie darker instincts?

4

In the previous section, I have asked if trains can contain the world. For Theroux, they are the ideal vehicle, the precise mobile frame of experience. This is spectacularly evident in *The Great Railway Bazaar* (1975) and *The Old Patagonian Express* (1979).

Railways are "irresistible bazaars," Theroux says in the earlier work. "If a train is large and comfortable you don't even need a destination; a corner seat is enough . . ." (*G,* 1). His corner seat takes him from London to Tokyo through southern Asia and back through Siberia. His corner seat is on marvelous or dismal trains, with magical names: the Direct Orient Express, the branch line to Simla, the spur through the Khyber Pass, the Mandalay Express, the North Star, the Trans-Siberian. But seeking trains, he also finds passengers, natives of every land he traverses, and meets wanderers like himself, Americans, Europeans, Australians. Riding trains, he encounters the whole strangeness of the world. And encounters himself.

The first interest of *The Great Railway Bazaar* lies in its panoramic virtuosity of observation. Trains pass, and everything passes through trains. Thus, traveling the earth with Theroux, we experience that dazzling variousness of the human condition, its outrage, hilarity, desolation, its *thereness* above all. We experience it in vivid and incongruous details: a hopping beggar in Calcutta who on one leg outraces Theroux; an immigration officer in Singapore who threatens to shear the visitor's longish hair; Tamil children who raid train toilets at every stop for a canful of water; American hippies copulating in train compartments before astonished Turkish women; a Canadian mistakenly put in a Kabul insane asylum, happy so long as his chocolates last; Ceylonese scholars who attend a U.S. Embassy seminar only because it offers lavish meals; blond "Vietnamese" babies, orphans of war, given away at street corners; demure Japanese schoolgirls who devour comic books, all gore and sexual mayhem, on aseptic bullet trains; Western derelicts of every kind, seeking societies more fragile or decayed than their own—the list is endless.

The Great Railway Bazaar, then, is no mere travelogue. It contains history, geography, sociology, literature, architecture, politics, contains, above all, knowing depictions of the human landscape—knowing but not always wise or deep. And it reflects continually on America nearly as much as on exotic or faraway places. Here is a pithy instance: "I went to Vietnam to take the train; people have done stranger things in that country" (*G*, 240). And a little later: "the truth was close and cruel: the Vietnamese had been damaged and then abandoned, almost as if, dressed in our clothes, they had been mistaken for us and shot at . . ." (*G*, 259). This same lethal absentmindedness of America seems dormant in the young drifters we meet, most of whom protested the Vietnam war before.

Cutting through languages, cultures, climes in a speeding train, Theroux discovers for us the unsavory facts of the world. But his observations are sometimes marred by sudden eruptions of bile or bigotry:

> Afghanistan is a nuisance. Formerly it was cheap and barbarous, and people went there to buy lumps of hashish. . . . Now Afghanistan is expensive but just as barbarous as before. The food smells of cholera . . . and the Afghans are lazy, idle, and violent. (*G*, 71f.)

At other times, Theroux's insights are shaped by amusing glibness, dismissive wit:

> The Japanese have perfected good manners and made them indistinguishable from rudeness. (*G*, 289)

> . . . a society without jaywalkers might indicate a society without artists. (*G*, 297)

For anyone who knows Japan, these statements are clever fiddle: they approach a point then swerve widely off the mark. More disturbing, perhaps, is the numbness, a kind of self-ignorance, these "insights" suggest in a writer quick to condemn in others their illiberal prejudices. Is a generalization about Afghans so different from one about class or race?

The question of Theroux's self-knowledge is more critical here than his satirical stance; for it engages both his personal and his artistic identity, what I have called his covert quest. Theroux leaves his wife and children, living on comfortless trains for four months—he does stop a few days in cities along the way to lecture for the USIA on American fiction. He knows from the start that travel is "flight and pursuit in equal parts" (*G*, 2); but he also admits that he is "embarked on a fairly aimless enterprise, the lazy indulgence of travel for its own sake" (*G*, 32). There is some evasion here, some waffling, a point unstated. Is he like the aimless hippies he encounters and condemns, "just traveling, man, just traveling"? Perhaps he is, more than he acknowledges, with one crucial difference: Theroux is an accomplished writer. Whatever drives him to board trains, and to board them again and again—call it freedom, curiosity, the lure of the unknown, the need to experience difficulty — the writer's motive inhabits that drive: train travel animates powerfully his imagination.

This imaginative release does not prevent Theroux from discovering that long travel also contracts the mind, encapsulates the self. Thus as the journey nears its end, his anxieties accrue. They accrue because it is ending *and* because it is not ending soon enough so that he can begin to write it up from notes. They accrue, too, because the journey brings no escape from the self: "The farther one traveled, the nakeder one got, until, towards the end, ceasing to be animated by any scene, one was most oneself, a man in a bed surrounded by empty bottles" (*G,* 297). Thus all travel writing, he says, becomes autobiography, "the embarrassed monologue in a deserted bazaar." Thus, also, travel and writing become a kind of circular exorcism. Theroux sickens himself on travel to free himself from it; he becomes free only by writing about it; he travels again in order to feed the imagination that empowers him to write. And so the book ends as it began:

> On my lap I have four thick notebooks. One has a Madras water stain on it, another has been slopped with *borscht,* the blue one (lettered, in gold, *Punjab Stationery Mart*) has the ring from a damp glass on its front, and the red one's color has been diluted to pink by the Turkish sun. These stains are like notations. The trip is finished and so is the book, and in a moment I will turn to the first page, and to amuse myself on the way to London will read with some satisfaction the trip that begins, *Ever since childhood, when I lived within earshot of the Boston and Maine, I have seldom heard a train go by and not wished I was on it. . . .* (*G,* 342)

This is not exactly self-ignorance; but neither does it finally probe the motive of Theroux's recurrent, *and recursive,* errands. It leaves us only with the fact of the finished book, a crackerjack best-seller.

The popularity of the book is due largely to its color, vivacity, pace, its crisp dialogue — Theroux can be brusque — and engrossing vignettes. These vignettes mix autobiography, reflection, character sketches, comic anecdotes, and stories within stories, blended into a single narrative, winding yet always on track. In this, the narrative is like a train that travels through time and space but maintains an illusion of unity, holding a few dramatis personae captive in a compartment; all the world becomes a narrow stage, still and moving. Thus *The Great Railway Bazaar* seems at once a couchette play, railroad picaresque, and iron-track adventure, all wit and grit and romance. This is not to say that Theroux is an "experimental" writer; he is a realist, steeped in the central tradition of European fiction, who considers most artistic experiments "formal hysteria." In the train book, he has simply found his form.

The book, however, finally takes its form not from a pair of iron rails but from the character, the obsession, of its author. Or is it his whimsy? The character, at any rate, seems brisk and savvy, yet brooding too and in odd ways passive. Theroux departs from Victoria Station and returns there, missing a train only once in Moscow—he calls this "duffilled," like poor old Mr. Duffill who misses his train, his opportunity, in mid-journey. Thus, despite his claim to cowardice, he considers himself "as intrepid as the next man" (G, 198)—are all men cowards then?—and enters every compartment ready for combat. The combat is for comfort and privacy, Theroux's privacy; that of his subjects he constantly invades. (He inspects brothels, for instance, and flirts with women, without ever admitting to having sex with any.) In the end, though, it is Theroux's obsession, his "wound," that shapes the book more than anything else. I refer to his guilt-ridden dreams, mounting angst, moments of panic, and above all, his need to repeat those long train journeys into the night. The external form is travel, travel at its crackling best; the form within is obsession, exorcism, flight and pursuit; or rather, the form is the same within and without, a form of travel compelled by its urgency into quest.

The same compulsion shapes *The Old Patagonian Express,* becoming almost formulaic. Here Theroux journeys longitudinally, from Boston to Esquel, in Patagonia, on rickety trains. The journeys are often harder than his Asian journeys and more perilous. Yet the book lacks the sprightliness of its predecessor, lacks a certain lightness of imaginative being. This may be due simply to repetition. But it may be due also to the sinister, volcanic setting, riven by riots and revolutions, leaden with misery and oppression.

This is not to say that Theroux forswears romance, seedy romance. Its ambiguous spirit pervades the book, starting with its two epigraphs.[10] And even the dedication adds to Theroux's family (Anne, Marcel, and Louis) "my Shanghai Lil," from the song of Ben Bernie and the Lads: "I've been looking high / I've been looking low / Looking for my Shanghai Lil" (O, 364). Doesn't Shanghai Lil evoke Shangri-la? Contrary as always, Theroux quotes a little later Dr. Johnson on the vice of "romantick absurdity, or incredible fictions" (O, 477).

Indeed, facts continually jostle fantasy in *The Old Patagonian Express.* The facts begin with a bone-chilling cold that grips North America in the winter of 1978, and the ashen faces of commuters on the subway to Boston's South Station, from which Theroux boards the train to Patagonia. (He wants to tell readers how he got there in the first place, from his bedroom in Medford all the way to Esquel.) The facts are concrete: a wrinkled department store bag on the subway; the whistle pitch of American trains, "*Hoo-wee*"; "pally names" on storefronts, Stars and Stripes in backyards;

a self-absorbed coed, folded in the lotus position, prattling about natural foods. The facts are also telling: they reveal America, its energy, cuteness, fakery, all the way from Boston to Laredo. And the facts are unsparing: seeing hundreds of "TV-mummies," all dressed to kill, board the train with their children in Oklahoma, Theroux thinks of Dinka women in southern Sudan, and wonders why, "in one of the most socially advanced countries on earth, here was a group behaving no different from the wariest folk society" (*O,* 39).

But the facts become grimmer across the Rio Grande. "Spanish America is cursed with the grandiosity of crooked statesmen; the Indians and peasants remain Indians and peasants" (*O,* 67), sums it all. Tyranny, violence, corruption, and privations beyond our conceiving, cross continually our sight. Something has gone "haywire" there, Theroux broods:

> it was as if New England had gone completely to ruin, and places like Rhode Island and Connecticut were run by maniacal generals and thuggish policemen; as if they had evolved into motiveless tyrannies and become forcing-houses of nationalism. It was no wonder that, seeing them as degenerate states, tycoons like Vanderbilt and imperial-minded companies like the United Fruit Company took them over and tried to run them. (*O,* 174)

Still, broken-down trains, clattering from one wasted town to another, pass through "marvels of erupted landscape," and this keeps Theroux's spirits up.

Traveling among the poorest of the poor — only *they* ride trains in Latin America — traveling among the inchoate and defeated, Theroux pays the price of his experiences. He becomes a stranger among strangers, nearly mute except in his journal, praying for hope. This enforces his isolation, the traveler's clearheaded solitude. I do not mean that Theroux never speaks. He knows enough Spanish to converse with assorted characters, from tubercular waifs dying in the cold streets of Armenia (Colombia) to affluent business relatives in Guayaquil, from a forlorn sailor called Ranaldo Davies in Esquel to Jorge Luis Borges in Buenos Aires. These conversations do convey a sense of the societies Theroux traverses. But it is a superficial, a fleeting sense. What persists is his alienation, and his impotent outrage at the unspeakable conditions he sees:

> Class warfare proceeds without bugle calls; it creates stinks and murmurs, not the noisy grandeur of armies heroically wrecking themselves on battlefields. (*O,* 352f.)

> Air travel has wished tourists on only the most moth-eaten countries in the world: tourism, never more energetically pursued than in static societies, is usually the mobile rich making a blind blundering visitation on the inert poor. (*O,* 355)

But Theroux is not a Marxist, not a revolutionary; he is keenly skeptical of both, even though he sometimes dreams of a Latin American liberator, like Bolivar or Guevara. His just anger, however, has no outlet except in writing. The anger smolders or flares throughout the book, igniting the reader's outrage. Because this last has no issue in writing or action, an irritated reader may well wonder: what exactly is this book? Travel, autobiography, quest? Or rather, sociopolitical muckraking, like Naipaul's cutting exposés of wounded civilizations, areas of darkness? The questions betray aesthetic discomfort, a sense of something artistically skewed.

Theroux's personal voice, though, carries us along. The voice is interesting from the start: "One of us on the sliding subway train was clearly not heading for work. . . . you can always tell a fugitive by his vagrant expression of smugness; he seems to have a secret in his mouth . . ." (*O*, 1). The secret is a *writer's* secret. For if travel is a "vanishing act, a solitary trip down a pinched line of geography to oblivion," a travel *book* is quite the opposite, "the loner bouncing back bigger than life to tell the story of his experiment with space" (*O*, 3). Even the motive of Theroux's journey is bound to his writer's art:

> I had nothing better to do. I was at a stage I had grown to recognize in my writing life. I had just finished a novel, two years of indoor activity. Looking for something else to write, I found that instead of hitting nails on the head I was only striking a series of glancing blows. I hated cold weather. I wanted some sunshine. I had no job. What was the problem? I studied maps and discovered that there was a continuous track from my house in Medford to the Great Plateau of Patagonia in southern Argentina. (*O*, 7)

Indeed, throughout the book, Theroux reads — Twain, London, Kipling, Dürrenmatt, Dr. Johnson, and above all Poe, quoting from *The Narrative of Arthur Gordon Pym* — and writes in his journal as he travels. He pretends to be a geography teacher in order to reassure his subjects; in fact, he remains always the writer-voyeur, as a prostitute in Nuevo Laredo jeers. And in his moments of self-doubt, he compares himself to another Massachusetts-born writer, Jack Kerouac, aging and weary, heading back to his mother's house.

In these dejected moments, Theroux admits he is no explorer; like Crusoe, he feels punished for his "selfishness" in leaving home. Yet he endures more than heat, dust, fatigue; he risks coups, cholera, sharks, rabid dogs, murderous muggers, and trigger-happy border guards. Why, then, is he braving all these dangers and discomforts? Certainly not to live cheaply, like some German skinflints who drift to South America only because it is cheap. Is it simply to procure materials for another book? Or is it a sentimental journey to Patagonia, for which his great-grandfather had set out from Italy before diverting to New York? Or is the voyage really a search for experience, autonomy, self-worth?

The answer is sometimes explicit, tucked in the middle of the book: "I craved a little risk, some danger, an untoward event, a vivid discomfort, an experience of my own company, and in a modest way the romance of solitude" (*O*, 200). But the answer also comes in the final chapter, suggesting a descent into hell and (prospective) return. Theroux reaches at last Patagonia, an arid, windswept region of thorn bushes, ribbed rocks, gaunt skies, the end of the line, the end of a world. When he alights from his "nest" on the train, it is 2 A.M. He thinks of himself as Ishmael:

> "And I only am escaped alone to tell thee." It was cold in this dismal place, but I had no choice but to wait four hours for the teeny-weeny steam train to Esquel. But I also thought: *It's perfect.* If one of the objects of travel was to give yourself the explorer's thrill that you were alone, that after fifteen or twenty thousand miles you had outrun everyone else and were embarked on a solitary mission of discovery in a remote place, then I had accomplished the traveler's dream. The train travels a thousand miles from Buenos Aires, stops in the middle of the desert, and you get out. You look around; you're alone. It is like arriving. In itself it is like discovery — it has that singularity. The sky was full of stars in unfamiliar constellations, and even the moon was distorted, like an antipodean version of the one I was used to. This was all new. In the best travel books the word *alone* is implied on every exciting page, as subtle and ineradicable as a watermark. The conceit of this, the idea of being able to report it — for I had deliberately set out to write a book, hadn't I? — made up for the discomfort. Alone, alone: it was like proof of my success. I had had to travel very far to arrive at this solitary condition. (*O*, 462f.)

This goes beyond the writer's motive; it is an ontic claim. Patagonia: a terrible, legendary, godforsaken place to die, to vanish in. But this "Nowhere is a place" (*O*, 477), as Theroux discovers in shocked revelation, the space of rebirth, a place to start over from again, a point of no return or, with luck, the very point of return. Theroux does not proceed from there to Antarctica, the farthest pole of experience. He can return now to Medford with an achievement, perhaps not like Scott's or Amundsen's, yet achievement enough for any man. Indeed, the return is so certain, so natural, that Theroux simply elides it; there is no need to describe the journey home, as he does in *The Great Railway Bazaar.*

The Old Patagonian Express is gloomier than its predecessor, more bitter, sometimes only more tedious. Its high points — for instance, dawn at Machu Picchu, an evening with Borges, the awesome emptiness of Patagonia — cannot relieve the gloom of this infernal journey, which consciously evokes Ishmael's and Arthur Gordon Pym's. Nor does the book rightly blend its moods, harmonize its lighter and duskier shades, or perceive its subject deeply. Yet it reveals the raw, disreputable motive of quest more than any other nonfictional work of Theroux.

Theroux's later travel books tend to be mainly travel, lacking the inner pressure that transforms a journey into quest. They subordinate the struggling self, the interior drama of hope, to precise observation, tart insight, the exotic brought home. In these works, Theroux relates himself differently to his narrative: his voice is less richly anxious, less poetic, as if (to paraphrase Yeats) in quarreling more with the world than with himself, Theroux is now content to create less poetry than rhetoric.

Sailing through China (1983), for instance, takes us on a Lindblad Tour down the Yangtze; it is a slim, sharp essay on American millionaires skimming the Great River. The Imperial Way (1985), gorgeously illustrated by Steve McCurry, is "neither a vacation nor an ordeal, but rather a kind of sedentary adventuring — an imperial progress along the railways of the old Raj" (I, 7), which Theroux had jauntily followed a decade earlier. The Kingdom by the Sea (1983) circumambulates Britain by foot and train. It is a salty, bristly book, sometimes mean-spirited, and the furore it created — the British become the "funny foreigners" they have themselves invented — concerns us little. The work does reflect shrewdly on travel, though, and sometimes on England, which it makes into a seedy, futuristic nightmare; but it is not quest. As Theroux says: "There were no blank spaces on the map of Great Britain, the best known, most fastidiously mapped, and most widely trampled piece of geography on earth. No country was easier to travel in . . ." (K, 3). Nor is Riding the Iron Rooster (1988) quest; chatty and profuse, it takes us across Asia by train again — this time with a tour group — and throughout China by "rooster." Whatever motives impel Theroux in his later peregrinations, they remain submerged, diffused, as if he had made peace with the "hot-eyed punk" in him, and now found greater freedom in a thousand fact-packed pages.

For quest, then, we must look elsewhere, look to his novels.

5

Theroux writes with both hands, fiction and nonfiction. To the fiction he has always accorded a special status — fiction is "pure joy" — without offering, however, any fresh insight into the novel as a literary form. In The Great Railway Bazaar, he identified "the difference between travel writing and fiction" as the "difference between recording what the eye sees and discovering what the imagination knows" (G, 341). And in The Old Patagonian Express, he associated travel with the work of memory, "skimming south" but recalling, writing everything from notes. Yet Theroux must also know that the imagination invades memory; moods shape what the eye sees. If fiction for him is pure joy, is it not rather because the "self" he creates in a novel is unencumbered by autobiography, because the narrative voice is other than his own?

This liberty is manifest in *Saint Jack* (1973). The speaker in this early novel is Jack Fiori, alias Flowers, born in the North End of Boston, a genial, hard-boiled Singapore hustler—or "ponce" as his alter ego, an Englishman called Leigh, says. Jack is an "institution" in the Orient, a character of extraordinary humor, competence, and moral vitality, a seeker who grows before our eyes and achieves an intangible grace.

The novel is neatly structured in three parts—call them antithesis, thesis, and synthesis; or present, past, and timeless future—highlighting stages in the progress of a secular saint. When the book opens, Jack is fifty-three, a ship chandler in Singapore, taking orders from a venal Chinese boss or *towkay*. Jack's arms are tattooed with floral patterns from elbow to wrist; everyone likes him, even if an aura of jovial defeat clings to his flower-print shirts. Out of each day's humiliations, he manages to rescue a measure of dignity; out of loneliness and drift, a sense of purpose. He has boarded in his life too many sinking ships. And so, after fourteen years in Singapore, he thinks: "To be this age and very far from where you started out, unconsoled by any possibility of miracle—that is bad . . ." (*SJ,* 11).

But William Leigh lands to his rescue. Also fiftyish, he is a disagreeable accountant come from Hong Kong to audit the ledgers of the *towkay,* Hing. He asks Jack: are you a ponce? and how can you stand it, this life of yours in Singapore? Leigh's own life in Hong Kong is desolate; he and his wife dream only of retirement to a cottage in Wiltshire. The dream comes to a sudden end in a Singapore bar, where Leigh dies of a heart attack, bequeathing to Jack the questions neither has answered for himself. There is some sympathy between the two men; Jack feels for the accountant "an inward clutching at self-pity" (*SJ,* 38). Thus when Leigh dies—Jack pays for the funeral, and watches the cremated body go up in "a black puff and ripples of stringy heat"—the latter feels the terror of his own exile and death, feels also a sort of peace: "Burning . . . was like deliverance; it was only bad on a hot day" (*SJ,* 83, 81), Jack thinks.

Flowers needed the shock of vicarious death to account for his own rambling existence. He has been kind. The sight of sensual joy "lifts his heart," that of glass shards bristling on top of a wall, to thwart interlopers, makes his "pecker ache"; he has avoided cruelty and lies. He has been brave and above all else sane. But he has also deceived himself. This we begin to see in the second part of the novel, which takes us back to Jack's arrival in Singapore—he jumps the *Allegro,* on which he is a paid steward. Once on the island, he hustles in his free time, whispering from doorways,

"It's kinda hot," or "Anything I can do for you, anything at all?" Later, he reflects on his decision to jump ship. Was it cowardice disguised as a promise of renewal?

Up to that time, Saint Jack's illusion was a special destiny, vouchsafed to him without effort or cost. He fancies letters in the mail, granting him fame and fortune. Saint Jack, Sir Jack, King Jack, President Flowers: "The letters were fantasy, but the impulse was real: a visceral longing for success, comfort, renown, the gift that could be handled, tangible grace" (*SJ*, 91). But Leigh's death awakens him to reality:

> My life was a pause; I lived in expectation of an angel.
>
> My vision was explicit, and no guilt hampered it; I wished away the ego of my past—I would not be burdened by my history. But I had a fear: that I might turn out to be one of those travelers who, unnerved by the unconscious boldness of their distance—the flight that took them too far—believe themselves to be off course and head for anything that resembles a familiar landmark. Only, up close, they discover it to be a common feature of a foreign landscape on which identical landmarks lie in all directions. They chase these signs, their panic giving the wheeling chase some drama, and very soon they are nowhere, travelers who never arrive, who do not die but are lost and never found, like those unfortunate Arctic explorers, or really any single middle-aged feller who dies in a tropical alien place, alone and among strangers who mock what they can't comprehend, the hopeful man with the perfect dream of magic, burned to ashes one hot day and negligently buried, who was lost long before he died. (*SJ*, 93)

The "hopeful man with the perfect dream of magic" is heir to the Great Gatsby, a visionary corrupted by his own dream. But what brings this hopeful American to board the *Allegro* in the first place, then hustle in Singapore, conveying twenty-three whores in a lighter, through a horrendous storm, to grateful, ship-bound sailors on a freighter? Jack Fiori became a freshman at thirty-five, studying English, after spending World War II behind a desk in Oklahoma. An aspiring writer, he is in search of experience; he will not sell insurance and settle down. But writing, he discovers, "bores" him; and education seems to him "inappropriate" to reality. That first year in Singapore, he feels his luck change. He finds "a rare kind of happiness, like the *accidental* [italics mine] discovery of renewal. . . . It was true power: mercy and boldness. I felt brave" (*SJ*, 115). But mercy runs out. Though he hustles with charity—his customers seem always full of false gratitude—his clowneries begin to take on the hues of despair. A Chinese secret society wrecks his "wang house" (brothel) and tattoos his arms with horrible maledictions which he, typically, transforms into *fiori*. Later, his R and R "resthouse," for GIs recovering from Vietnam, runs out of army funds. And with the vicious new ethos of pornography, im-

ported from America, business becomes hard. Yet Jack Flowers survives
with humor and deferred grace.

The third section of the novel resolves quest into questlessness. Jack
drives away from Leigh's funeral, remembering his own "season of flights."
He understands now why he has never risen; he demands from himself
"an altered rendering of a previous hope" (*SJ,* 229f.). He must act, expect-
ing nothing. The action comes when Shuck, a tough U.S. intelligence agent,
offers Jack a fortune to frame a certain Major General Andrew Maddox,
responsible for prolonging the war in Vietnam. Reluctantly, Jack tapes and
photographs the sexual frolics of the general in a hotel room. But General
Maddox, though implicated in some dubious deals, seems quite ordinary:
"Shuck held him responsible for a war. I could not speak for that outrage,
but in one respect [i.e., erotically], the only one I had seen, the man was
gentle. I had spied on innocence" (*SJ,* 272). Jack refuses to sell the pictures. Here is the last scene with Shuck:

> I wanted no part of the graceless distortion. I was a person of small virtue;
> virtue wasn't salvation, but knowing that might be.
> "I don't believe he's guilty," I said at last.
> "How do you know?"
> "Because *I'm* not."
> . . . I had panicked and acted. I shouldn't have panicked; but the act re-
> leased me. I was a lucky feller. . . .
> I was no exile. There were fast planes west, and I knew the cosiest ships.
> Being away can make you a stranger in two places, I thought; but it wasn't a
> country I needed, and not money, though I knew some cash would improve
> my backward heart. (*SJ,* 275–77)

At the end, Jack Flowers feels tranquil enough to toss himself into the
harbor but decides "to live for a hundred years" instead. He walks in a
crowded Singapore street, recognized and reconciled, and blesses children
holding bright colored lanterns with a simple nod. And to a pretty American tourist, pretending to be lost, who asks if he has a minute, he answers
with a warble: "Lady, believe me. . . . I've got all the time in the world"
(*SJ,* 278). The time he "has" is a timeless present, time almost redeemed.

In Jack Flowers, Theroux has created a colorful, wayward, and compassionate character. Flowers also gives a new, realistic sense to quest: acquainted with danger, he eschews heroics, and answerable to others, he
learns to save himself. His pursuit of experience in the shady byways of
life becomes a search for self-worth, an inner calm that voids the quest
itself. Clearly Theroux shares some of Jack's attitudes—toward politics,
religion, morality, sex—and this helps Theroux's readers identify with his
hero. Readers, though, may experience another difficulty, arising from Jack's
voice.

The first-person story of a ponce requires some plausible, if not rigorous, explanation: why is the story so well written, and how does it fall into our hands? This is always the problem of personal narratives; Poe's Pym, Melville's Ishmael, Bellow's Henderson, and Mailer's D.J. face the same problem in different ways. Theroux solves it in part by making Jack Flowers an incipient novelist and avid reader, and by making him conscious of writing a "memoir" from the rather clumsy start. At later points, Jack fears that he may be "practicing satire or self-mockery" in his story, and that his fantasies, "squatting like trepanned demons in the padded privacy of an idle mind," may seem "the extravagant ravings of a crackpot" (*SJ,* 90), once they are committed to print. Still, the discrepancy between the convoluted idiom of introspection and slangy, tangy lingo of the street often jars, like a sustained conceit. In the end, though, the voice works because Jack does not insist on his presence, because his natural delicacy saves him from ethical as from aesthetic gaffes.

Tightly structured, finely attuned to the sounds of American and foreign speech, rich in postcolonial lore, deft in developing the iconography of sainthood, the "priestly vocation" of Jack, jiving here and somber there as the mood requires, above all open to experience, *Saint Jack* may not possess the sweep and darker energies of *The Mosquito Coast,* but it aspires to unite right action and belief in the form of art. This was, judging from the novel's epigraph, precisely the charge Theroux had given himself.

Most of Theroux's novels are set abroad, dramatizing cultural contrasts; not all are quest. But *The Mosquito Coast* is preeminently a labor of quest, and it confronts the destructive element of quest without qualm. The novel actually tells two simultaneous stories which become one: that of Allie Fox's quest and that of his son's initiation. Thus, though Allie — nearly everyone calls him Father — dominates hugely the novel, the narrator is Charlie, a thirteen-year-old boy of steady vision who recounts the disintegration of his childhood world, the breakup of his father.

Allie Fox is a Yankee original, a comic Ahab, though no less lethal for that, and the novel is largely his rant. An amateur inventor with nine patents and six pending, he embodies heroic American virtues brought to the point of vice. He beggars our adjectives — brave, brilliant, bombastic, erudite, monstrously egotistic — subsumes all passions in his hubris of invention, improving nature with his art. This is a complex, a mastering obsession, full of crotchets and contradictions. For Allie himself can be both practical and visionary, fair and fanatical, generous and vindictive, at once reverential and ruthless in his use of "appropriate technology." Thus he appears as a daemon, more than "the last man in America," in search of some ultimate freedom. Allie simply calls it "elbow room." But this "room" is a world of his own making after civilization has annihilated itself, as he thinks it must—shades of Dickey's Lewis Medlock here.

Allie Fox finds America "in gridlock," and never tires of condemning its greed, corruption, injustice, kitsch, sleaze. Everything particular he says seems right, yet it all somehow adds up to something hideously wrong. Perhaps this is in the nature of obsession, that it converts insight into blindness. In any case, Allie deserves to be heard at some length:

> We drove past Tiny Polski's mansion house to the main road, and then the five miles into Northampton. Father talking the whole way about savages and the awfulness of America—how it got turned into a dope-taking, door-locking, ulcerated danger zone of rabid scavengers and criminal millionaires and moral sneaks. And look at the schools. And look at the politicians. And there wasn't a Harvard graduate who could change a flat tire or do ten pushups. And there were people in New York City who lived on pet food, who would kill you for a little loose change. Was that normal? If not, why did anyone put up with it? (*M*, 3)

> And Father said, ". . . I'm sick of everyone pretending to be old Dan Beavers in his L. L. Bean moccasins, and his Dubbelwares, and his Japanese bucksaw—all these fake frontiersmen with their chuck wagons full of Twinkies and Wonderbread and aerosol cheese spread. Get out the Duraflame log and the plastic cracker barrel, Dan, and let's talk self-sufficiency!" (*M*, 40)

> "Good-bye, America," he said. "If anyone asks, say we were shipwrecked. Good-bye to your junk and your old hideola! And have a nice day!" (*M*, 67)

American will soon go up in flames anyway—is this prophetic vision or the personal grudge, secret wound, of apocalyptics? Allie decides to save himself and his family, composed of Mother, Charlie, Jerry, the little twins, April and Clover. Honduran migrant workers whom he befriends on an asparagus farm in Massachusetts inspire him with an idea: he will swap countries with them. He bequeathes to them his invention, a machine that makes ice from fire, and they give him a machete as a parting gift. The Foxes then ship out on a banana boat to Le Ceiba. On board, atheist Allie lectures sanctimonious missionaries on the Bible, which he considers a failed manual for humanity, and instructs the captain to balance his listing freighter. When the family reaches the Mosquito Coast, Charlie sees only a brown sea, chicken huts, dead dogs, flapping vultures, roads leading to nowhere. But Allie, scorning this scavenger's coast, buys Jeronimo for four hundred dollars an acre. It is a jungle village, a few ramshackle huts up a clogged river, to which he hauls his family and supplies in a tattered launch. He had warned his family: this quest would require "not ordinary gumption, but four-o'clock-in-the-morning courage" (*M*, 10).

Dodging truant officers in America, Allie had kept all his children out of school; he himself had dropped out of Harvard. Now is the chance for all the Foxes to prove their mettle. Jeronimo was just a name, "the muddy end of the muddy path" (*M,* 130), but they transform it, with stintless labor and ingenuity, into a hard-earned tropical paradise. Even the local Indians admire it, awed by Allie's great, extravagant masterpiece, a machine larger than a silo for making ice, an "oddity of such magnificence that it was a thing in itself, like an Egyptian pyramid" (*M,* 153). The Foxes call it Fat Boy. The name is appropriate: the thing blows up, pulverizing Jeronimo and poisoning the jungle—the family takes refuge in the Acre, a secret hideout the children made—and blows up with it three armed renegades who had threatened to take over the village. Is this murder, Charlie and his mother wonder, or self-defense? To the end, this terrible ambiguity will remain.

From this point on, however, Allie will lead his family through horrendous hardships, from one nameless place to another, including a storm-swept sandbank by a lagoon—lead them to his own doom. This man who rarely sleeps, who goes hungry to think better, who knows it all and takes charge of everything, who never stops until he gets there, who abhors liars, cheats, scavengers of every kind, ends by sealing himself and his family in a devastating fantasy—America no longer exists—in order to justify his mad search. For what? Freedom, self-sufficiency, a simple way of life? Or is it, rather, a quest for nothingness, the tabula rasa of existence, the deep blankness within Allie's soul that compels him to recreate everything, perpetually, from scratch? He describes God as "the dead boy with a spinning top" (*M,* 278), but the phrase may describe Allie better. For there is always something absent in him, something abstract, even when he plays Prometheus to the Indians, brings them useless gifts, not fire but ice that melts before it reaches their hands. And though he detests Christian missionaries, he acts like a deranged Angel of Reason himself, blighting everything he touches—again, like Ahab, Kurtz, Fitzcarraldo. In the end, we are left with Allie's bare egotism: "I want to penetrate where they've [missionaries, explorers] never been" (*M,* 176).

The quest of Allie Fox has energy, demented splendor. What puts it in perspective is Charlie's voice, his initiation or counterquest. In this counterquest, Mother—no one ever calls her otherwise—holds the moral center of the action, since Charlie himself can not be presumed an unbiased, a flawless narrator.

Charlie Fox begins with complete trust in his father. But as Charlie tells it in his own language, a language neither too bare nor too novelistic to be credible in a thirteen-year-old boy, the shadow of doubt falls early on the son. Charlie, for instance, is more conformist than Allie; he worries about what other boys who attend school might think of him; he quietly yearns to be in school himself. Moreover, Charlie listens to old Polski, a former employer of the Foxes, who warns him about his father, and tells him about a notorious murderer, Spider Mooney, who bit off *his* crazy father's ear before hanging: "He spit it out, and *then* he says, 'That's for makun me what I am'" (*M,* 55). Charlie also recalls various physical ordeals that Allie imposes on him, like sitting on a rock as the tide rushes in, shinnying up the shrouds of a rolling ship, diving for a sunken propeller in a muddy river infested with alligators, and climbing through the tubing of Fat Boy:

> Just as I said to myself *Don't look down,* I looked down. And kept looking. I recognized what I saw. This was no belly—this was Father's head, the mechanical part of his brain and the complications of his mind, as strong and huge and mysterious. It was all revealed to me, but there was too much of it, like a book page full of secrets, printed too small. Everything fitted so neatly and was so well bolted and finely fixed it looked selfish. I could see that it had order, but the order—the size of it—frightened me. (*M,* 160)

More than all these ordeals, however, it is the widening gap of perception that separates father and son. Charlie experiences this gap first as a difference of values, then as a conscious lie that his father perpetrates about the end of civilization, and finally as Allie's madness. Hence the deepening loneliness of Charlie, the onset of his manhood, which permits him to see through his father:

> His movements, his travel, were inventions, too. When it looked to him as though America was doomed, he invented a way out. Leaving the country on the banana boat was one of his most ingenious schemes. And Jeronimo had been full of examples of his ingenuity, gadgets he had devised to make life— his life—easier. These schemes and tactics were his answer to the imperfect world. But I sometimes pitied him. Discomfort and dissatisfaction made his brain spin. . . . Selfishness had made him clever. (*M,* 277)

But *The Mosquito Coast* is neither a fiction of happy initiation nor one of triumphant quest. The novel keeps all its terrors alive, and leaves the taste of truth and fear in the mouth. Shot by a missionary whose camp he had set on fire—that same missionary whom he had harangued on the banana boat—crippled from the waist down, Allie is finished off by vultures despite all the care of his starving family, the transcendent loyalty of his wife. Charlie finally attests: "Once I had believed in Father, and the world had seemed very small and old. He was gone, and now I hardly believed in myself, and the world was limitless. . . . No, he was not here. But the pain was so strong I could not mourn him" (*M,* 374). Still, the physical world itself remains; it had not all gone up in flames, after all.

Interestingly, Theroux dedicates the novel "To 'Charlie Fox,' whose story this is and whose courage showed me that the brave cannot be killed. With grateful thanks for many hours of patient explanation and good humor in the face of my ignorant questions." Are we then faced with yet another "nonfiction novel"? The term, like the question, may be otiose: whatever the source of the biographical material, it enjoys the full *re*sources of art. This is first evident in the style which compounds the author's with the narrator's vision. Thus when Allie throws a useless outboard motor into the river, Charlie says: "It sank into the weeds and began bleeding rainbows" (*M,* 343). Elsewhere, the style demonstrates clipped power, like Allie's forefinger hacked to a stump, jabbing at the world, naming all creatures in its sickly paradise, all objects down to the rustiest cotter pin.

The novel's craft is also manifest in its subtle interplay of views. *The Mosquito Coast* is, after all, a torrid family romance, drenched in oedipal violence and guilt. The twin girls are too small to feature in this drama, though they do tend to side with their father. Jerry hates his father, and at times conspires to kill him, but Charlie—first born, and closest of the children to Allie—manages always to restrain him. The mother never flinches in her loyalty to Allie, never abandons him, though she perceives his lowering paranoia. Indeed, from the very start, she provides the most terse and cutting insights into her husband, insights compatible still with her amazing love. "Don't pretend to be better than you are," she says; or "Don't bully us, Allie"; or at the end, at the hairline of dementia, when he proposes to turn the whole family into human torches, she laughs, "Allie, we're too wet to burn." At the same time, she inspires a deep calm in her family, injects "a solution of love and sadness" in Charlie's blood, because she knows both more and less than they do about Father. Without her, the reader could not take the full measure of Allie Fox, of his raging mind, indomitable spirit, and weird humanity—a humanity in demonic risk. And it is she, after all, who finally saves the family, after the children save their parents in their hideout, the Acre, a microcosm utopia, topos of childhood desires and dreams, more organic and more beneficent than the place Allie built only to see blown up into ammonia clouds and smithereens. She saves them because she possesses the love they all lack, that even Charlie lacks, tempted as he is to bite off his dying father's ear, following the example of Spider Mooney.

Swollen as it may be with Allie's incessant rant, that paranoia of the Logos which threatens to supplant the world with words, emphatic and repetitive beyond its needs, *The Mosquito Coast* is still a major American novel, dense with ideas and compelling characters, a tribute to its author's consummate craft. It gathers symbolic echoes, mythic resonances, from every quarter—from Christ, Faust, Prometheus, Crusoe, Ahab, and Frankenstein, from Walden Pond, Brook Farm, and Noah's Ark, from *Huckleberry Finn, Heart of Darkness,* and *Lord of the Flies*—gathers these allusions sometimes glibly, yet ends by fashioning an original, comic, and terrifying work on the fate of the American Self in the nuclear age. And what it says about quest seems irrefutable, informed by history and keen self-recognition at the same time.

6

The characters of Theroux, including his own itinerant personae, give a contemporary sense of quest. They situate it in conditions palpably our own; traveling with them, we feel a stronger grip on the earth. Their landscape stretches south and east; their time spans the sixties and eighties; their social climate includes the turbulences of America and of the third world. Thus, in Theroux's work, the common and the marvelous blend, and geopolitics crackles in lived, concrete details. Thus, too, motion becomes experience, and experience meaning—travel becomes quest.

In the opening of his great essay "Experience," Emerson asks: "Where do we find ourselves? In a series of which we do not know the extremes, and believe that it has none."[11] Something of this sentiment lives in Theroux's journeys, in his ferret curiosity and itch for experience. But something in Emerson's sentiment also escapes him, the feeling that spirit "is its own evidence." What Theroux renders in his quests, fictional or factual—these quests thrive on generic ambiguities as on cultural contrasts—is the comic, seedy, wounded hope of existence, a celebration of shabby whimsies, coaxed grudgingly into spirit or art. Here is Saint Jack on religion, and here, I would wager, Theroux himself:

> I liked my religion to be a private affair ashore, a fire by a stone, a smoky offering; one necessary at night, the light giving the heavens fraternal features to surprise me with the thrill of agreeable company. It was to make the authority of ghosts vanish by making holiness a friendly human act and defining virtue as joy, and grace as permission granted. (*SJ,* 80)

This is as convincing as is on the whole the work of Paul Theroux. But a dyspeptic critic may still want to carp. He may find Theroux rather too prolific and casual; lacking in that imaginative stringency, that inner pressure of mind, which nourishes great art; short often on compassion, and given to gratuitous verbal violence, especially in his nonfictional works; and so much at ease with his own prejudices—say against Hemingway or the Falklands War—as to court bigotry.[12] Such a critic may be speaking from partial knowledge or indulging too much his carping mood. Though

I myself have made space to discuss only five of Theroux's many works, I hope I have given a different sense of his writerly achievement, its variousness, vivacity, acumen, humor, and craft, its openness to experience, the thrill and guilt of motion in it, the zing of its language, a dry-eyed prayer to a polyglot earth.

Chapter Nine
Peter Matthiessen:
The Fullness of Quest

In other days, I understood mountains differently, seeing in them something that abides. Even when approached respectfully (to challenge peaks as mountaineers do is another matter) they appalled me with their "permanence," with that awful and irrefutable *rock*-ness that seemed to intensify my sense of my own transience. Perhaps this dread of transience explains our greed for the few gobbets of raw experience in modern life, why violence is libidinous, why lust devours us, why soldiers choose not to forget their days of horror; we cling to such extreme moments in which we seem to die, yet are reborn. In sexual abandon as in danger, we are impelled, however briefly, into that vital present in which we do not stand apart from life, we *are* life, our being fills us; in ecstasy with another being, loneliness falls away into eternity. But in other days, such union was attainable through simple awe.

                                        —Peter Matthiessen

1

IN PETER MATTHIESSEN, the ideal of quest finds its fullness. Motion, peril, hope, a self at risk, encounters with otherness, urgent spiritual pursuits, meet at the heart of his work. In that work, also, the several personae of Matthiessen—artist, naturalist, explorer, conservationist, social activist, mystic of the real—often blend into a prose writer of unchallengeable distinction.

We first enter Matthiessen's world through that luminous prose, luminous but also thick with shadows. It is a subtle, sinewy prose, resplendent and sometimes surreal, yet also bare and spare when the naturalist speaks, naming the land, the people, the fauna and the flora of the earth. It is the prose of a "closet poet," as Matthiessen modestly allows, perhaps a haiku poet who can see with the eyes of both the Zen adept and the Western scientist. It is a prose, however particular in description, that never loses sight of the whole, a sacramental order of existence. Indeed, at its best, the prose aspires to become a human whale song, about which Matthiessen wrote: "No word conveys the eeriness of the whale song, tuned by the ages to a purity beyond refining, a sound that man should hear each morning to remind him of the morning of creation" (*B*, 11).[1]

Though Matthiessen does not wear his spirituality on his sleeve, the qualities of his explorations, very much like those of his style, refer us back to the domain of nature and spirit conjoined. William Styron once wondered about his friend of nearly forty years: "From whence sprang this amazing obsession to plant one's feet upon the most exotic quarters of the earth, to traverse festering swamps and to scale the aching heights of implausible mountains?"; the motive, Styron supposed, a motive beyond wanderlust or adventure, is that of "a man in ecstatic contemplation of our beautiful and inexplicable planet."[2] Call it a visionary ecology, to which the self seeks lyric and elemental reconciliation.

Is there too much primitivism, romanticism, sentimentalism in all this? Of the last, there is very little in Matthiessen, neither in his prose nor in his stance, unless everything primitive or romantic be considered sentimental from the start. Indubitably, though, Matthiessen reveals much sympathy for the primitive, everything wild, simple, intact; indubitably, he manifests a romantic temper, which he avows and, in his best work, complicates or qualifies.[3] There is no shame, moral or intellectual, in a sensibility so sensuous and answerable to all things live. Nor can civilization banish from itself the spirit of quest, which is the spirit of romance.

2

Questers and shamans also have a biography, a scattering of facts along their life's path. Peter Matthiessen is born in New York in 1927 to affluent parents; his father, a successful architect, has a strong interest in wildlife and serves as trustee to the National Audubon Society. Matthiessen attends the Hotchkiss School, then Yale, with a stint in the U.S. Navy (1945–47), and a junior year at the Sorbonne (1948–49). In 1951, he marries Patricia Southgate, the beautiful daughter of a socially prominent diplomat; they take an airy apartment in Montparnasse. That same year, Matthiessen founds, together with Harold L. Hume, the celebrated and indestructible *Paris Review,* acting as its fiction editor. Paris is becoming a movable feast again after the war, and the "Paris Review crowd"—Matthiessen, Hume, James Baldwin, William Styron, Richard Wright, George Plimpton, Terry Southern, Irwin Shaw—is a bright and talented crowd, not lost like an earlier and perhaps more talented generation.

But the break, the turning point, comes for Matthiessen in 1958: divorce, the journey home. The glittering life, à la Fitzgerald, is not for him. Earlier, in 1956, he visited every wildlife preserve in the United States; he also worked on Long Island with commercial fishermen, and in the summer he skippered charter boats. Now he commences to wander the world, cozier with death than any writer in this study. He travels to the Arctic, Alaska, Amazonia, Africa, Nepal, New Guinea, and on a converted whaler sails through several oceans in search of the Great White Shark. These are scientific expeditions, sponsored by the Sierra Club or the Harvard-Peabody Museum, not reckless adventures or flamboyant larks. These are also the journeys that give Matthiessen the firsthand experiences, the uncanny details, which thicken his work.

The books, more than twenty of them to date, achieve popularity and recognition — prizes, medals, National and American Book Awards, membership in the American Academy and Institute of Arts and Letters — but they fail, somehow, to enter the academic canon. This is predictable. Though many of the books espouse current social and ecological causes — the titles are revealing: *Wildlife in America* (1959), *Sal si puedes: Cesar Chavez and the New American Revolution* (1970), *In the Spirit of Crazy Horse* (1983), *Indian Country* (1984), *Men's Lives: The Surfmen and Baymen of the South Fork* (1986) — none conforms to current academic ideologies, "materialist" or otherwise.

But matter and spirit have never been separable in the practical ethos of Zen. As I have noted, Matthiessen is most reluctant to "brandish" his Zen: "It's just a quiet little practice, not a religion . . . just a way of seeing the world that is closely tied in with the way American Indian people see the world."[4] For him, Zen practice is simply "life practice"; self-conscious spirituality is what masters call the "stink of Zen." The "life practice" informs Matthiessen's journals, which yield some autobiographical insight.

Nine-Headed Dragon River: Zen Journals, 1969-1982 (1987) is informative, sometimes revealing, finally disappointing — it does not penetrate or cohere enough. Two figures, or perhaps emanations, pervade it: Deborah Love, Matthiessen's second wife, dying of metastatic cancer, and Eihei Dogen, the great thirteenth-century Soto Zen master. The tension between these two figures, between error and aspiration, guilt and atonement, is never resolved in Matthiessen's life; the ability to rest in the present in a state of wondrous simplicity is only sporadically, shadowily achieved.

In a preface, Matthiessen admits that his book is not really "his" at all; it is a compendium of teachings and so properly belongs to the Zen community of New York. This may explain, despite some numinous poems, its labored quality as it struggles to become autobiography, history of Zen, exposition of Buddhism, description of natural scenes (often the best in the book), and account of a pilgrimage to the great Zen monasteries of Japan all at once. Still, autobiographical rays break through clouds of learning, often with painful clarity; these illumine Matthiessen's past and present quests.

In 1968, after seven months in Africa, Matthiessen returns to his home in Sagaponack, Long Island, to find three inscrutable Japanese Zen masters in his driveway. Deborah Love, it seems, has been studying The Way for a number of years, and Matthiessen now decides to take it up in the spirit more of challenge than of devotion. (It turns out, in fact, that his great-grandfather was senior partner in the firm that hosted the first visit of a Zen master, Soyen Shaku, to America in the 1890s.) Zen and marriage, in any case, become intimates; for though husband and wife seem profoundly in love, their marriage approaches a crisis which they try to avert through spiritual discipline. Matthiessen succeeds in making some breakthroughs, minor illuminations or *kensho*s. He writes: "Then I let my breath go, gave my self up to immersion in all things, to a joyous *belonging* so overwhelming that tears of relief poured from my eyes. For the first time since unremembered childhood, I was not alone, there was no separate 'I.' Wounds, ragged edges, hollow places were all gone. . . . *Nothing was needed* . . ." (*N,* 21).

But this partial "state of grace" does not endure, though it recurs. Nor can these *kensho*s finally assuage the fear and rage of Deborah's dying, the ugly paranoia of death, the ravaging pains of terminal cancer, as Matthiessen renders them in the most moving, the most harrowing, the most human chapter in the book. Forgiveness, surcease from remorse, these the couple finds in transfiguring moments; grace remains, to the end, more doubtful. As Matthiessen himself dolefully notes: "The opening [or *kensho*] had been premature, and its power seeped away, month after month" (*N,* 27). The "monkey mind" clings, yearns, will not stay still. Thus, in one of the many haikus that dot the text, Matthiessen mourns:

> *Here I am in Sagaponack,*
> *Yet my heart longs for Sagaponack*   (*N,* 29)

In *Nine-Headed Dragon River*—the title alludes to the mystic wisdom of the dragon as well as to the valley in which Dogen founded his great monastery in Japan—Matthiessen reveals himself to be an indefatigable aspirant; he never pretends to have attained enlightenment. He will sit fourteen hours a day in *zazen* (the orthodox posture of meditation); he will go on sleepless pilgrimages to remote monasteries in Japan or Nepal. But he will not sweep his failures, his conflicts, under a Zen mat. Thus he acknowledges the tension between the "silence" of Zen and his own discursiveness, between the dispassion of the former and his social activism, between monastic obedience and his innate rebelliousness, between Japanese and American values — or, as I have said, simply between Dogen and Deborah, emblems of his love.

The man, resisting to shave his head like a monk, the engaged publicist, above all the artist — all of them strain continually against Zen, and the journals are themselves both cause and result of that strain. The man says: "After four years of hard *zazen,* my right knee is suddenly so sore that I must tape it. I use aspirin, heat pads, liniment, but can not bring myself to do *zazen* in a chair. Alas, this is no evidence of grit or dedication but only ineradicable male vanity" (*N,* 60). And the artist considers his addiction to literature a kind of mental greed, an impediment to his holy progress, yet prefers to write up his notes on a previous Himalayan journey — the result is a National and American Book Awards winner, *The Snow Leopard* (1978) — over intense Zen practice. Still, Matthiessen completes his training, qualifies technically as a Soto Zen monk with the Dharma name of Muryo, and his American-born teacher, Tetsugen Glassman-sensei, to whom the journals are dedicated, officiates in 1981 over his third marriage to Maria Eckhart.

If *Nine-Headed Dragon River,* then, is the record of a spiritual quest, a quest that both as literature and as religion leaves a bittersweet taste, the work nonetheless discloses a powerful and abiding motive in its author's life, perhaps in all our lives. Matthiessen puts it at the end in the form of a natural parable:

> The nymph is a mud-colored water dweller of forbidding aspect and rapacious habit that preys on small fish and other creatures until the day comes when it hauls its heavy body from the water, affixes itself to wood or stone, and struggles to cast off its thick carapace, permitting its translucent, sunfilled dragon-fly nature to take wing.
>
> At sunrise, the new dragonfly was almost free, a beautiful golden thing, silvered by dew, resting a little, twitching its transparent wings, yet not quite liberated from the crude armor of its former life. When I gasped like the young monk on the mountain, unable to repress a delighted comment, Soen-roshi pointed sternly at the meditation hall: "Now do your *best!*" (*N,* 255)

3

Matthiessen, however, did not spend his life in meditation halls. Some of his nonfictional works chronicle adventures; some, like *The Snow Leopard,* turn adventures into quests; nearly all reveal a radical restlessness, an unappeased primal need. The need, however intimate, finally claims Nature as ally, and claims all those who live in her harsh embrace: game wardens, migrant workers, commercial fishermen, conservationists, explorers, primitives.[5] Thus most of Matthiessen's expeditions meld personal, social, scientific, philosophic, and, above all, *literary* interests—the *New Yorker* did sponsor his earliest peregrinations.

But where is quest in all this? It remains virtual, implicit, in most of his earlier nonfictions. Full of engrossing actions and versatile knowledge, these works strike us finally as allegories of reconciled or, more often, failed existence: that is, allegories of man and beast in their natural element, of a wildness receding continually before civilization and nations wavering in the glare of history, of life itself, evolving or devolving in the invisible corridors of time—allegories of the human race, in all its unimagined variety, seeking to make sense of its destiny. Predictably, the allegories take on the hues of myth, prophecy, elegy, and monition all at the same time, as in this unattributed passage from *Indian Country:*

> One thing we know which the white man may one day discover. Our God is the same God. You may think now that you own Him as you wish to own our land. But you cannot. . . . The whites too shall pass—perhaps sooner than other tribes. Continue to contaminate your bed, and you will one night suffocate in your own waste. When the buffalo are all slaughtered, the wild horses all tamed, the secret corners of the forest heavy with the scent of many men, and the view of the ripe hills blotted by talking wires, where is the thicket? Gone. Where is the eagle? Gone. And what is it to say good-by to the swift and the hunt, the end of living and the beginning of survival? (*I,* 8)

We can not take this to be Matthiessen's own view, which in a Westerner today may seem a little tender. But we can take it as a view the West has proven unable to replace or even to mediate. "My hope is that these Indian voices," Matthiessen says in his introduction, "eloquent and bitter, humorous and sad, will provide what history and statistics cannot, a sense of that profound 'life way' which could illuminate our own dispirited consumer culture" (*I,* xii). This, at least, is the beginning, if only a beginning, of mediation.

The sentiment, in any case, expresses the intent of Matthiessen whose work always reaches for meaning, value, belief, even in the most descriptive, the most impersonal of narratives. *Under the Mountain Wall* (1962), for instance, set in the highlands of New Guinea, reads like an anthropological novel about Papuan chieftains, their warriors, families, enemies. Presumably, as Matthiessen says, the expedition offers a "unique chance, perhaps the last, to describe a lost culture in the terrible beauty of its pure estate" (*U,* xiv). But the third-person narrative, blending local myths, ethnographic detail, and dramatic actions (nearly always violent), also raises overwhelming questions. The questions center, first, on the disturbing alterity of "Stone Age" Papuans and on their equally disturbing sameness to any reader, center also on the history of Dutch-Indonesian colonization and the future of all "natives." Above all, the book powerfully evokes cosmic rhythms, the "wax and wane of ice-age seas."

The same cosmic rhythms beat through *The Tree Where Man Was Born* (1972). Vibrant with Eliot Porter's photographs, the work takes us on a spiritual safari through East Africa. As usual, Matthiessen has a pretext for starting out: in this case, an invitation from Jack Owen, director of Tanzania's National Parks, to observe wildlife at the Serengeti Research Institute. There, true geophile, Matthiessen acts as witness to the earth, noting with wondrous concreteness its vital evidence, noting more sadly the ruin of vast ecosystems. There, too, as in all his journeys, he meets humanity on its own terms, meets the maimed, the indigent, the dispossessed, meets them as they submit — even the indomitable Masai! — to the trials of civilization.

Matthiessen observes accurately, without rote. He can be hard on unprivileged nations, he can be hard on himself; he has taught himself to regard death with clarity. Watching a dying lioness, he unexpectedly declares his sympathies "with the predator, not with the hunted," then goes on to note:

> Still grunting, she licked passionately at the grass, and her haunches shuddered in long spasms, and this last abandon shattered the detachment I had felt until that moment. I was swept by a wave of feeling, then a pang so sharp that, for a moment, I felt sick, as if all the waste and loss in life, the harm one brings to oneself and others, had been drawn to a point in this lonely passage between light and darkness. (*T,* 138)

There is nothing false here, nothing scanted. Nor is there anything false in this passage, at once radiant and poised, with which the book — The Tree of Man? — starts:

> The tree where man was born, according to the Nuer, still stood within man's memory in the west part of the south Sudan, and I imagine a great baobab thrust up like an old root of life in those wild grasses that blow forever to the horizons, and wild man in naked silhouette against the first blue sky. That bodeful man of silence and the past is everywhere in Africa. One hears the silence, hears one's step, and stops . . . and he is there, in the near distance. I see him still: a spear point glitters in the sun. (*T,* 22)

The foregoing works suggest the ambience but not the particular character of quest in Matthiessen. Hints of that character, though, appear in two narratives, both told with the imminence of first-person experience.

In *The Cloud Forest* (1961), Matthiessen undertakes one of his earliest voyages into the wilderness, prodigious Amazonia. Subtitled a "chronicle" again, the journey seeks, like future journeys, to penetrate time even more than space. Certainly he attends minutely to his spatial environment: a freighter is "warped swiftly from her berth," a stevedore lets "the last hawser slap into the water" (C, 1). But the sense of disjunction, time jarred out of its course, affects him even more deeply: "Now the tug is gone, and there comes a sense of uncertainty, of loss. This is not entirely homesickness; a continuity has been broken with the desertion of that tug, as if life must now start up all over again" (C, 2). This could have been the commencement of quest, its beginnings in a metaphysical twinge.

But the narrative, though rich in factual and poetic interest — Marston Bates has compared it to H. M. Tomlinson's *The Sea and the Jungle* and Peter Fleming's *Brazilian Adventure,* paragons of Amazonian travel literature — the narrative proceeds without any awareness of itself as a personal quest.[6] It proceeds, rather, as an adventure upon which the hero is almost too modest to intrude. Matthiessen perceives; unlike Theroux, he does not rush to judge. Thus, though repelled by the cluttered vulgarity of church interiors in South America, he typically admits his inability to comment fairly on colonial Spanish architecture. Thus also, while braving genuine dangers — jaguars, anacondas, alligators, piranhas, murderous rapids, aroused Indians — dangers in the Urubamba and Ucayali basins, he describes himself as neither explorer nor seeker but simply a man on an "outing."

Hints of quest nonetheless flicker throughout the story. These do not refer to secret pre-Colombian ruins or giant prehistoric fossils (the *mandibula* of some extinct monster) that Matthiessen "discovers," or at least photographs. The hints pertain rather — since he is no Indiana Jones — to the mystery of human existence, his own. Matthiessen learns something about his moodiness, stubbornness, fits of garrulous jollity, about his fear as well as need for risk. He learns much about nature, and about his attitude to nature; at one point, "drunk with power," he cuts down crocodiles with a rifle, knowing in advance that he will keenly regret the impulse. Above all, he learns a unique kind of happiness, an intuition of a world seemingly complete, delivered from time, from death. The passage deserves to be given whole:

> I haven't said that I've had a magnificent morning. I have. And curiously, the magnificence did not consist of finding what we were after — more poor old bones, and thus a certain scientific confirmation of the site — but lay instead in the purity of this jungle stream. Only a few woodcutters like Juan Pablo, seeking the isolated *cedro* and *caoba* trees, may ever have ascended this *quebrada,* and there is no mark of the white man's heavy hand upon it. Its still banks are laced with the tracks of tapir, capybara, and other creatures, and its clear water, running quietly on sandy shoals, sparkles with the flash of the pretty *sabalo.* In the bends the water runs beneath stone banks and is a pure,

limpid green, and the trees which lend their leaf color to the water soar away in great white columns. The queer and clumsy hoatsin huffs everywhere in the lower branches, and hidden birds of unknown shape and color whistle and answer down the cool silences, in counterpoint and incredible clear harmonies. The tree frogs loose their prodigious croaks, and from a mile away resounds one of the mightiest sounds in nature, like nothing so much as an ominous moan of wind, the community howl of the *mono colorado* — the red howler monkey. In the stream itself lie the striking shells of a variety of mollusks, including a gastropod so large — the size of a very large pear — that it is difficult to believe it is not a marine creature. (Louis Agassiz, a century ago, pointed out the marine character of the dolphins, fishes, and other aquatic fauna of the Amazon basin.) We paused to breakfast on a kind of nut, the Indian name for which has now escaped me, and I wondered why the stream itself was so much more exciting than the bones we had found in it — more exciting than the first sight of the great jaw itself the night before. And it occurred to me that, aside from its beauty — for it is precisely this inner, mysterious quality of the jungle, represented so well by this lost stream, that I have been searching for and feel I have found at last — there was an adventure here, an exploration, however timid. (*C,* 239f.)

Deliverance, we see, is momentary; it only serves to renew the promise of adventure, the whisper of a perilous quest almost fulfilled. Certainly *The Cloud Forest* simulates the form of classic journeys in "the heart of darkness," simulates the form without its density of allusions, its duskier self-apprehensions. For Matthiessen, the full achievement of quest was yet to come.

It does not come in *Blue Meridian: The Search for the Great White Shark* (1971), which nonetheless gestures at quest. Here Peter Gimbel, organizer of the expedition, holds the center. Another scion of affluence, Gimbel is a banker turned adventurer, and shares with Matthiessen, another Peter, many impulses — they both skydive, for instance, during the fifties, when skydiving was hardly a sport, and they both roam, independently, the Amazon. Gimbel longs for a confrontation with the formidable shark, "the white death," as challenge and exorcism; Matthiessen admits only to the challenge. Both are eager, indeed anxious, to test their limits, swimming with sharks — *not* the Great White — even in their feeding frenzy. Gimbel puts it simply: "We came, really, when you get right down to it, to see what the limits are, just how wildly — that's the wrong word — just how openly a man can expose himself in the water with excited sharks and still maintain control" (*B,* 160f.). And Matthiessen concurs: ". . . I am sympathetic with Peter [Gimbel]'s need to find out what the limits are; the original motivations may be ambiguous but attacks upon this [dangerous] life style are often ambiguous as well, as if the need to attack betrayed a fear in the attacker that his own life seeps away from him unlived" (*B,*

162). (Matthiessen has particularly in mind a woman who vehemently calls risk takers "silly and childish.")

Blue Meridian ends with terrific and terrifying scenes of encounter with the "white death," filmed underwater from flimsy aluminum cages, and so proves itself, despite shades of psychic failure and fleeting introspection, a rousing adventure tale, not a focused human quest. Still, at the close of the book, Gimbel — *not* Matthiessen — reflects: "I was filled with a terrible sadness that we had indeed determined precisely the limits we sought, that the mystery was at least partly gone because we knew that we could get away with anything, that the story — and such a story! — has an end" (*B*, 204). This is indeed the sadness of quest, a quest hinted more than realized.

4

The preceding texts, I have already noted, delimit the interior landscape of Peter Matthiessen, the terrain of his imagination. Against their background, his best quest, one of the most compelling in this study, takes shape.

The journey in *The Snow Leopard* is both real, painstakingly real, and also mythic, both personal and universal. The work itself is rooted at every level in autobiography. Dedicated to three Zen *roshis* whom Matthiessen portrays reverently in *Nine-Headed Dragon River,* permeated by memories of Deborah Love whose agonizing death we have witnessed there, written in the first person as a series of diary entries, the book testifies to its author's felt self, his full life. Its incentive is also practical: Matthiessen accompanies the wildlife biologist George Schaller — they met at the Serengeti Research Institute in Africa — who wants to observe the November rutting of Himalayan blue sheep, and perhaps glimpse that shyest, rarest, and "most beautiful of cats," the snow leopard. At the same time, the space of the journey teems with mountain gods and legendary beasts, monks, mystics, lunatics, and bandits roaming at altitudes of more than seventeen thousand feet, prophets riding the icy winds, astride snow leopards sometimes, and *bodhisattvas* who look like lowly porters. Then again, the destination of Matthiessen, the Crystal Monastery at Shey Gompa in Nepal's Inner Dolpo, appears on any good map of the region.

The journey does not begin auspiciously. Matthiessen himself starts in a troubled state. Deborah has just died, leaving him with two children. The widower nonetheless resolves to undertake his pilgrimage, as if to cleanse himself, come to terms with his wound. The snow leopard becomes for him a symbol of spiritual knowledge or attainment, though he never manages to see it — Schaller, a "stern pragmatist," does. Matthiessen's Zen teacher had warned him back in New York: "Do not expect too much";

that is, "You may not be ready to see the leopard."[7] But in Zen, the admonition could also mean: "To see or not to see the leopard is the same; *satori* simply comes." In any case, the journey begins ominously with thirty hours of continuous rain in Kathmandu. Later, a group of shrouded figures bearing a corpse crosses the path of his Land Rover, arousing in him feelings of "dim, restless foreboding." And a little later on the road, he sees an ancient Hindu, propped up on a basket, entirely "ravened from within": "I nod to Death in passing," Matthiessen soberly notes, "aware of the sound of my own feet upon my path" (*S,* 13).

Death attends this journey, attends it as awareness not simply quietus, though Matthiessen keeps his foot steady at the edge of dizzying mountain chasms. The journey itself proceeds in several dimensions: horizontal (from Kathmandu to the Crystal Mountain), vertical (from valleys, through mountain passes, close to unassailable peaks), temporal (present to past, modern to medieval), cultural (West to East and back again), generic (alternating between the forms of autobiography, didactic essay, theological tract, ecological disquisition, naturalist catalogue, poetic and philosophical meditation), and spiritual (a "journey of the heart," toward enlightenment). Taken as a whole, the diary appears as a continuous dialogue of heterocosms, straining for peace between the One and the Many in all their manifestations.

Matthiessen, however, does not write abstractly, and this is the triumph of his book. Though he hears "whispers of a paradisal age" in the mountains, his boots are full of blood from walking. Altogether *there,* he does not look away from children with broken legs or swollen bellies; nor will he allow himself, and us, to forget the face of the loveliest child he has ever seen, sitting with others in a circle, drinking buffalo blood. One day's trek may take him a century back; but he also recalls the turmoils of America in the sixties. And though he may read the universe as scripture like any good Zen or Christian adept, he can record each and every finite detail in its unalterable quiddity. A haunting immediacy characterizes his depictions of actions as well as objects. Here is Matthiessen, after crawling along a foot-wide ledge, waiting for the porters to catch up:

> For some time now, the chattering, laughing voices of the B'on-pos have been coming up behind. At that dangerous point of the cliff, an extraordinary thing happens. Not yet in view, the nine fall silent. . . . Then one by one, the nine figures round the point of rock in silhouette, unreal beneath big bulky loads that threaten each second to bump the cliff and nudge them over the precipice. On they come, staring straight ahead, as steadily and certainly as ants, yet seeming to glide with an easy, ethereal lightness, as if some sort of inner concentration was lifting them just off the surface of the ground. Bent far forward against the tump lines around their foreheads, fingers spread wide by

way of balance, they touch the cliff face lightly to the left side, stroke the north
wind to the right. Light fingertips touch my upper leg . . . but their intensity
is such that they seem not to distinguish between cold rock face and warm
blue jeans. Mute, unknowing, dull eyes glazed, the figures brush past . . . leaving behind in the clear air the smell of grease and fires. When the bad stretch
is past, the hooting instantly resumes, perhaps at the point that they left off,
as if all had awakened from a trance. (*S,* 155f.)

Personal and social insights also root the book into the world. Thus,
for instance, Matthiessen comments on his companion, George Schaller,
in a moment of strain:

Hunched in a cold and soggy sleeping bag amongst the puddles, I have envied the owner of the·crisp blue tent next door, and perhaps these base feelings fired our first argument, this dark morning, when GS tossed used cans
and papers into the schoolyard. He asserted that he did so because the local
people are always avid for containers, which is true. But why not set the cans
upon the wall instead of littering the place, and making the people pick them
up out of the mud? (*S,* 36)

The comment yields quickly, magnanimously, to others on Schaller's dedication, intelligence, and great stamina.

Matthiessen also portrays with deft sympathy the Nepalese. Predictably,
he most admires the Sherpas for their courage, dignity, altruism, their
"merry defencelessness." His journey puts him in constant interaction with
various natives, including porters, tribesmen, villagers, monks, lamas, who
form a tacit hierarchy—lamas and Sherpas at the top precisely because
they are the most selfless. He favors one particularly, Tukten by name, a
rogue Sherpa who demeans himself by serving as porter. Part trickster and
part *bodhisattva,* Tukten radiates an inner repose, the aura of a "crazy
wisdom," a shade disreputable. In him, nonetheless, Matthiessen finds a
kindred spirit, speaking an alien tongue.

But the worldliness of the book comes also from its roots in America,
Matthiessen's own "psychedelic years." His eerie mountain environment,
inhabited by the simplest human needs, acts on him as a mute critique
of his own society, its "corrosive money rot," its "retreat from wonder,"
its "proliferations without joy" (*S,* 42). Thus, indirectly, Matthiessen remarks on race, sex, drugs, power, violence in America during the sixties,
perceived now from the austere, wholly essential perspective of the Himalayas. Not that Asians appear altogether feckless, true innocents like the
sennin or solitary mountain idiots. Repeatedly, Matthiessen shows that if
Western colonialism seems inexpugnable, even in the remotest Himalayan
ranges, so is Asian caste prejudice, so is human venality, greed.

The world, in fact, may be too much with Matthiessen: continually, he recalls his wife, his children, his friends. The pangs of Deborah's love persist, an unfinished passion, though five months before her death the couple had decided to divorce. Matthiessen also recalls Alex, their youngest son, who once stood rapt in his sandbox, "as doves and redwings came and went on the warm wind, the leaves dancing, the clouds flying, birdsong and sweet smell of privet and rose. The child was not observing; he was at rest in the very center of the universe . . ." (*S*, 41). But then, at eight, Alex has already begun to shut away "the wildness of the world," begun to fall into a more common day—precisely that dull, quotidian day from which his father, in the faraway Dolpo, is trying to awake.

Hence, despite all its worldliness, *The Snow Leopard* remains the quest of one man for another reality, another "day," or at least for a way to mediate between worlds. Matthiessen concedes at the start that he carries with him several "I's": one who observes, another who recalls, a third, exhausted, lies down to sleep . . . but always, somewhere, the one who pursues. He suspects that he may have contracted the Kierkegaardian "sickness of infinitudes," the wanderer's curse: "I only knew that at the bottom of each breath there was a hollow place that needed to be filled" (*S*, 43). And so, in a ritual of dispossession—we have seen this gesture in other writers before—he removes his watch, shedding time; for the true *yeti*, "homegoing" is always Now.

Not that the journey lacks movement, difficulties to overcome. The dangers of snow blindness, frozen toes, rolling boulders, lost supplies, and sheer, transfixing heights are omnipresent. Nor are the dangers physical only. True to its moment, the quest swarms with ambiguities. Matthiessen recalls earlier *kensho*s, instants of provisional insight, only to relapse into black moods. When he reaches the remote Crystal Monastery, from which nothing is visible but snow and sky, he finds it deserted. He never glimpses the leopard, never answers the pertinent *koan*. He even begins to suspect that the willed act of searching may preclude the finding. And he worries that entrusting his experiences to the written word may falsify them irrevocably. Finally, in Patan, after journey's end, he awaits Tukten at a Buddhist monastery, waits at the rendezvous in vain. Thinking that he may have been spared the "desolation of success," Matthiessen looks, on the last day of his three-month journey, at his face in the mirror: "In the gaunt, brown face in the mirror—unseen since last September—the blue eyes in a monkish skull seem eerily clear, but this is the face of a man I do not know" (*S*, 328).

That stranger's face may be the face behind every human face, a face in and out of time. For even in the high, sublunary landscape of the Dolpo, where lungs gasp with each breath and life itself seems but a thin stain on eternity, history and politics continually obtrude. The wounded, whimsical Western seeker finds himself, recurrently, *between* worlds. All around him, the evidence of poverty is excruciating, and dogs eat human excrement. As Matthiessen puts it: "Confronted with the pain of Asia, one cannot look and cannot turn away" (*S,* 12). This may be the penultimate word on the interface between certain cultures, less interface than hideous scar which only a *bodhisattva* could steadily contemplate. As for the rest of us — perhaps even for Matthiessen — the ultimate word may be inconclusive quest, intermittent pain.

To say that *The Snow Leopard* may be inconclusive, however, is not to say that it fails as either spiritual quest or literary work. Indeed, the stunning achievement of the book is that it convinces a sympathetic reader that he has attained a measure of enlightenment himself; that he, too, could wake up some morning from a dream of white, supernal light. It all seems so near at hand, as in this epiphany of a wafted feather:

> A white down feather, sun-filled, dances before me on the wind: alighting nowhere, it balances on a shining thorn, goes spinning on. Between this white feather, sheep dung, light, and the fleeting aggregate of atoms that is "I," there is no particle of difference. There is a mountain opposite, but this "I" is opposite nothing, opposed to nothing.
>
> I grow into these mountains like a moss. I am bewitched. The blinding snow peaks and the clarion air, the sound of earth and heaven in the silence, the requiem birds, the mythic beasts, the flags, great horns, and old carved stones, the rough-hewn Tartars in their braids and homespun boots, the silver ice in the black river, the Kang, the Crystal Mountain. Also, I love the common miracles — the murmur of my friends at evening, the clay fires of smudgy juniper, the coarse dull food, the hardship and simplicity, the contentment of doing one thing at a time: when I take my blue tin cup into my hand, that is all I do. (*S,* 238)

As a literary work, though, *The Snow Leopard* falls short of the perfection it seeks. The failure is largely due to its massive interpolations of Oriental religion and personal history, homily and flashback, crammed in. This forced quality stems from the ambition of the work itself. Written as a journal, beginning September 28, 1973, and every day thereafter into December, the book unfolds, Paul Zweig saw, "not as a story but as a filled space of perception."[8] Matthiessen wants to jam his whole existence into three months. And he nearly succeeds, rendering his story in the present tense, that eternal present of Zen. Yet with a little more reticence toward his illuminations — these, in all but the greatest masters, skirt always narcissism — Matthiessen might have consecrated his high moments in a finer, tauter form. Still, *The Snow Leopard* must perdure as a landmark in the literature of quest; for, in addition to all its spiritual virtues, it gives immaculate attention to the phenomenal world, to the abrupt glory of things as they are. Paradoxically, the seeker, a self at risk, comes closest to his end when he loses all self-concern, attending to attention and to the created world. With death the book began, with another kind of death it hopes to transfigure the quest.

5

As a young man in Paris, Matthiessen commenced his literary career by writing short stories, one of which won the prestigious *Atlantic* Prize in 1951. Since then, he has written five novels, *Race Rock* (1954), *Partisans* (1955), *Raditzer* (1961), *At Play in the Fields of the Lord* (1965), and *Far Tortuga* (1975), and has never ceased to cherish that genre. As he says about a forthcoming novel: "I'm extremely happy that I'm back to fiction—it's been a *very* long time—and I hope to stay there. I prefer writing fiction; I find it exhilarating. . . . I'm worn out by nonfiction."[9] (This recalls Paul Theroux.) Certainly Matthiessen's earlier fiction is accomplished if sometimes ornate, written with the autobiographical intensity of youth, touching on themes—marital discord, the psychology of misfits, utopian or existential politics—rife in the fifties and early sixties. Only two of these novels, however, bear on quest; they are his last two and by far his best.[10]

Far Tortuga is the more original, the more astonishing achievement—and the less pertinent to quest. The book has some aspects of a postmodern literary "experiment": typographic variations and blank spaces on the page, ink drawings and boat diagrams, lists. Its visual effects, as some critics have noted, recall Pound's *Cantos* or Olson's *Maximus Poems,* though Matthiessen himself adduces the influences of *sumi* brush painting, haiku poetry, the spare, direct self-presentation of screenplays. Thus he describes his work:

> *Far Tortuga* is based on a sea turtle fishing voyage off Nicaragua: *tortuga* is the Spanish word for sea turtle, and sometimes refers to a cay where green turtles are found. I started work on the book in 1966, and since then, it's been put aside many times, but I never tired of it. I was moved by the stark quality of that voyage, everything worn bare by wind and sea—the reefs, the faded schooner, the turtle men themselves—everything so pared down and so simple that metaphors, stream-of-consciousness, even such ordinary conventions of the novel as "he said" or "he thought," seemed intrusive, even offensive, and a great impediment, besides. So from the start I was feeling my way toward a spare form, with more air around the words, more space: I wanted the descriptions to be very clear and flat, to find such poetry as they might attain in their very directness and simplicity. In fact, I can only recall one simile in the whole book. And eventually, I attempted using white space to achieve reso-

nance, to make the reader receive things intuitively, hear the silence in the wind, for instance, that is a constant presence in the book.[11]

The lone simile refers to Far Tortuga, "like a memory in the ocean emptiness" (*F,* 336), a blessed isle, teeming with turtles, marked on old sea charts as the Misteriosa Cay which may have worn off in hurricanes, but was more probably "a mere dream and legend of the turtle men" (*F,* 3). Between a vanishing past and an elemental present, the *Lillian Eden* sails with Captain Raib and assorted derelicts, till it founders on the Misteriosa reefs—allegorically, Eden foundering on its own dream—leaving nothing behind except wind, sky, sun, stars, sea, leaving no one behind except a black Honduran Ishmael, known as Speedy. That, in starkest outline, constitutes the action of *Far Tortuga,* its skeletal myth.

The myth, though, is fleshed in Matthiessen's fiction; the story, narrated in the present tense, dramatically recapitulates both cosmic process and personal destiny. The characters live first in the cadences of Caribbean speech, the twang and slur of native dialects.[12] They live, too, in the illusion of a sheer "objective" presence—the author interprets nothing, quotes no one—like self-evident facts of nature. But this is an artistic illusion, the effect of a virtuoso verbal performance. For the characters live, above all, in their private obsessions, tacit identity—Speedy, particularly, a survivor, quick of understanding and swift with a knife, determined to get back to his "fifty-five acres, mon, and cows," and Captain Raib Avers, the central tragic figure of the book.

Captain Raib is one of the last "wind captains" in the Caribbean, descendant of generations of turtlers. He is brave, demanding, cruel sometimes, yet stubbornly human and a high achiever. But history—the novel's refrain is "modern times, mon"—has passed him by. Diesel has supplanted sail; tourists are everywhere; the green turtles have departed. The schooner he commands has no running lights, no life jackets, no fire equipment; its shrouds are frayed, its catboats leak; and its radio, out of joint with the times, can only receive messages. The crew of eight is ragged, mostly drunk or thievish, coming apart at the seams. And the voyage itself, belated, starts tardily in the turtling season.

The voyage of the *Lillian Eden* may echo myth and a long tradition of fated sea journeys.[13] But it is not a voyage of quest; nor is Captain Raib really a seeker. Above all, he wants to preserve, vindicate, the past; maniacally, he refuses to become a living anachronism. As two of his men, discussing him behind his broad ominous back, say:

> I don't know, mon. As a coptin, he okay. Got to give de mon dat much; he know de sea. It only de way he treat de men—dat de back-time way.

He a wind coptin, dass de trouble. He a sailin mon, and he used to de old-time way. All his life he been ziggin and zaggin, he don't know how to go straight. (*F,* 127)

The "ziggin and zaggin" give Raib his bitterly human quality. In a rare unguarded moment, he admits the acrid loneliness of his life to Speedy. Raib's sons, except Buddy — inept and seasick always, with a deep, unrequited love for his father — desert him to work in Tampa or Miami; his crews abandon him, finding him too hard a taskmaster; the fisheries have lost their purpose. Still, what gives him tragic stature is his hard, unforgiving vision of existence. For Raib does not see himself merely as a victim of history, "modern times, mon"; he is a battler in an inhuman universe. Here is the essential vision, in an interchange between Byrum, a recalcitrant deckhand, and Raib:

> Time is changin, mon. De old days a mon burn de johnnycake, he walk de plank. Dese days we got unions and all of dat. A mon got rights.

A long silence. Then Raib speaks quietly.

> You hear dat rushin out dere, Byrum? De wind and de sea comin together? Dat de sound of *hell,* boy, dat de sound of *hell!* You way out on de edge, boy, you out on de edge of de world. No mon! Ain't no unions on de turtle banks, I tellin you dat! Ain't no rights out here! Ain't nothin out here but de reefs and de wind and de sea, and de mon who know de bleak ocean de best has got to be de coptin, and de men don't listen to de coptin, dey stand a very good chance of losin dere lifes! (*F,* 225f.)

Far Tortuga is unquestionably a grand and brilliant achievement, inviting comparisons with Conrad's *The Nigger of the Narcissus* and prompting James Dickey to say that its "passionate impressionism" has given American fiction a new vision. Its unique, elliptical style, a tour de force some may deprecatingly claim, excludes nothing vital. The book teems with characters, anecdotes, actions — arson, murder, piracy, shipwreck — family quarrels, the lore of the islands, the natural history of the Caribbean, its birds and fish, winds and currents, its ever-changing sea. Still, the terms of quest apply to it only obliquely. If the captain and crew of the *Lillian Eden* search for mysterious Far Tortuga, a treacherous Eden sunk barely beneath the surface of the sea, they bring to their search no awareness of its larger sense, its place in their lives or its ultimate meaning. This is true even of Captain Raib Avers who only flickers into a consciousness of quest. The last judgment of the book is "Far Tortuga sinks beneath the sea" (*F,* 380). This elemental sentence may serve as fit epitaph to a way of life; it can not inspirit quest. However grand, the novel remains eccentric to the concern of *Selves at Risk* — hence my truncated discussion of it here.

This is not the case with *At Play in the Fields of the Lord.* Though more traditional in form, the novel engages directly, amply, the subject of quest. Set in deep Amazonia, it revels in contrasts: Nature and Civilization, South and North America, Animist and Christian religions, Catholic and Protestant missionaries, the Indian and the White Man. The novel, though, like its lush, jungle-green setting, finally overcomes its own antinomies. Thus, for instance, though Protestant missionaries — Leslie Huben, Martin and Hazel Quarrier — seem far more bigoted than the Dominican priest, Father Xantes, it is Martin Quarrier who achieves knowledge, a kind of bungling martyrdom in the rain forest. And though Indians seem guileless compared with the fanatic, genocidal White Man, they too, the Niarunas and kindred Yurimahas, can prove stupid, greedy, and murderous: at an earlier time, they enslaved the "filthy Tiro" tribe. There is no paradise in this novel, no Edenic world that does not contain its Serpent, contain already its Cains and Abels.

The real focus of ambiguity in the novel, however, the real focus of its energy, is Lewis Meriwether Moon, a halfbreed Cheyenne-Canuck turned outlaw. Together with another soldier of fortune, Wolfie, a squat, knife-wielding, bearded Jew, he flies into Madre de Dios — Matthiessen does not identify the nation — in an old, pocked, stolen Mustang marked "Wolfie & Moon, Inc. Small Wars and Demolitions." Moon belongs to no world; his icy rage has closed his heart and snapped his teeth shut. Thus he appears the metaphysical drifter par excellence, owning nothing except bitter memories of humiliation and injustice, traveling always and traveling light. Even his sidekick, Wolfie, fears him, yet intuits an implacable contradiction in his character, a "beautiful" side and another "meaner than catshit" (*AP,* 69).

Still, something stirs in Moon's spirit. Even in the jungle, where no personal past or future counts, he thinks of himself, ironically, as the "great halfbreed of the world," precursor of a miscegenated earth. In a village latrine, recalling all the latrines he has visited, he broods that none has yielded him an answer; or "rather that it always came up with the same answer, a suck and gurgle of unspeakable vileness, a sort of self-satisfied low chuckling: Go to it man, you're pissing your life away. / Standing there, swaying pleasantly, he grinned. I do not care, he thought, I no longer care" (*AP,* 58). Yet Moon cares, continues to care. He grins and yippees with fierce delight when a naked Niaruna warrior shoots an arrow at his plane, flying high above the tree line. And unlike Wolfie, he refuses to bomb the Indian village at the behest of Comandante Guzmán who wants to "clear" the forest. In this refusal, Moon tries to define himself, a northern halfbreed among Amazonian Indians, an outcast of Western civilization, neither in nor out of its history.

The novel's action, however, remains always in context, a context rendered in various dramatic ways. Through Moon, for instance, Matthiessen can dramatize the plight of the Cheyennes as well as the Niarunas, the situation of each reflecting on that of the other. Through the missionaries, he can reveal how cultures, even in their idealistic moment, violate one another; as Leslie Huben puts it: "Before we are through, we hope to have an airplane survey, so that we may hunt out the last lost soul in this great wilderness. Not one will escape the great net of our Lord" (*AP,* 18). Through Comandante Guzmán, Matthiessen can show how power still brutalizes human beings in the name of progress. Through Wolfie, half nice Jewish boy and half hippie turned thug, he can probe American society, its vices and antics. And through the women in the novel—Andy Huben, pretty and compassionate; Hazel Quarrier, ugly and devious; Pindi, the young Niaruna who becomes for a time Moon's "wife"—he can follow the transformations of eros, its blockage and flow in human life.

The central dramatic fact of the novel, though, is individual awakening, degrees of "conversion." Wolfie realizes his dependency on Moon, realizes his spiritual fatigue and solitude. Andy recognizes, without consummation, her desire for Moon, and his desire for her. Young Billy Quarrier, a child beautiful in face and soul, sees through his mother's deceits, through the strange injustices of an adult world. And Martin Quarrier, mediocre in so many obvious ways, yet dogged, even strenuous in probity, rises to painful perceptions of himself, his wife, his lust for Andy, even his Christian mission and faith. After his contact with Catholics ("the Enemy," as Protestant missionaries say) and Indians, after his son's death of blackwater fever, he finds no solace in inert Christian pieties. Courageously, he assumes the full burden of his doubts as of his duties, till a venal twice-converted (Catholic then Protestant) Indian cuts him down with a machete.

The Wandering Jew, the Wandering Christian, the Wandering Half-breed—none of them can affirm any value except in violent gestures of dispossession. Moon, who provides the dark, central energy of the novel, begins his dispossession in a three-day hunger vigil as a boy in the Dakotas, and continues it through his college career, his drunken rages and assaults, his psychedelic madness.[14] "He had flung himself away from life, from the very last realities, had strayed to the cold windy reaches of insanity. This perception was so clear and final that he moaned; he would not find his way back" (*AP,* 110). Under the influence of an Indian herb, *ayahuasca,* Moon steals Wolfie's plane and Quarrier's Niaruna dictionary, throws away his watch, and flies at dawn straight into the sun, then parachutes into impassable Niaruna country. The signs in his life, which once said Nowhere, suddenly point Now Here. Before leaving, he had said to Andy: "That's the only way to do it—*go.* When there's a jungle waiting,

you go through it and come out clean on the far side. Because if you struggle to back out, you get all snarled, and afterwards the jungle is still there,
still waiting" (*AP,* 130). That is how he plays in the fields of the Lord, not
at all the missionary's way.

Among the Niarunas, Moon is considered a descendant of Kisu, the
Great Rain Spirit, whom they ironically confuse with Jesu. Only Aeore,
that same truculent warrior who had earlier shot an arrow at the sky, remains hostile to Moon. The latter, nonetheless, spends three idyllic months
in the rain forest: "Days opened out, and furled again at night like jungle
flowers" (*AP,* 200). Obscurely, though, he senses that he is at a "beginning
and an end," a crux in his dread existence. Among the Indians, their myths
and rituals, Moon recovers some atavistic knowledge of the blood, and
begins to perceive the wilderness as host to multitudinous powers, neither
benevolent nor malevolent only, but interdependent, and in this interde-
pendence complete. The unabashed sensuality of the Niarunas, especially
Pindi's, frees his instinctual energies. And, oddly enough, Aeore—jungle
mentor, spiritual rival and brother, mortal enemy—imparts to Moon a sense
of the great mystery which the former, also a "jaguar shaman," strains to
realize.

But the idyll ends at gun and spear point; the world closes in. Lewis
Meriwether Moon can not finally identify with the Niaruna whom he perceives as irrational and primitive, more primitive than his own Plains Indians. Still alien in his adopted tribe, he carries from Andy, in a naked,
sexually unconsummated scene, the flu virus that decimates the tribe; in
the end, he must also shoot the relentless Aeore dead. Nor can Moon relate to Quarrier, though they share a certain doom:

> "I'm not really afraid of anything that may happen." Quarrier raised his
> eyebrows, as if surprised by this realization. "I've made such a disaster of my
> life that I'm not afraid of anything—that is, any change is welcome. Maybe
> you've never reached that point."
>
> "I've been there, all right. My trouble is, I never left it. I even *like* it." He
> turned the manioc tubers in the embers. (*AP,* 358)

Quarrier dies, stubborn to the last in his effort to make sense of a crumbling existence. Is Moon reborn? "Lewis Meriwether Moon: die soon" (*AP,*
396). In a long, hallucinating scene, drifting downriver prone in a funer-
ary canoe, feverish with malaria, his legs intertwined with the corpse of
Aeore, the smell of putrefying Indians wafted with every breath of wind,
he expresses a pride equal to Ahab's: "He stared straight upward. Kill me
or spare me as you like, but either way expect no thanks for it" (*AP,* 395).
Yet the next moment, looking at the decomposing face of Aeore, he feels
an immense compassion, "and a well of sadness for things irredeemable

and gone flowed over him. . . . He wept and wept, and though toward the end he began to smile, he kept on weeping until at last he breathed a tremendous sigh and laughed quietly, without tears" (*AP,* 397). Reborn in his tears, at last, denying no part of himself, he drinks from the glittering river and bathes his heart; he rolls in the shallows like an otter and scrubs his skin with sand. Thus the book ends:

> The wind was bright. Laid naked to the sun and sky, he felt himself open like a flower. Soon he slept. At dark he built an enormous fire, in celebration of the only man beneath the eye of Heaven. (*AP,* 399)

Is this lasting rebirth, or simply a lambent pause, like legendary moths drawn to the moon, in an endless search? Matthiessen, of course, does not say; he only tells us, through every inflection of his novel, that Moon incarnates a radical human drive even as he radically threatens us all: "He don't care about nothing nobody else cares about" (*AP,* 377), Wolfie says, and he ought to know.

Sexual, political, ecological, religious themes crowd the novel; but its form is finally mythic, the shape of death and rebirth. Hence the recurrent biblical leitmotif: "He that loseth his life for my sake shall find it" (Matthew 10:39). The narrative form, though omniscient, also focuses on the mythic figure of Lewis Meriwether Moon who commands, even as an anonymous "he", the first and last sections of the novel, and much that is in between. His ironic words to Leslie Huben over the radio, just before he bails out into the jungle, give the novel its title. And Moon's tribulations, a self desperately at risk, give the novel its haunting interest.

This is not to say that the novel is flawless. Some of its unfavorable portraits—Comandante Guzmán, Leslie Huben, Hazel Quarrier—seem caricatures. The action sometimes chokes on "colorful" anthropological details, and sometimes crawls—it takes us two pages to see Father Xantes consume an egg. The novel, in places, also flaunts its verbal power, full of "fine writing" as Matthiessen himself admits, especially in the long hallucinatory sections when characters succumb to drugs or delirium—one wonders then if style does not substitute for narrative structure and dramatic insight. Yet repeatedly, when the novel finds again its true passion and pace, such insights strike through the foliage to take our breath away. Then the words become one with their green, dangerous setting, one also with the more dangerous human heart. And Indian and Christian myth blend into an utterance, stuttering the name of the unnameable.[15]

6

In this study's perspective—notably in *The Snow Leopard* and *At Play in the Fields of The Lord*—Peter Matthiessen comes close to realizing the form of quest, the ideal of selves at richest risk. This attainment reflects on both man and artist.

As a man, Matthiessen reveals extraordinary courage, moral stamina, a true longing of the soul. Modest too, lacking in the spiritual vulgarity of many adventurers, devoid of the grating egoism — though not of the egoism itself! — of many writers, he possesses a certain genial charm of self-presentation. The whim of the seeker is evident in him, the wound too. But the discipline of style, a style at home in alien cultures, attentive to the natural world, makes both whim and wound occasions for dramatic empathy. Man and artist also invite us to enduring mysteries. For as I have noted, Matthiessen seeks to penetrate time as he travels in space, and his allegories of reconciled existence put squarely before us the enigma of human, indeed of cosmic, evolution.

The question of belief thus becomes crucial to his work: what, in the decaying ecology of our values, remains still vital, worthy of our commitment and faith? Matthiessen's answer begins with nature, the history and future of the given world, its presence in us all. The answer reaches finally for an ecological vision, at worst intrusively didactic, at its best the vision of an artist and mystic of the real, casting the wide net of language on a universe he can never capture or own.

But there are really no answers, only ways. Matthiessen's way through Nepal or Amazonia, through ecology or Zen, may not be our way. It is nonetheless an emblematic way through our perplexities in the West.

In-Conclusion

No, you know better than that, friends. The hidden Yes in you is
stronger than all Nos and Maybes that afflict you and your age like
a disease; and when you have to embark on the sea, you emigrants,
you, too, are compelled to this by—a faith.
— Friedrich Nietzsche

QUESTS HAVE no conclusion—that's the start of mine,
which will repeat the book's argument only briefly, and
try to take one small step beyond. Quests are extreme enactments of our
fate in the universe. Everything is gathered in them, from personal whim
or wound to geopolitics, from the mythic experience of America to the
facticity of Western societies, from narrative genre and protagonist gender
to the nature of ultimate reality. As a symbolic option in the contemporary world, quests recover something essential to human life, sometimes
in encounters with animals (lion, grizzly, leopard), often in encounters between cultures, almost always in encounters with nature—let us simply say
with the Other. However ravaging or equivocal, quests somehow pluck the
nerve of existence; they dispel the amnesia and anesthesia, the complacent
nihilism, of our cosseted lives. And they do so most vividly in contemporary American and British letters. In the end, they simply yield to an indefectible perception of an individual alone, edging cultures, hedging histories, acting riskily on a vision of himself, or herself, and the world, a
perception that from our best selves speaks to all.

An individual alone, yet not quite alone. In this study, I have tried to
suggest the openness of quest to our largest concerns. For quests are com-
mitments, desperate exercises in belief; their long desire, itch of a radical
want, seems to reach beyond the grave, beyond the conclusive worm. More
to the point, they focus the problems of existence; they constitute much
in our quotidian lives, partaking in that ambiguous economy of struggle
which is the world. In the pattern of their return, they reveal their true
end: home; they are quests for America itself, however alien their ground,
distant their reach. At their best, then, they are not escapes but critiques,
not rejections but aspirations; at their very best, they are invocations of
being under the signs of risk.

There is, of course, something perversely or peculiarly American in all this: the pursuit of the "self in its wholeness" (D. H. Lawrence), of a "condition of complete simplicity" (T. S. Eliot), of a "pragmatic equivalent" (William James) to real experience. For the American form, whether novel or romance, is, like quest, autobiography in motion, a *symbolic* autobiography wherein the heroic journey becomes a testament of some greater power, a song of a creative, universal self (Whitman); or else the journey becomes, more darkly, the fierce exigency to "strike through the pasteboard mask" of existence (Melville). In any case, as Americans once moved West in search of frontiers, and later moved East (to Europe) in search of roots, they now move everywhere in a planetized, in a tribalized world, following their needs at a compass's whim.

But has this motion now faltered, has the American vision closed in life or letters? In every age, I think, as one horizon closes, another opens; human beings stand perpetually on the brink of things. In literature, however, the argument for closure seems more plausible. Certainly we have witnessed error, aimlessness, constriction, a rhetoric of terror, guilt, spiritual fatigue in contemporary texts of quest; we have witnessed fragmentation, the blurring of genres. Yet the traditional form of quest, like myth itself, returns, revised or revived, in our skeptical clime; and in this "eternal return" authors invent new styles to suit current urgencies. Hence works like Mailer's *Why Are We in Vietnam?* and Bellow's *Henderson the Rain King,* Matthiessen's *The Snow Leopard* and Zweig's *Three Journeys.*

Paul Zweig took the brighter view. "The possibility of adventure lies within our grasp," he wrote before his premature death. "Perhaps not the exploits of Odysseus in the magic countries, but the irruptive, dazzling intensities of inner venture which flit by us in the margins of our lives. We need only value them and take them with high seriousness, to possess them, and to be possessed by them."[1] In literature, this inward turn creates a space at once mythic and ironic, sometimes parodic, creates episodic structures, mortal or magic encounters, a language both comic and numinous which recovers for literary narrative an ancient dramatic energy. Story returns, picking the debris of postmodern experiments; or rather, Story, which never really left, reorganizes contemporary sensibilities in ways, according to protocols and *beliefs,* that postmodernism tended to ignore.

Belief is indeed central to quest, belief sacred or profane. Mircea Eliade thought that the sacred "camouflages" itself in modern arts. "The West," he wrote, "can no longer create a 'religious art'. . . . This doesn't mean, however, that the sacred has entirely disappeared from modern art. But the sacred has become *unrecognizable;* it has camouflaged itself in forms, intentions, and significances that appear to be 'profane.' The sacred is no longer in full view. . . ."[2] This is also the view of Joseph Campbell, elaborated throughout his mythography. The view sometimes carries implications of premature universalism, a mythic confidence at once gnostic and utopian, as in this passage:

> It is — and will forever be, as long as our human race exists — the old, everlasting, perennial mythology, in its "subjective sense," poetically renewed in terms neither of a remembered past nor of a projected future, but of now: addressed, that is to say, not to the flattery of "people," but to the waking of individuals in the knowledge of themselves, not simply as egos fighting for place on the surface of this beautiful planet, but equally as centers of Mind at Large — each in his own way at one with all, and with no horizons.[3]

"Mind at Large" may define a limit of quest, a concern, as we have seen, at the edge of a seeker's consciousness; but other concerns, calling for profane beliefs, for actions in context, are more proximate. These concerns arise from a large curiosity about self, about others, about the world, a curiosity, nonetheless, that seeks to distill from every passing day the meaning of the universe. It is a traveling curiosity, perhaps a mainspring of our moral nature. It is a constitutive curiosity, akin to myth, music, and memory, as Claude Lévi-Strauss thinks in *Tristes Tropiques*, a structural principle of human existence. It is a curiosity that may not always alter the world, attended as it is by all the dangers of a failed Prometheanism, often promising disappointment at the end of its journey; yet it remains imperative, cardinal, touched by what poets and philosophers call the Sublime. And it assumes always, even in a skeptical age and amid all our "deconstructions," the impulse both to know and to believe.

Emerson understood that "it is not what we believe concerning the immortality of the soul or the like, but *the universal impulse to believe,* that is the material circumstance and is the principal fact in the history of the globe."[4] This is also a key theme of William James who radically remarks, "we have the right to believe *at our own risk* [italics mine] any hypothesis that is live enough to tempt our will," then clarifies: "Our faculties of belief were not primarily given us to make orthodoxies and heresies withal; they were given us to live by."[5] Thus the greatest epochs of expansion in culture prove friendliest to the inward necessity of its denizens, as if saying to each and all: "The inmost nature of the reality is congenial to *powers* which you possess."[6] In a sense, this is precisely the proposition that all seekers *test,* test dangerously and sometimes in extremis. Intuitively, they seem to know what Nietzsche went mad knowing: that, gradually, "man has become a fantastic animal that has to fulfill one more condition of existence than any other animal: man *has to* believe, to know, from time to time *why* he exists; his race cannot flourish without a periodic trust in life. . . ."[7]

Belief is crux to quest, to knowledge and action in the world. But the quests of *Selves at Risk* are *literary* quests, narratives in words. There belief is crucial too, though in more artful and secretive ways. Beliefs are vital to literature, Ben Belitt argues in a subtle essay, "because they create the occasion for the practice of literature and minister to its momentum"; conversely, literature "can bring belief to order, not by reducing life, but by exceeding it," by projecting "the mystery of which the artist himself may remain unaware."[8] Either way, literature and belief cohabit, nowhere more intimately than in the literature of quest which, in its implacable pursuit of meaning in the contemporary world, puts all pieties of belief or disbelief in question.

I say the "literature of quest," though I have offered only a pragmatic definition of it, a tangential definition by lapse, allusion, and example. Yet this, I think, has ever been the mission of literature: to exceed not only life but also itself, to confuse or refuse its own genres. We may indeed posit an ideal text of quest, and gesture at *Henderson the Rain King* or *The Snow Leopard.* But how much richer — more useful and interesting — is that other "definition" which works through particular texts, recognizing the discrete imperatives of each, while laboring to perceive, and partially to construct, a pattern of quest. How much livelier — and more edifying — to observe how the general pattern breaks down, shifts, alters in, say, Dillard's *Pilgrim at Tinker Creek* or Morris's *Nothing to Declare.* (As we have seen, so many quests seem truant, truncated, adventitious; so many seem to defy their own purpose.) This is perhaps only to say that criticism must be aesthetic, polymorphous, and sometimes perverse, not theoretical only or ideological. For as Walter Benjamin tersely put it: "An author who teaches *writers* [italics mine] nothing, teaches no one."[9]

The authors here, I do believe, teach writers and readers a great deal and, since they can teach *writers,* delight us all. In any case, the authors are, most of them, adventurers incidentally, and seekers mainly *within their literary art.* This does not diminish — it enhances! — their capacity to give us back the world. They give it back amply, give us America with all its brilliance, dreck, and distractions, give us our interactive planet, in its full glory and indigence, give us the suffering earth, green, brown, blue, its spiritual ecology fierce and fragile — give us all this in a verbal magnificence of questing selves at risk.

Notes

Index

Notes

In-Quest: A Synoptic Introduction

1. See Trip Gabriel, "One Man vs. Everest," *New York Times Magazine,* August 10, 1986, p. 41; and Salman Rushdie, "Adventures and Epics," *New York Times Magazine,* March 16, 1986, Part 2, p. 26.

2. *Phoenix: The Posthumous Papers of D. H. Lawrence,* ed. with intro. by Edward D. McDonald (London: William Heinemann, 1936), p. 141.

3. Michael Nerlich, *Ideology of Adventure: Studies in Modern Consciousness, 1100–1750,* trans. Ruth Crowley, foreword Wlad Godzich, 2 vols. (Minneapolis: University of Minnesota Press, 1987), 1:xx.

4. Ibid., p. xxi. The violent "integration" of others is also called colonialism, imperialism, which I discuss in Chapter 4.

5. Tzvetan Todorov, *The Conquest of America,* trans. Richard Howard (New York: Harper and Row, 1984), p. 4. See also Claude Lévi-Strauss, *Tristes Tropiques,* trans. John Russell (New York: Criterion Books, 1961), p. 78.

6. See, for instance, *Reconstructing American Literary History,* ed. Sacvan Bercovitch (Cambridge: Harvard University Press, 1986).

7. Myra Jehlen, *American Incarnation: The Individual, the Nation, and the Continent* (Cambridge: Harvard University Press, 1986), pp. 5, 7.

8. Gert Raeithel, "Philobatism and American Culture," *Journal of Psychohistory* 6, 4 (Spring 1979): 461–96. The same personality may also relish stress; see David Brion Davis, "Stress-seeking and the Self-Made Man in American Literature," in *Why Man Takes Chances: Studies in Stress-seeking,* ed. Samuel Z. Klausner (Garden City, N.Y.: Doubleday Anchor Original, 1968), pp. 104–31.

9. Martin Green, *The Great American Adventure* (Boston: Beacon Press, 1984), p. 18. See also Janis P. Stout, *The Journey Narrative in American Literature: Patterns and Departures* (Westport, Conn.: Greenwood Press, 1983), which develops the theme of journey narratives as mediators "between history and aesthetic traditions and between the peculiarities of being American and the embracing generalities of larger human history and a larger literary context," p. xiii.

10. Green, *Great American Adventure,* p. 110.

11. Richard Slotkin, *Regeneration through Violence: The Mythology of the American Frontier, 1600–1860* (Middletown, Conn.: Wesleyan University Press, 1973), pp. 5, 22. See also Slotkin's *The Fatal Environment: The Myth of the Frontier in the Age of Industrialization* (New York: Atheneum, 1985); Richard Maxwell Brown, *Strain of Violence* (New York: Oxford University Press, 1975); Richard Drinnon, *Facing West: The Metaphysics of Indian-hating and Empire-building* (Minneapolis: University of Minnesota Press, 1980); and Annette Kolodny, *The Lay of the Land:*

Metaphor as Experience and History in American Literature (Chapel Hill: University of North Carolina Press, 1975).

12. See also Annette Kolodny, *The Land before Her: Fantasy and Experience of the American Frontiers* (Chapel Hill: University of North Carolina Press, 1984).

13. Stout, *Journey Narrative in American Literature,* p. 12.

14. D. H. Lawrence, *Studies in Classic American Literature* (Garden City, N.Y.: Doubleday Anchor, 1955), p. 15.

15. For an interesting feminist analysis of the relation between American men and women on the frontier, see John Mack Faragher, *Women and Men on the Overland Trail* (New Haven: Yale University Press, 1979). For British women adventurers, see the numerous works published in the Virago/ Beacon Travel Series.

16. Elizabeth Fagg Olds, *Women of the Four Winds* (Boston: Houghton Mifflin, 1985), p. 2.

17. See, for instance, Barbara Land, *The New Explorers: Women in Antarctica* (New York: Dodd, Mead, 1981).

18. Paul Zweig, *The Adventurer: The Fate of Adventure in the Western World* (Princeton: Princeton University Press, 1974), p. 72.

19. See Lionel Tiger, *Men in Groups* (New York: Random House, 1969), and Lionel Tiger and Robin Fox, *The Imperial Animal* (New York: Holt, Rinehart, and Winston, 1971).

20. See Robert May, *Sex and Fantasy: Patterns of Male and Female Development* (New York: W. W. Norton, 1980).

21. Walter J. Ong, *Fighting for Life: Contest, Sexuality, and Consciousness* (Ithaca: Cornell University Press, 1981), especially pp. 15f., 40-115, 187-208.

22. Ibid., p. 62.

23. Ibid., pp. 196, 203.

24. There is no paucity of "interior" or spiritual quests, quests without physical effort, peril, and displacement, in women's literature. See, for instance, Carol P. Christ, *Deep Diving and Surfacing: Women Writers on Spiritual Quest* (Boston: Beacon Press, 1980, 1986), or, for a more "heroic" concept, Lee R. Edwards, *Psyche as Hero: Female Heroism and Fictional Form* (Middletown, Conn.: Wesleyan University Press, 1984).

25. Ong, *Fighting for Life,* p. 190. See also Ann Douglas, *The Feminization of American Culture* (New York: Avon Books, 1978).

26. Zweig, *Adventurer,* p. 246.

27. David Riesman, *The Lonely Crowd: A Study of the Changing American Character* (New Haven: Yale University Press, 1950); Peter F. Drucker, *The Age of Discontinuity: Guidelines for Our Changing Society* (New York: Harper and Row, 1969); Charles A. Reich, *The Greening of America* (New York: Random House, 1970); Daniel Bell, *The Coming of Post-Industrial Society: A Venture in Social Forecasting* (New York: Basic Books, 1973); Christopher Lasch, *The Culture of Narcissism: American Life in an Age of Diminishing Expectations* (New York: W. W. Norton, 1978); and Jean Baudrillard, "Astral America," *Artforum* 23, 1 (September 1984), who concludes: "This American universe thoroughly rotten with wealth, with power, with senility, with indifference, with puritanism and mental hygiene, with misery and waste, with technological vanity and useless violence — I can not stop myself from seeing in it the morning of the world," p. 74.

28. See Willard Gaylin, *The Rage Within: Anger in Modern Life* (New York: Simon and Schuster, 1984).

29. See C. L. R. James, *Mariners, Renegades, and Castaways: The Story of Herman Melville and the World We Live In* (London: Allison and Busby, 1985).

30. A. Alvarez, *The Savage God: A Study of Suicide* (New York: Random House, 1972), p. 262.

31. Arnold Gehlen, *Man in the Age of Technology,* trans. Patricia Lipscomb, with a foreword by Peter L. Berger (New York: Columbia University Press, 1980), p. 67.

32. See Jean-François Lyotard, *The Postmodern Condition: A Report on Knowledge,* trans. Geoff Bennington and Brian Massumi, with a foreword by Fredric Jameson (Minneapolis: University of Minnesota Press, 1984); and Ihab Hassan, *The Postmodern Turn: Essays in Postmodern Theory and Culture* (Columbus: Ohio State University Press, 1987).

33. Jean Baudrillard, *In the Shadow of the Silent Majorities,* trans. Paul Foss, Paul Patton, and John Johnston (New York: Semiotext(e) Foreign Agent Series, 1983); *Simulations,* trans. Paul Foss, Paul Patton, and Philip Beitchman (New York: Semiotext(e) Foreign Agent Series, 1983); and "What Are You Doing after the Orgy?" *Artforum* 22, 2 (October 1983). For another view of mass culture and society, see Patrick Bratlinger, *Bread and Circuses: Theories of Mass Culture and Social Decay* (Ithaca: Cornell University Press, 1983).

34. Mary Louise Pratt, "Scratches on the Face of the Country; or, What Mr. Barrow Saw in the Land of the Bushmen," *Critical Inquiry* 12, 1 (Autumn 1985): 122.

35. Dean MacCannell, *The Tourist: A New Theory of the Leisure Class* (New York: Schocken Books, 1976), pp. 5, 3.

36. Ibid., p. 40; and Denys Finch-Hatton, in Errol Trzebinski, *Silence Will Speak: A Study of Denys Finch-Hatton and His Relationship with Karen Blixen* (Chicago: University of Chicago Press, 1977), p. 274. It is ironic, and perhaps symbolic, that Finch-Hatton, who survived countless encounters with lions, buffaloes, elephants, should have died by machine, in a plane accident. It is also interesting that Finch-Hatton always stayed at the Conservative Club in London, evincing no contradiction between his ecological, antiracist, sacramental outlook and a certain strain of English conservatism.

37. See Lloyd L. Morain, *The Human Cougar* (Buffalo: Prometheus Books, 1976); and Robert N. Bellah, Richard Madsen, William M. Sullivan, Ann Swidler, and Steven M. Tipton, *Habits of the Heart* (New York: Harper and Row, 1985).

38. Ralph Keyes writes: "The implicit lesson of televised, simulated, and artificial risks of all kinds is that there is no danger of actual loss involved in taking a chance. Fear does not anticipate danger. Having separated fear from danger and made it into a leisure activity, we learn to treat being scared as a green light of excitement, not a yellow light of caution. But no matter how much they make our palms sweat and hearts flutter, no-risk risks neither teach nor test anything of consequence. If theme parks, computer games, and "That's Incredible!" are our primary source of information about risks, where do we ever learn that they can be lost? Or better yet, that actual risks with real stakes can be *won,* with much greater satisfaction than winning the simulated variety?" *Chancing It: Why We Take Risks* (Boston: Little, Brown, 1985), p. 272.

39. William James, *Pragmatism* (New York: Meridian Books, 1955), p. 61. See also the superb essay of Ben Belitt "Literature and Belief," *Salmagundi* 72 (Fall 1986): 5–21.

40. I elaborate on this question of ideology in literature in "Fictions of Power: A Note on Ideological Discourse in the Humanities," *American Literary History* 1, 1 (Spring 1989).

Chapter 1. Quest as a Literary Mode

1. See Leo Braudy, *The Frenzy of Renown: Fame and Its History* (New York: Oxford University Press, 1986), pp. 19–22.

2. Yukio Mishima, *Sun and Steel,* trans. John Bester (New York: Grove Press, 1970), p. 74.

3. Alastair Fowler, *Kinds of Literature: An Introduction to the Theory of Genres and Modes* (Cambridge: Harvard University Press, 1982), p. 11.

4. Ibid., p. 24.

5. The term "carnivalization" is of course M. M. Bakhtin's; see, for instance, *Rabelais and His World,* trans. Helena Iswolsky (Cambridge: Harvard University Press, 1968). But see also, on carnivalization, hybridization, Gary Saul Morson, *The Boundaries of Genre: Dostoyevsky's "Diary of a Writer" and the Traditions of Literary Utopia* (Austin: University of Texas Press, 1981), esp. pp. 48–50, 107–8, and 142–43.

6. Jacques Derrida, "*La Loi du genre* / The Law of Genre," *Glyph* 7 (1980): 204, 206. See also his "Living On: Border Lines," in *Deconstruction and Criticism,* ed. Geoffrey Hartman (New York: Seabury Press, 1979), pp. 83f.

7. Giambattista Vico, *The New Science of Giambattista Vico,* trans. from the Third Edition by Thomas Goddard Bergin and Max Harold Fisch, revised and abridged (Ithaca: Cornell University Press, 1970), p. 5.

8. Ibid., pp. 64, 90, 123.

9. Ibid., p. 224.

10. Thomas Mann, "Freud and the Future," *Essays,* trans. H. T. Lowe-Porter (New York: Vintage Books, 1957), p. 317. See also Jeffrey M. Perl, *The Tradition of Return: The Implicit History of Modern Literature* (Princeton: Princeton University Press, 1984).

11. Joseph Campbell, *The Masks of God: Primitive Mythology* (New York: Viking, 1959), p. 15.

12. Joseph Campbell, *The Hero with a Thousand Faces* (New York: Meridian Books, 1956), pp. 381, 30.

13. Ibid., p. 40.

14. *The Epic of Gilgamesh,* ed. and trans. N. K. Sandars (London: Penguin Books, 1972), pp. 105f.

15. Ibid., p. 61. Raw action may not be essential to epic quests but danger and violence indeed are. With the Assyrian Friezes of Ashurbanipal (called the "Lion Hunt") in mind, Leo Bersani and Ulysse Dutoit discover "a complicity between narrativity and violence." See *The Forms of Violence: Narrative in Assyrian Art and Modern Culture* (New York: Schocken Books, 1985), p. v. See also pp. 40, 125, 131.

16. Paul Zweig, *The Adventurer: The Fate of Adventure in the Western World*

(Princeton: Princeton University Press, 1974), p. 4. The German sociologist Georg Simmel makes a similar point when he says that the adventurer gains access to "a higher unity, a super-life, as it were . . . a transcendent existence," which permits him to reconcile chance and necessity, opportunity and risk. See *On Individuality and Social Forms: Selected Writings,* ed. Donald N. Levine (Chicago: University of Chicago Press, 1971), pp. 191f.

17. Zweig, *Adventurer,* p. 36.

18. Jessie L. Weston, *From Ritual to Romance* (Garden City, N.Y.: Doubleday Anchor Books, 1957), pp. 203, 209.

19. Northrop Frye, *Anatomy of Criticism: Four Essays* (Princeton: Princeton University Press, 1957), p. 215. Considering his other uses of the word "myth," the term "quest-myth" seems somewhat misleading; perhaps "total quest" would do better. Frye gives his succinct view of myth as a *literary* device in the essay "Myth, Fiction, and Displacement," collected in Northrop Frye, *Fables of Identity: Studies in Poetic Mythology* (New York: Harcourt, Brace, and World, 1963).

20. Frye, *Anatomy of Criticism,* p. 193.

21. Ibid., pp. 197, 188, 195.

22. Northrop Frye, *The Secular Scripture: A Study of the Structure of Romance* (Cambridge: Harvard University Press, 1976), pp. 9, 6.

23. Ibid., p. 30.

24. Ibid., p. 188.

25. Walter Benjamin, *Illuminations,* trans. Harry Zohn, ed. and intro. Hannah Arendt (New York: Harcourt, Brace, and World, 1968), pp. 86f. See also Albert Lord, *The Singer of Tales* (Cambridge: Harvard University Press, 1960), and Walter J. Ong, *Rhetoric, Romance, and Technology: Studies in the Interaction of Expression and Culture* (Ithaca: Cornell University Press, 1971).

26. Benjamin, *Illuminations,* p. 93.

27. Ibid., pp. 108f.

28. Zweig, *Adventurer,* p. 82. Simmel also calls the adventurer "the extreme example of the ahistorical individual, of the man who lives in the present," p. 190.

29. For a sane discussion of these and other terms of narrative, see Robert Scholes and Robert Kellogg, *The Nature of Narrative* (New York: Oxford University Press, 1966).

30. Zweig, *Adventurer,* p. 14.

31. See Scholes and Kellogg, *Nature of Narrative,* pp. 73-81.

32. Percy G. Adams, *Travel Literature and the Evolution of the Novel* (Lexington: University of Kentucky Press, 1983), p. 284. One might also adduce the works of other writers, from Melville to Malraux, who transform travel and adventure into a new order of literature.

33. Janis P. Stout, *The Journey Narrative in American Literature: Patterns and Departures* (Westport, Conn.: Greenwood Press, 1983), p. 12.

34. See Wright Morris, *The Territory Ahead* (New York: Harcourt, Brace, 1958); Richard Poirier, *A World Elsewhere: The Place of Style in American Literature* (New York: Oxford University Press, 1966; rpt. Madison: University of Wisconsin Press, 1985); Richard Chase, *The American Novel and Its Tradition* (Garden City, N.Y.: Doubleday Anchor Books, 1957), p. viii; and D. H. Lawrence, *Studies in Classic American Literature* (Garden City, N.Y.: Doubleday Anchor Books, 1955), p. 17.

35. Stout, *Journey Narrative in American Literature,* p. 247.

36. Morris, *Territory Ahead,* p. xvi. For an opposite view, see Leslie A. Fiedler, *The Return of the Vanishing American* (New York: Stein and Day, 1968).

37. Robert Byron, *The Road to Oxiana,* intro. Paul Fussell (New York: Oxford University Press, 1982), p. v.

38. *Granta* 10 (1984): 7.

39. Paul Fussell, *Abroad: British Literary Traveling Between the Wars* (New York: Oxford University Press, 1980), p. 39. Witty and perceptive, Fussell sometimes yields to a spirit more snobbish than elite.

40. Ibid., p. 30. Fussell also argues that the travel writer is often more affluent than his readers; hence "pastoral"—in William Empson's sense, "a beautiful relation between rich and poor"—is a "powerful element in most travel books," p. 210.

41. Jonathan Raban, "Wanderlust," *Departures* (November–December, 1985): 10. See also Zweig, *Adventurer,* p. 95.

42. Stout makes this point about American quests in particular (*Journey Narrative in American Literature,* p. 90), while Frye observes a larger pattern in the shift of focus from "heroes and other elements of narrative toward the process of creating them. The real hero becomes the poet. . . . In proportion as this happens, the inherently revolutionary quality in romance begins to emerge from all the nostalgia about a vanished past." *Secular Scripture,* p. 178.

43. Michel Butor, "Travel and Writing," *Mosaic* 8, 1 (Fall 1974): 14.

44. Ibid., p. 15.

45. Works on autobiography continue to proliferate. I cite here only two excellent introductions to the topic, with helpful bibliographies and notes: James Olney, *Metaphors of Self: The Meaning of Autobiography* (Princeton: Princeton University Press, 1972); James Olney, ed., *Autobiography: Essays Theoretical and Critical* (Princeton: Princeton University Press, 1980).

46. See J. Gerald Kennedy, "Roland Barthes, Autobiography, and the End of Writing," *Georgia Review* 35, 2 (Summer 1981): 381–98; and Mishima, *Sun and Steel,* pp. 8f., 18, 85f.

47. Alfred Hornung, "The Autobiographical Mode in Contemporary American Fiction," *Prose Studies* 8, 3 (December 1985): 81.

48. Alfred Kazin, "The Self as History: Reflections on Autobiography," in *Telling Lives: The Biographer's Art,* ed. Marc Pachter (Washington, D.C.: New Republic Books, 1979), p. 76. The links between American individualism, democratic pluralism, and autobiography are also a major theme in Albert E. Stone, *Autobiographical Occasions and Original Acts: Versions of American Identity from Henry Adams to Nate Shaw* (Philadelphia: University of Pennsylvania Press, 1982).

49. See William C. Spengemann, *The Forms of Autobiography: Episodes in the History of a Literary Genre* (New Haven: Yale University Press, 1980), which also provides an extended bibliographic essay, and Paul Jay, *Being in the Text: Self-Representations from Wordsworth to Roland Barthes* (Ithaca: Cornell University Press, 1984).

50. See John Barth, "The Literature of Exhaustion," *Atlantic Monthly* (August 1967): 29–34; and "The Literature of Replenishment: Postmodernist Fiction," *Atlantic Monthly* (January 1980): 65–71. Barth's concept of "replenishment," however, remains limited to certain examples drawn mainly from Latin American fiction.

51. Michel Foucault, "What is an Author?" which Malcolm Bradbury takes as

his epigraph in a brilliant satire of faddish "absences," *My Strange Quest for Mensonge: Structuralism's Hidden Hero* (London: André Deutsch, 1987).

Chapter 2. The Subject of Quest

1. Paul de Man, "Autobiography as De-Facement," *The Rhetoric of Romanticism* (New York: Columbia University Press, 1984), p. 81. Other recent works that affirm, deny, or simply review the textualization of the self include Paul Jay, *Being in the Text: Self-Representations from Wordsworth to Roland Barthes* (Ithaca: Cornell University Press, 1984); Janet Varner Gunn, *Autobiography: Toward a Poetics of Experience* (Philadelphia: University of Pennsylvania Press, 1982); Paul John Eakin, *Fictions in Autobiography: Studies in the Art of Self-Invention* (Princeton: Princeton University Press, 1985); Elizabeth W. Bruss, *Autobiographical Acts: The Changing Situation of a Literary Genre* (Baltimore: Johns Hopkins University Press, 1976); and James Olney, ed., *Autobiography: Essays Theoretical and Critical* (Princeton: Princeton University Press, 1980).

2. De Man, "Autobiography as De-Facement," p. 70.

3. Ibid., p. 76.

4. Gunn, *Autobiography*, p. 19.

5. Sigmund Freud, *The Standard Edition of the Complete Psychological Works of Sigmund Freud*, trans. James Strachey, vol. 17 (London: Hogarth Press, 1955), pp. 49f.

6. Gregory S. Jay, "Freud: The Death of Autobiography," *Genre* 19 (Summer 1986): 105, 124. See also Paul Jay, *Being in the Text*, pp. 23–26; Michael Sprinker, "Fictions of the Self: The End of Autobiography," in *Autobiography*, ed. Olney, pp. 321–42; Richard Rorty, "Freud and Moral Reflection," and Richard H. King, "Self-Realization and Solidarity: Rorty and the Judging Self," both in *Pragmatism's Freud: The Moral Disposition of Psychoanalysis* ed. Joseph H. Smith and William Kerrigan (Baltimore: Johns Hopkins University Press, 1986), pp. 1–51. The last two essays are provocative discussions of the decentered self in Freud, its implications for politics and morality.

7. Francis R. Hart, "Notes for an Anatomy of Modern Autobiography," *New Literary History* 1, 3 (Spring 1970): 492.

8. See J. Gerald Kennedy, "Roland Barthes, Autobiography, and the End of Writing," *Georgia Review* 35, 2 (Summer 1981): 383, 391–98.

9. Albert E. Stone, *Autobiographical Occasions and Original Acts: Versions of American Identity from Henry Adams to Nate Shaw* (Philadelphia: University of Pennsylvania Press, 1982), p. 13. James Olney also defends the metaphoric qualities of such an ideal self in his signal *Metaphors of Self: The Meaning of Autobiography* (Princeton: Princeton University Press, 1972).

10. Leo Braudy, *The Frenzy of Renown: Fame and Its History* (New York: Oxford University Press, 1986), pp. 7, 9.

11. Paul Zweig, *The Heresy of Self-Love: A Study of Subversive Individualism* (Princeton: Princeton University Press, 1968), p. vii.

12. Ibid., p. 268.

13. Useful works on this subject include Georges Gusdorf, *La Découverte de soi* (Paris: Presses Universitaires de France, 1948); Colin Morris, *The Discovery of the Individual: 1050–1200* (New York: Harper and Row, 1972); Sacvan Berco-

vitch, *The Puritan Origins of the American Self* (New Haven: Yale University Press, 1975); Karl Joachim Weintraub, *The Value of the Individual: Self and Circumstance in Autobiography* (Chicago: University of Chicago Press, 1978); and Stanley Corngold, *The Fate of the Self: German Writers and French Theory* (New York: Columbia University Press, 1986), as well as Paul Jay (*Being in the Text*) and Eakin (*Fictions in Autobiography*) for historical discussions of the self as applied to autobiography.

14. See Sprinker, "Fictions of the Self," pp. 329–33, for a discussion of Kierkegaard, autobiography, masks, and repetition, in which Sprinker concludes: "Kierkegaard . . . refuses to assume the traditional responsibility of an author for his text, and in so doing he undermines the conventional notions of author and text, self and discourse," p. 332. See also Mark C. Taylor, *Kierkegaard's Pseudonymous Authorship: A Study of Time and the Self* (Princeton: Princeton University Press, 1975).

15. Søren Kierkegaard, *Fear and Trembling and The Sickness unto Death,* trans. with intro. and notes by Walter Lowrie (Garden City, N.Y.: Doubleday, 1954), p. 163.

16. Karl Marx, "Theses on Feuerbach," in Karl Marx and Friedrich Engels, *Basic Writings on Politics and Philosophy,* ed. Lewis S. Feuer (Garden City, N.Y.: Doubleday, 1959), p. 244. See also the critique of this doctrine in Robert L. Heilbroner, *Marxism: For and Against* (New York: W. W. Norton, 1980), pp. 162–66; and in Joel Whitebook, who acknowledges a certain "awkwardness" of Marxism "toward the autonomous individual," in "Saving the Subject: Modernity and the Problem of the Autonomous Individual," *Telos* 50 (Winter 1981–82): 80f., 84f.

17. Friedrich Nietzsche, *The Will to Power,* trans. Walter Kaufmann and R. J. Hollingdale, ed. with commentary by Walter Kaufmann (New York: Random House, 1967), pp. 200, 270.

18. Friedrich Nietzsche, *The Birth of Tragedy and The Genealogy of Morals,* trans. Francis Golffing (Garden City, N.Y.: Doubleday, 1956), p. 218.

19. Sigmund Freud, *Civilization and Its Discontents,* trans. and ed. James Strachey (New York: Norton, 1962), p. 69.

20. Ibid., p. 66. The hypothesis of the death instinct was first presented in Sigmund Freud, *Beyond the Pleasure Principle,* trans. James Strachey (New York: Liveright, 1950), originally published in 1920.

21. Jacques Lacan, *Écrits: A Selection,* trans. Alan Sheridan (New York: Norton, 1977), p. 2.

22. Jacques Lacan, *The Four Fundamental Concepts of Psycho-Analysis,* ed. Jacques-Alain Miller, trans. Alan Sheridan (New York: Norton, 1978), p. 221. See also pp. 218, 222–29.

23. Emile Benveniste, *Problems in General Linguistics,* trans. Mary E. Meek (Coral Gables, Fla.: University of Miami Press, 1971), p. 224. See also the excellent discussions in David Carroll, *The Subject in Question: The Languages of Theory and the Strategies of Fiction* (Chicago: University of Chicago Press, 1982), pp. 14–26.

24. Claude Lévi-Strauss, *The Naked Man,* vol. 4 of *Introduction to a Science of Mythology,* trans. John Weightman and Doreen Weightman (New York: Harper and Row, 1981), p. 625. Elsewhere, Lévi-Strauss says: "Not merely is the first person singular detestable: there is no room for it between 'ourselves' and 'nothing.'"

In *Tristes Tropiques,* trans. John Russell (New York: Criterion Books, 1961), p. 398.

25. Roland Barthes, "The Death of the Author," in *Image-Music-Text,* trans. and ed. Stephen Heath (New York: Hill and Wang, 1977), pp. 143, 145.

26. Jacques Derrida, "Living On: Border Lines," in *Deconstruction and Criticism,* ed. Geoffrey Hartman (New York: Seabury Press, 1979), pp. 83f.

27. Jacques Derrida, *La Carte postale: De Socrate à Freud et au-delà* (Paris: Flammarion, 1980), p. 382.

28. J. Hillis Miller, *Poets of Reality: Six Twentieth-Century Writers* (Cambridge: Harvard University Press, 1965), p. 3. Mark C. Taylor gives a theological twist to the argument when he says: "God, self, history, and book are, thus, bound in an intricate relationship in which each mirrors the other. . . . The echoes of the death of God can be heard in the disappearance of the self, the end of history, and the closure of the book." In *ERЯing: A Postmodern A/theology* (Chicago: University of Chicago Press, 1984), pp. 7f.; on the "disappearance of the self," see pp. 34–51.

29. Marcel Mauss, *Sociology and Psychology,* trans. Ben Brewster (London: Routledge and Kegan Paul, 1979), p. 61.

30. Clifford Geertz, *Local Knowledge: Further Essays in Interpretive Anthropology* (New York: Basic Books, 1983), p. 16; see also pp. 8f., 45, 50–54.

31. Benveniste, *Problems in General Linguistics,* p. 225. See also Carroll, *Subject in Question,* pp. 22–25. See also Lévi-Strauss, *Naked Man,* p. 630.

32. See some of the contributions in two issues of *Critical Inquiry* 12, 1, and 13, 1, "'Race,' Writing, and Difference" (Autumn 1985 and Autumn 1986), as well as Tzvetan Todorov's critique of these essays, in "'Race,' Writing, and Culture," *Critical Inquiry* 13, 1 (Autumn 1986): 171–81.

33. Trinh T. Minh-ha, "Introduction," *Discourse* 8, "The Inappropriate/d Other" (Fall–Winter 1986–87): 9. Some essays in this volume also combine insight with tendentiousness.

34. Barbara Johnson, *The Critical Difference: Essays in the Contemporary Rhetoric of Reading* (Baltimore: Johns Hopkins University Press, 1980), p. x.

35. Lyotard, for instance, admits, perhaps in an excess of scruple: "I must be a bad reader, not sufficiently sensitive or 'passive' in the greater sense of the word, too willful, 'aggressive,' not sufficiently espousing the supposed organic development of the other (?), in a rush to place it in the light of my own concerns." Jean-François Lyotard, "Interview," *Diacritics* 14, 3 (Fall 1984): 17. But isn't this more than most of us find the grace to admit?

36. Foucault partially recognizes this. In discussing the disappearance of the author, he concludes that the "subject should not be entirely abandoned," but rather considered "stripped of its creative role and analysed as a complex and variable function of discourse." See Michel Foucault, "What Is an Author?" *Language, Counter-Memory, Practice: Selected Essays and Interviews,* ed. Donald F. Bouchard, trans. Donald F. Bouchard and Sherry Simon (Ithaca, N.Y.: Cornell University Press, 1977), pp. 137f. Foucault goes farther in exploring "new kinds of subjectivity" in "The Subject and Power," *Critical Inquiry* 8, 4 (Summer 1982): 777–96.

37. Paul de Man, "The Sublimation of the Self," *Blindness and Insight: Essays in the Rhetoric of Contemporary Criticism* (New York: Oxford University Press, 1971), p. 39.

218   Notes to Pages 42–44

38. Norman Holland, *The I* (New Haven: Yale University Press, 1985), pp. x–xii, 23.

39. Ibid., pp. 75f. Holland, I might note, sees psychoanalysis evolving in three stages: first as psychology of the unconscious, next of the ego, and most recently of the self, each larger, more inclusive in its frame. See the excellent appendix, pp. 331–63.

40. Sharon R. Kaufman, *The Ageless Self: Sources of Meaning in Late Life* (Madison: University of Wisconsin Press, 1986), p. 25.

41. Ibid., pp. 19f.

42. J. Hillis Miller observes: "The aporia of Nietzsche's strategy of deconstruction is a version of the universal aporia of deconstruction. It lies in the fact that Nietzsche must use as the indispensable lever of his act of disarticulation a positing of the entity he intends to demolish. He must affirm the thing he means to deconstruct in order to deconstruct it. The deconstruction therefore deconstructs itself. It is built over the abyss of its own impossibility. . . . This reversal, whereby deconstruction deconstructs itself, and at the same time creates another labyrinthine fiction whose authority is undermined by its own creation, is characteristic of all deconstructive discourse. The way in which the fiction of selfhood survives its dismantling, or is even a necessary presupposition of its own dismantling, is a striking example of this." See "The Disarticulation of the Self in Nietzsche," *Monist* 64, 2 (April 1981): 260f.

43. Michel Leiris, *Manhood: A Journey from Childhood into the Fierce Order of Virility,* trans. Richard Howard (San Francisco: North Point Press, 1984), p. 157; and Georg Simmel, *On Individuality and Social Forms: Selected Writings,* ed. Donald N. Levine (Chicago: University of Chicago Press, 1971), pp. 189, 197.

44. Thomas C. Heller, Morton Sosna, and David E. Wellbery, eds., *Reconstructing Individualism: Autonomy, Individuality, and the Self in Western Thought* (Stanford: Stanford University Press, 1986), p. 2.

45. Ibid., pp. 10, 15. One of the more striking transpositions of the individual is by Niklas Luhmann, a systems philosopher, who defines the self as an autopoietic, self-referential system. He concludes: "Autopoietic systems reproduce themselves; they continue their reproduction or not. This makes them individuals. And there is nothing more to say," p. 325.

46. Fredric Jameson, *The Prison-House of Language: A Critical Account of Structuralism and Russian Formalism* (Princeton: Princeton University Press, 1972), pp. 139–41.

47. Fredric Jameson, *The Political Unconscious: Narrative as a Socially Symbolic Act* (Ithaca: Cornell University Press, 1981), pp. 153f. Nevertheless, Jameson would base his "positive hermeneutic" on social class, distinguishing it from those "'negative hermeneutics' still limited by anarchist categories of the individual subject and individual experience," p. 286.

48. Walter Benjamin, *Reflections: Essays, Aphorisms, Autobiographical Writings,* trans. Edmund Jephcott (New York: Harcourt Brace Jovanovich, 1978), p. 179.

49. Simmel, *On Individuality and Social Forms,* p. 188.

50. Ibid., p. 195.

51. Freud, *Civilization and Its Discontents,* pp. 14f.

52. *Emerson in His Journals,* ed. Joel Porte (Cambridge: Harvard University Press, 1982), p. 285.

53. Ralph Waldo Emerson, *The Complete Essays and Other Writings,* ed. with intro. by Brooks Atkinson (New York: Random House, 1940), pp. 155, 355, 6.

54. Ibid., p. 151.

55. Ibid., pp. 342, 350, 206.

56. Mauss, *Sociology and Psychology,* p. 90.

57. William James, *The Will to Believe and Other Essays in Popular Philosophy and Human Immortality* (New York: Dover Publications, 1956), p. 96. Of all modern thinkers, James best understood how teleological the self is, setting, serving, and evaluating ends at the behest of biological imperatives and personal "over-beliefs."

58. William James, *Essays in Radical Empiricism* (New York: Longmans, 1912), pp. 3, 4, 44, 45.

Chapter 3. The Motives of Quest

1. Countless works attest to the unflinching will and awesome stamina of adventurers; for one signal example, see Alfred Lansing, *Endurance: Shackleton's Incredible Voyage* (New York: Carroll and Graf, 1986). For excellent introductions, with useful bibliographies, to the subject, see Chris Bonington, *Quest for Adventure* (New York: Clarkson N. Potter, 1982); Eric Newby, ed., *A Book of Travellers' Tales* (New York: Viking Press, 1986); and Daniel J. Boorstin, *The Discoverers: A History of Man's Search to Know His World and Himself* (New York: Random House, 1983). For works on women particularly, see Leo Hamalian, ed., *Ladies on the Loose: Women Travellers of the Eighteenth and Nineteenth Centuries* (New York: Dodd, Mead, 1981); Elizabeth Fagg Olds, *Women of the Four Winds* (Boston: Houghton Mifflin, 1985); and Mary Russell, *The Blessings of a Good Thick Skirt* (London: Collins, 1986).

2. Quoted by Newby, *Book of Travellers' Tales,* pp. 544f.

3. Bonington, *Quest for Adventure,* pp. 124, 129.

4. Ibid., pp. 11f. See also the strikingly similar statement of Doug Scott on the sheer face of El Capitan, p. 418.

5. Ibid., p. 418. Georg Simmel also emphasizes the adventurer's discontinuity with normal existence, his dreamlike memory of events. *On Individuality and Social Forms: Selected Writings,* ed. Donald N. Levine (Chicago: University of Chicago Press, 1971), pp. 187f.

6. Bonington, *Quest for Adventure,* p. 111. Colin Thubron gives a more personal and romantic, finally a weaker, version of this sentiment when he says: "I travel in order to fall in love: in the hope of recovering, in a new place or a new people, some lost sense of wholeness. Of course, I know by now that no permanent love will result. . . . Is the travel writer, then, a permanent adolescent?" In "Wanderlust," *Departures* (June–July 1985): 11.

7. Quoted by Caroline Moorehead, *Freya Stark* (New York: Viking Press, 1985), p. 44. But see also Leo Braudy, *The Frenzy of Renown: Fame and Its History* (New York: Oxford University Press, 1986), which documents well the trials of fame and paradoxes of immortality.

8. See Evan S. Connell, *A Long Desire* (New York: Holt, Rinehart, and Winston, 1979), for engaging accounts of wanderers in history.

9. Quoted by Bonington, *Quest for Adventure,* p. 420.

220   Notes to Pages 51–55

10. Ibid., p. 424.

11. See Paul Colinvaux, *Why Big Fierce Animals Are Rare: An Ecologist's Perspective* (Princeton: Princeton University Press, 1978), pp. 213–33; Ralph Keyes, *Chancing It: Why We Take Risks* (Boston: Little, Brown, 1985), p. 32; Walter J. Ong, *Fighting for Life: Contest, Sexuality, and Consciousness* (Ithaca: Cornell University Press, 1981), p. 15.

12. Robert Ardrey, *The Hunting Hypothesis* (New York: Bantam Books, 1977), pp. 9f.

13. Quoted by José Ortega y Gasset, *Meditations on Hunting,* trans. Howard B. Wescott (New York: Charles Scribner's Sons, 1985), p. 132.

14. Ibid., p. 130.

15. Konrad Lorenz, *On Aggression,* trans. Marjorie Kerr Wilson (New York: Harcourt, Brace, and World, 1966), p. 278. See also Sigmund Freud, *Civilization and Its Discontents,* trans. James Strachey (New York: W. W. Norton, 1962), pp. 55–69; and Willard Gaylin, *The Rage Within: Anger in Modern Life* (New York: Simon and Schuster, 1984), a popular work on the anger response. For the sociobiological value of combativeness, see also Ong, *Fighting for Life,* pp. 118–209.

16. Paul Zweig, *The Adventurer: The Fate of Adventure in the Western World* (Princeton: Princeton University Press, 1974), p. 43.

17. Robert Gardner and Karl G. Heider, *Gardens of War: Life and Death in the New Guinea Stone Age,* intro. Margaret Mead (New York: Random House, 1968), p. 114. Coincidentally, Peter Matthiessen and Michael Rockefeller, who later disappeared in the Pacific, were members of this three-year expedition.

18. See, for instance, René Girard, *Violence and the Sacred,* trans. Patrick Gregory (Baltimore: Johns Hopkins University Press, 1977), and Leo Bersani and Ulysse Dutoit, *The Forms of Violence: Narrative in Assyrian Art and Modern Culture* (New York: Schocken Books, 1985). With characteristic severity, Freud thought that wars would not be abolished, and asked: "Is it not we who must give in, who must adapt ourselves to them? Is it not for us to confess that in our civilized attitude towards death we are once more living psychologically beyond our means, and must reform and give truth its due?" Sigmund Freud, "Thoughts for the Times on War and Death," *Collected Papers,* Vol. 4, ed. Ernest Jones (London: Hogarth Press, 1956), p. 316.

19. William Broyles, Jr., "Why Men Love War," *Esquire,* November 1984, p. 57. See also, for a more literary discussion, Peter G. Jones, *War and the Novelist: Appraising the American War Novel* (Columbia: University of Missouri Press, 1976).

20. Samuel Z. Klausner, ed., *Why Man Takes Chances: Studies in Stress-seeking* (Garden City, N.Y.: Doubleday Anchor Books, 1968), pp. 164, vii, and 141–45. See also Chuck Yeager and Leo Janos, *Yeager: An Autobiography* (New York: Bantam Books, 1985), in which the author, the first pilot to crack the speed of sound, speaks of living off fear, as one might live off a high-energy candy bar.

21. Michael Balint, *Thrills and Regressions* (New York: International Universities Press, 1959), p. 23.

22. Sigmund Freud, *Beyond the Pleasure Principle,* trans. James Strachey (New York: Liveright, 1950), p. 15.

23. Ibid., p. 50.

24. Freud, *Civilization and Its Discontents,* p. 69.

25. Writing about travelers, Bill Buford says: "They seem — every single one of them — to have some kind of disease; a fever, certainly." See his "Editorial," *Granta* 10 (1984): 6. But Buford barely realizes the consequences of this "fever" or "disease," which Malcolm Cowley suggests in "Hemingway's Wound — and Its Consequences for American Literature," *Georgia Review* 38, 2 (Summer 1984).

26. Friedrich Nietzsche, *The Gay Science, With a Prelude in Rhymes and an Appendix of Songs,* trans. with commentary by Walter Kaufmann (New York: Vintage Books, 1974), pp. 273f. See also Zweig, *Adventurer,* p. 191, on the logic of recurrence in adventure.

27. Nietzsche, *Gay Science,* p. 32. Absolute pain, as in torture, is world destroying, Elaine Scarry argues brilliantly in *The Body in Pain: The Making and Unmaking of the World* (New York: Oxford University Press, 1985), missing the worth of a pain overcome or endured; this prompts her to see only "magisterial pretense" in Nietzsche's claim to have "at last gained the upper hand" on his "dog pain," p. 11.

28. Nietzsche, *Gay Science,* p. 199.

29. Ibid., p. 214.

30. Friedrich Nietzsche, *The Will to Power,* trans. Walter Kaufmann and R. J. Hollingdale, ed. with commentary by Walter Kaufmann (New York: Random House, 1967), p. 366. On the next page Nietzsche writes: "It can be shown most clearly that every living thing does everything it can not to preserve itself but to become *more —*."

31. Ibid., p. 71.

32. Ibid., pp. 396, 494, 499, 519.

33. Zweig, *Adventurer,* p. 219. All this did not prevent Nietzsche from ironizing about himself: "A seeker, I? Oh, please be still! / I'm merely *heavy* — weigh many a pound. / I fall, and I keep falling till / At last I reach the ground." *Gay Science,* p. 59.

34. William James, *Pragmatism and Four Essays from The Meaning of Truth* (New York: Meridian Books, 1955), p. 108.

35. Ibid., pp. 190f.

36. William James, *The Will to Believe and Human Immortality* (New York: Dover Publications, 1956), p. 9.

37. Ibid., p. 47.

38. Ibid., p. 75.

39. Jacques Barzun, *A Stroll with William James* (Chicago: University of Chicago Press, 1983), p. 19. See also pp. 178 and 269 for examples of James's heroic predilection for risk, challenge, disaster, and his distaste for tepid utopian thought, "this atrocious harmlessness of all things."

40. Ibid., p. 34.

41. See Erik H. Erikson, *Young Man Luther: A Study in Psychoanalysis and History* (New York: W. W. Norton, 1958), pp. 40–48; Simmel, *On Individuality and Social Forms,* p. 189. The point is picked up in journalistic accounts of adventure; see David Falkner, "Adventurers Busily Explore Final Frontier: Imagination," *New York Times,* February 8, 1988, p. A1.

42. *Why Man Explores,* A Symposium sponsored by NASA, with Ray Bradbury, Norman Cousins, Jacques-Yves Cousteau, James Michener, and Philip Morrison (Washington, D.C.: U.S. Government Printing Office, 1976), pp. 54, 20. "The

discoverer simply uncovers, but the explorer opens. The discoverer concludes a
search; he is a finder. The explorer begins a search; he is a seeker. And he opens
the way for other seekers," writes Daniel J. Boorstin in *The Exploring Spirit: America and the World Then and Now* (New York: Vintage Books, 1977), p. 20. Suggestive as it may be, the distinction is not easy to maintain, as Boorstin himself
finds in *The Discoverers.*

43. Robert Byron, *The Road to Oxiana,* intro. Paul Fussell (New York: Oxford
University Press, 1982), p. viii. For some striking affinities between adventure, sen-
suous perception, and spiritual insight, see David McCullough, "Aviator Authors,"
New York Times Magazine, October 12, 1986, pp. 82f.

44. Jonathan Raban, "Wanderlust," *Departures* (November–December 1985):
p. 9.

45. Ibid., p. 10.

46. Arthur Rimbaud, *A Season in Hell and The Drunken Boat,* trans. Louise
Varèse (New York: New Directions, 1961), pp. 96, 97, 100, 101.

47. Charles Baudelaire, *Flowers of Evil: A Selection,* ed. Marthiel Mathews and
Jackson Mathews (New York: New Directions, 1955), pp. 142f. The translation of
"Le Voyage" in this volume is by Roy Campbell.

48. Quoted by Newby, *Book of Travellers' Tales,* p. 15; and in *The Complete
Essays and Other Writings of Ralph Waldo Emerson,* ed. Brooks Atkinson (New
York: Random House, 1940), p. 165.

49. Italo Calvino, *Invisible Cities,* trans. William Weaver (New York: Harcourt
Brace Jovanovich, 1974), p. 28.

50. Ibid., p. 98.

51. T. S. Eliot, *Four Quartets* (New York: Harcourt, Brace, 1943), pp. 25f.

52. Zweig, *Adventurer,* pp. 246f.

Chapter 4. The Space of Quest

1. Martin Heidegger, *On the Way to Language,* trans. Peter D. Hertz (New
York: Harper and Row, 1971), pp. 15, 16. More recently, Octavio Paz also writes
with sharper historical acumen in *One Earth, Four or Five Worlds,* trans. Helen R.
Lane (New York: Harcourt Brace Jovanovich, 1985).

2. Heidegger, *On the Way to Language,* p. 44.

3. Jean-François Lyotard, *Le Différend* (Paris: Éditions de Minuit, 1984), especially pp. 24f., 29f., 54, 90f.

4. The entire colloquy between Jean-François Lyotard and Richard Rorty appears in *Critique* 456 (May 1985): 559–85; the brief quotation from Rorty, which
I have paraphrased from the French back into English, appears on p. 575.

5. Giovanni Vattimo, "Difference and Interference: On the Reduction of Hermeneutics to Anthropology," *Res* 4 (Autumn 1982): 91.

6. Claude Lévi-Strauss, *The Naked Man,* vol. 4 of *Introduction to a Science
of Mythology,* trans. John Weightman and Doreen Weightman (New York: Harper
and Row, 1981), pp. 690, 636.

7. Claude Lévi-Strauss, *Tristes Tropiques,* trans. John Russell (New York: Criterion Books, 1961), p. 32. See also Michel Leiris, "L'Ethnographe devant le colo-
nialisme," reprinted in *Brisées* (Paris: Mercure de France, 1966).

8. Lévi-Strauss, *Tristes Tropiques,* p. 41.

9. Ibid., p. 42.

10. Ibid., p. 43.

11. Ibid., p. 45. See also Clifford Geertz, "'From the Native Point of View': On the Nature of Anthropological Understanding," *Local Knowledge* (New York: Basic Books, 1983), pp. 55–71; and James Clifford and George E. Marcus, eds., *Writing Culture* (Berkeley and Los Angeles: University of California Press, 1986), which argues for a "post-modern" anthropology, textual, political, dialogical, transgeneric, and self-reflexive, an anthropology that *writes,* even constructs, not merely represents, cultures without pretense of holism, pp. 1–26.

12. Lévi-Strauss, *Tristes Tropiques,* p. 388.

13. Clifford and Marcus, *Writing Culture,* p. 23. Acutely, M. A. Abbas argues that "fascination" derives from a recognition of otherness within ourselves, in "On Fascination," a paper delivered at a conference entitled "Interfaces of Culture: The West and Its Others," Center for Twentieth Century Studies, University of Wisconsin-Milwaukee, September 19, 1986.

14. Lévi-Strauss, *Tristes Tropiques,* pp. 391, 392.

15. Ibid., p. 397.

16. See also Vattimo, "Difference and Interference," pp. 87–89.

17. William Barrett, *Irrational Man: A Study in Existential Philosophy* (Garden City, N.Y.: Doubleday, 1958), p. 53. See also William Rubin, ed., "Primitivism," in *Twentieth-Century Art* (New York: Museum of Modern Art, 1984), and Jeffrey M. Perl, *The Tradition of Return* (Princeton, N.J.: Princeton University Press, 1984).

18. Norman Lewis claims that countries are still preserved "for the discerning traveler by their inaccessibility, their bad roads, by neglectful governments, the malarial mosquito, guerrillas in the mountains, and bureaucratic inflexibility . . ."; yet he admits, "'When the going was good —.' Looking back in 2005 at this remaining handful of threatened years, surely there will be no doubt *this* was the time?" In "Wanderlust," *Departures,* March–April 1985, p. 10. More wryly, Pico Iyer writes: "It is the first secret conceit of every voyager to imagine that he alone has found the world's last paradise; it is the second to believe that the door has slammed shut right behind him." In "How Paradise Is Lost — and Found," *Time,* June 9, 1986, p. 82.

19. Salman Rushdie, "Adventures and Epics," *New York Times Magazine* March 16, 1986, Part 2, p. 27.

20. Bernard Lewis, *The Muslim Discovery of Europe* (New York: W. W. Norton, 1982), p. 29.

21. Even the great Moslem empires, Lewis notes, showed little interest in naming races and territories of the world. Ibid., pp. 60, 68. But now, Said avers, postcolonial writers, like Ngũgĩ and Salih, reclaim the topoi of quest and journey to speak their experience. See Edward W. Said, "The Post-Colonial Intellectual," *Salmagundi,* nos. 70–71 (Spring–Summer 1986), pp. 54f.

22. Barry Menikoff, *Robert Louis Stevenson and "The Beach at Falesá": A Study in Victorian Publishing with the Original Text* (Stanford: Stanford University Press, 1984), p. 186. Menikoff's careful study of the bowdlerization of this text shows all the racial, sexual, and political prejudices of Victorian England.

23. For examples of biased critique, see Ngũgĩ wa Thiong'o, *Decolonizing the Mind: The Politics of Language in African Literature* (London: James Curry, 1986),

and Abdul R. JanMohamed, *Manichean Aesthetics: The Politics of Literature in Colonial Africa* (Amherst: University of Massachusetts Press, 1983). Though informed and astute, such critiques of colonialism often lapse into fictions of revenge or self-exoneration, begetting nasty counterstatements, as in Pascal Bruckner, *The Tears of the White Man: Compassion as Contempt,* trans. William R. Beer (New York: Free Press, 1986). Some admirable works, however, do manage to avoid tendentiousness of any kind; see, for instance, Tepilit Ole Saitoti, *The Worlds of a Masai Warrior: An Autobiography* (New York: Random House, 1986).

24. Frantz Fanon, *The Wretched of the Earth,* with a preface by Jean-Paul Sartre, trans. Constance Farrington (New York: Grove Press, 1968), pp. 218f. Michel Leiris preceded Fanon in colonial demystification in *L'Afrique fantôme* (Paris: Gallimard, 1934).

25. Edward W. Said, *Orientalism* (New York: Vintage Books, 1979), p. 3. See also pp. 12, 19–25, 201–4.

26. *The Letters of Gustave Flaubert, 1830–1857,* ed. and trans. Francis Steegmuller (Cambridge: Harvard University Press, 1980), p. 80.

27. Quoted by Lewis, *Muslim Discovery of Europe,* p. 68. Elsewhere, Lewis also discusses racist attitudes of Arabs toward African blacks. See Bernard Lewis, "The Crows of the Arabs," *Critical Inquiry* 12, 1 (Autumn 1985): 88–97. As for the Hindu's sense of superiority to Europeans, see V. S. Naipaul, *An Area of Darkness* (New York: Random House, 1981), pp. 64f., 75, and passim.

28. Lewis, *Muslim Discovery of Europe,* p. 296. Said, however, is quite right to call for an epistemological critique of a Western discourse that combines historicism and imperialist ideologies. See Edward W. Said, "Orientalism Reconsidered," *Cultural Critique* 1 (Fall 1985): 101, as well as Mary Louise Pratt's interesting essay "Scratches on the Face of the Country; or, What Mr. Barrow Saw in the Land of the Bushmen," *Critical Inquiry* 12, 1 (Autumn 1985): 119–43.

29. "Self-Reliance," *The Complete Essays and Other Writings of Ralph Waldo Emerson,* ed. Brooks Atkinson (New York: Random House, 1940), pp. 145, 149.

30. Valerie Pakenham, *Out in the Noonday Sun: Edwardians in the Tropics* (New York: Random House, 1985), p. 10. Another English author wonders: "What was the impulse which drove middle-class Victorians to leave the country they loved so chauvinistically, and the company of the race they considered God's last word in breeding, to travel in discomfort, danger, illness, filth, and misery among Asiatics whose morals and habits they despised?" See Phillip Glazebrook, *Journey to Kars* (New York: Holt, Rinehart, and Winston, 1984), p. 9.

31. "Immediately after World War II, then, the Orient became [for the U.S.], not a broad catholic issue as it had been for centuries in Europe, but an administrative one, a matter of policy," Said notes in *Orientalism,* p. 290.

32. For a literate view of the afflictions of the third world, see Clifford Geertz, *The Interpretation of Culture* (New York: Basic Books, 1973), pp. 193–341.

33. Ibid., p. 258.

34. See p. 13, above.

35. Dean MacCannell, *The Tourist: A New Theory of the Leisure Class* (New York: Schocken Books, 1976), p. 8.

36. Ibid., p. 13.

37. George Steiner, "The Archives of Eden," *Salmagundi,* nos. 50–51 (Autumn 1980–Winter 1981), pp. 70f.

38. *Familiar Letters of John Adams and His Wife Abigail Adams during the Revolution,* ed. Charles Francis Adams (Boston: Houghton Mifflin, 1875), pp. 191f.

39. Geertz, *Local Knowledge,* pp. 8f. and 36–54.

40. Rasselas—an Oriental, though himself a figment of the Western imagination—expresses a mood very different from Emerson's Whim in his Happy Valley: "'That I want nothing,' said the Prince, 'or that I know not what I want, is the cause of my complaint.'" Samuel Johnson, *Rasselas* (Oxford: Clarendon Press, 1954), p. 44.

Chapter 5. Faces of Quest: Fact

1. Abbreviations and page numbers refer to the following editions of works cited in this chapter: Michael Collins, *Carrying the Fire: An Astronaut's Journey,* with a foreword by Charles A. Lindbergh (New York: Ballantine Books, 1975), abbr. as *C;* Annie Dillard, *Holy the Firm* (New York: Harper Colophon Books, 1984), abbr. as *H,* and *Pilgrim at Tinker Creek* (New York: Bantam Books, 1975), abbr. as *P;* Alex Haley, *Roots: The Saga of an American Family* (New York: Doubleday, 1976), abbr. as *R;* Michael J. Arlen, *Exiles* and *Passage to Ararat* (New York: Farrar, Straus, and Giroux, n.d.), abbr. as *E;* Eleanor Clark, *Tamrart: Thirteen Days in the Sahara* (New York: Stuart Wright, 1984), abbr. as *T;* John McPhee, *Coming into the Country* (New York: Bantam Books, 1979), abbr. as *CC;* Edward Hoagland, *African Calliope: A Journey to the Sudan* (Harmondsworth, England: Penguin, 1981), abbr. as *A;* Mary Morris, *Nothing to Declare: Memoirs of a Woman Traveling Alone* (Boston: Houghton Mifflin, 1988), abbr. as *N;* Paul Zweig, *Three Journeys: An Automythology* (New York: Basic Books, 1976), abbr. as *TJ.*

2. Elsewhere, Haley also speaks of his "two-year quest involved in the establishment of the family lineage." See his "Foreword" to *From Freedom to Freedom: African Roots in American Soil,* ed. Mildred Bain and Ervin Lewis (Milwaukee: Purnell Reference Books, 1977), p. xiv.

3. Ibid., p. xvi.

4. Coincidentally, Russian Armenians have now begun violently to agitate for the unification of the Nagorno-Karabakh Armenians, in adjoining Azerbaijan, with the Soviet Armenian Republic, creating a crisis for Gorbachev's policy of *glasnost.*

5. Note the interesting contrasts between McPhee the writer and another, unrelated, John McPhee, a bush pilot and fish-and-game warden, in John McPhee, "North of the C.P. Line," *Table of Contents* (New York: Farrar, Straus, and Giroux, 1985).

6. Michael Parfit, *South Light: A Journey to the Last Continent* (New York: Macmillan, 1985), p. 295; and Barry Lopez, *Arctic Dreams: Imagination and Desire in a Northern Landscape* (New York: Scribners, 1986), p. xxix.

7. Paul Zweig, *The Heresy of Self-Love* (Princeton: Princeton University Press, 1968, 1980), pp. xii, 265.

8. Paul Zweig, *The Adventurer: The Fate of Adventure in the Western World.* (Princeton: Princeton University Press, 1974), pp. 16, 31, 95f.

9. Paul Zweig, *Departures: Memoirs,* intro. Morris Dickstein (New York: Harper and Row, 1986), p. 19.

10. Ibid., pp. 62, 116, 218, 217.

Chapter 6. Faces of Quest: Fiction

1. Abbreviations and page numbers refer to the following editions of novels quoted in this chapter: Harriet Doerr, *Stones for Ibarra* (New York: Penguin Books, 1984), abbr. as *S;* Joan Didion, *A Book of Common Prayer* (New York: Pocket Books, 1978), abbr. as *B;* Eleanor Clark, *Camping Out* (New York: Putnam's, 1986), abbr. as *C;* James Dickey, *Deliverance* (Boston: Houghton Mifflin, 1970), abbr. as *D;* Norman Mailer, *Why Are We in Vietnam?* (New York: Putnam's, 1967), abbr. as *W;* Saul Bellow, *Henderson the Rain King* (New York: Viking, 1959), abbr. as *H.*

2. Some critics have interpreted D.J.'s going off to "see the Wizard" in Vietnam as a defeat; see, for instance, Robert Solotaroff, *Down Mailer's Way* (Urbana: University of Illinois Press, 1974), pp. 179–207. I interpret exactly the reverse, as does John W. Aldridge, "From Vietnam to Obscenity," in Robert F. Lucid, ed., *Norman Mailer: The Man and His Work* (Boston: Little, Brown, 1971), pp. 180–92.

3. See Nina Steers, "Successor to Faulkner?" *Show* 4 (November 1964): 38.

Chapter 7. Paul Bowles

1. Abbreviations and page numbers in the text refer to the following editions of Paul Bowles's works: *The Sheltering Sky* (New York: New American Library, 1951), abbr. as *SS; Let It Come Down* (New York: Signet, 1953), abbr. as *LCD; The Spider's House* (Santa Rosa, Calif.: Black Sparrow Press, 1987), abbr. as *SH; Yallah!* (New York: McDowell, Obolensky, 1957), abbr. as *Y; Their Heads Are Green and Their Hands Are Blue: Scenes from the Non-Christian World* (New York: Ecco Press, 1963), abbr. as *THA; Up Above the World* (New York: Ecco Press, 1982), abbr. as *UAW; Without Stopping: An Autobiography* (New York: Ecco Press, 1985), abbr. as *WS;* and *Collected Stories,* intro. Gore Vidal (Santa Barbara, Calif.: Black Sparrow Press, 1979), abbr. as *CS.*

2. The title refers to Edward Lear's poem "The Jumblies," which Bowles takes for his epigraph. Bowles's use of alien cultures as a critique of Western civilization is discussed perceptively throughout Wayne Pounds, *Paul Bowles: The Inner Geography* (New York: Peter Lang, 1985).

3. Harvey Breit, "A Talk with Paul Bowles," *New York Times Book Review,* March 9, 1952, p. 19. After living for three decades in Tangier, Bowles would still comment on the difficulties of relating to Moroccans who seemed to have "whole sections missing in their psyche." See "The Art of Fiction LXVII: Paul Bowles," interview with Jeffrey Bailey, *Paris Review* 23, 81 (Fall 1981): 92.

4. Richard F. Patteson, *A World Outside: The Fiction of Paul Bowles* (Austin: University of Texas Press, 1987), p. 71. Elsewhere, Patteson rightly concludes: "The literature of exploration and cultural interaction has changed over the past century as the alien and the outside have come to seem closer, more a part of our lives. What Bowles has done is to marshal and direct his own personal imaginative experience in such a way as to make himself the most eloquent contemporary analyst of the terror that, in Greene's words, lies 'pressed against the windows,'" p. 60.

5. Quoted by Patteson, ibid., p. x.

6. Reproached about the prevalence of violence in his work, Bowles answered: "If I'm persuaded that our life is predicated upon violence, that the entire struc-

ture of what we call civilization . . . can collapse at any moment, then whatever I write is going to be affected by that assumption." See "Art of Fiction LXVII," p. 80.

7. Daniel Halperin, "Interview with Paul Bowles," *TriQuarterly* 33 (Spring 1975): 170f.

8. "Art of Fiction LXVII," pp. 68, 81, 70.

Chapter 8. Paul Theroux

1. Abbreviations and page numbers refer to the following editions of works by Paul Theroux cited in this chapter: *V. S. Naipaul: An Introduction to His Work* (New York: Africana Publishing, 1972), abbr. as *N; Sunrise with Seamonsters: Travels and Discoveries, 1964–1984* (Boston: Hougton Mifflin, 1985), abbr. as *SS; The Great Railway Bazaar: By Train through Asia* (New York: Ballantine Books, 1976), abbr. as *G; The Old Patagonian Express: By Train through the Americas* (New York: Pocket Books, 1980), abbr. as *O;* Paul Theroux and Steve McCurry, *The Imperial Way: By Rail from Peshawar to Chittagong* (Boston: Houghton Mifflin, 1985), abbr. as *I; The Kingdom by the Sea: A Journey around Great Britain* (Boston: Houghton Mifflin, 1983), abbr. as *K; Saint Jack* (New York: Pocket Books, 1984), abbr. as *SJ; The Mosquito Coast* (New York: Avon Books, 1983), abbr. as *M.* Theroux's "nonfiction novel," *My Secret History* (New York: Putnam's, 1989), appeared too late for inclusion in this chapter.

2. James Atlas, "The Theroux Family Arsenal," *New York Times Magazine,* April 30, 1978, pp. 24f. This article gives an interesting overview of the Theroux clan.

3. See the epigraph to this chapter, from James T. Yenckel, "The Wanderlust World of Paul Theroux" (An Interview), *Washington Post,* December 30, 1984, sec. G, p. 1.

4. Atlas, "Theroux Family Arsenal," p. 54.

5. Yenckel, "Wanderlust World of Paul Theroux," p. 1.

6. Quoted by Samuel Coale, *Paul Theroux* (Boston: Twayne, 1987), p. 8.

7. Ibid., p. 27.

8. In his essay "The Exotic View," Theroux recognizes that the "exotic dream, not always outlandish, is a dream of what we lack and so crave" (*SS,* 146), and that it is a cruel irony such dreams are located now in poor or blighted regions of the world. Thus the exotic remains a Western category of illusion, without parallel, say, in Chinese travel literature.

9. One of Theroux's most flawed essays, downright silly at times, is called "Being a Man," and turns on the dubious proposition: "I have always disliked being a man" (*SS,* 309). Yet, despite all its inverted machismo and cant, the essay offers some insights into American manhood.

10. In Bruce Chatwin and Paul Theroux, *Patagonia Revisited* (Boston: Houghton Mifflin, 1986), both authors dwell on the fabled aura and curious splendors of Patagonia, if not of all South America. Moreover, Theroux admits: "When I think of going anywhere, I think of going south. I associate the word 'south' with freedom, and at a very young age I bought Sir Ernest Shackleton's book *South* for the title alone," p. 11.

11. *The Complete Essays and Other Writings of Ralph Waldo Emerson,* ed. with intro. by Brooks Atkinson (New York: Random House, 1940), p. 342.

12. An instance of verbal violence and wit in poor taste is Theroux's review of Erica Jong's *Fear of Flying,* admittedly a shabby book. Theroux writes in part: "With such continual and insistent reference to her cherished valve, Erica Jong's witless heroine looms like a mammoth pudendum, as roomy as the Carlsbad Caverns, luring amorous spelunkers to confusion in her plunging grottoes" (*SS,* 5).

Chapter 9. Peter Matthiessen

1. Abbreviations and page numbers refer to the following editions of Peter Matthiessen cited in this chapter: *Blue Meridian: The Search for the Great White Shark* (New York: Random House, 1971), abbr. as *B; Nine-Headed Dragon River: Zen Journals, 1969–1982* (Boston: Shambhala Press, 1987), abbr. as *N; Indian Country* (New York: Viking Press, 1984), abbr. as *I; Under the Mountain Wall: A Chronicle of Two Seasons in Stone Age New Guinea* (New York: Penguin Books, 1987), abbr. as *U; The Tree Where Man Was Born,* with Eliot Porter, *The African Experience* (New York: E. P. Dutton, 1972), abbr. as *T; The Cloud Forest: A Chronicle of the South American Wilderness* (New York: Penguin Books, 1987), abbr. as *C; The Snow Leopard* (New York: Bantam Books, 1979), abbr. as *S; Far Tortuga* (New York: Vintage Books, 1984), abbr. as *F; At Play in the Fields of the Lord* (New York: Bantam Books, 1976), abbr. as *AP.*

2. William Styron, *This Quiet Dust and Other Writings* (New York: Random House, 1982), pp. 251f.

3. Critics of the left as of the right tend to decry Matthiessen's alleged romantic primitivism, construing it as a powerful oedipal antagonism to Western civilization. Their disapprobation even extends to Matthiessen's interest in Zen. Thus, for instance, Bruce Bawer: "More than anything else he has written, the Zen journals reflect the profundity and perverseness of Matthiessen's antagonism toward America, toward Western civilization, and toward the Christian idea of God; to read them is a tiresome and dismaying experience." In "Nature Boy: The Novels of Peter Matthiessen," *New Criterion* 6, 10 (June 1988): 37.

4. Quoted by Wendy Smith, "Peter Matthiessen," *Publisher's Weekly* 229, 19 (May 9, 1986): 241.

5. Matthiessen forthrightly says: "I like the values of traditional people who are closer to the earth. It's an attitude which I think is very precious and is in very serious danger of being lost, stamped out entirely." Ibid., p. 241.

6. Marston Bates, "Fortune Smiled on the Traveler in an Unmapped Part of the Earth," *New York Times Book Review,* October 15, 1961, p. 3.

7. In *Nine-Headed Dragon River,* which reprints in chapters 7 and 8 long sections on Buddhism and Hinduism from *The Snow Leopard,* Matthiessen also mentions that his teacher, Eido-shi, gives him a particular *koan* for the trip: "All the peaks are covered with snow — why is this one bare?" p. 47. Matthiessen confesses to great disappointment after he fails to attain illumination.

8. Paul Zweig, "Eastern Mountain Time," *Saturday Review* 15 (August 1978): 44. Both Zweig and Edward Hoagland, encountered earlier in this book, highly esteem *The Snow Leopard* while regretting its jimmied interpolations. See Edward Hoagland, "Walking the High Himalayas," *New York Times Book Review,* April 13, 1978.

9. Smith, "Peter Matthiessen," p. 241.

10. See Styron, *This Quiet Dust,* p. 251, who also prefers, like many critics, the last two novels.

11. Peter Matthiessen, "The Craft of Fiction in *Far Tortuga:* An Interview," *Paris Review* 15, 60 (Winter 1974): 79, 81.

12. Matthiessen, who has an excellent ear for dialects, also used a tape recorder in the Caribbean. "But mainly," he says, ". . . you can't really write dialect until you can speak it yourself." See Smith, "Peter Matthiessen," pp. 241f.

13. See Bert Bender, *"Far Tortuga* and American Sea Fiction since *Moby Dick,"* *American Literature* 52, 2, (May 1984): 227–48.

14. Leslie Fiedler sees psychedelic derangement as the opposite of nostalgic primitivism, and sees Moon, in this regard, as a presage of the New Western Hero. See *The Return of the Vanishing American* (New York: Stein and Day, 1968), pp. 172–75.

15. Quite rightly, Frederick R. Karl remarks about this work: "The only comparable novel to deal with such crucial issues is Bellow's *Henderson the Rain King,* also a marvel of language and cultural insights." See *American Fictions, 1940–1980* (New York: Harper and Row, 1983), p. 59.

In-Conclusion

1. Paul Zweig, *The Adventurer: The Fate of Adventure in the Western World.* (Princeton: Princeton University Press, 1974), p. viii.

2. Quoted by Matei Calinescu in Mircea Eliade, *Youth without Youth and Other Novellas,* ed. with intro by Matei Calinescu (Columbus: Ohio State University Press, 1988), p. xvi.

3. Joseph Campbell, *Myths to Live By* (New York: Viking, 1972), p. 266.

4. *The Complete Essays and Other Writings of Ralph Waldo Emerson,* ed. with intro. by Brooks Atkinson (New York: Random House, 1940), p. 358.

5. William James, *The Will to Believe and Other Essays in Popular Philosophy and Human Immortality* (New York: Dover Publications, 1956), pp. 29, 56. See also for other nuances on the topic of belief, pp. 11, 25, 55, 61f., 86, 93, 110, 116f.

6. Ibid., p. 86.

7. Friedrich Nietzsche, *The Gay Science,* trans. Walter Kaufmann (New York: Vintage Books, 1974), p. 75. See also his *Will to Power,* especially books 1 and 3, on the necessity of belief.

8. Ben Belitt, "Literature and Belief," *Salmagundi* 72 (Fall 1986): 18, 20.

9. Walter Benjamin, *Reflections: Essays, Aphorisms, Autobiographical Writings,* ed. with intro. by Peter Demetz, trans. Edmund Jephcott (New York: Harcourt Brace Jovanovich, 1978), p. 233.

Selective Index of Authors and Titles

The Wisconsin Project on American Writers

A series edited by Frank Lentricchia